DOUBLE YOUR MONEY
in America's Finest Companies®

DOUBLE YOUR MONEY
in America's Finest Companies®

THE UNBEATABLE POWER OF
RISING DIVIDENDS

Bill Staton, MBA, CFA

Foreword by Jeffrey A. Hirsch
Editor-in-Chief, *Stock Trader's Almanac*

WILEY

John Wiley & Sons, Inc.

Published by John Wiley & Sons, Inc., Hoboken, New Jersey.
Published simultaneously in Canada.

For general information on our other products and services or for technical support, please
contact our Customer Care Department within the United States at (800) 762-2974, outside
the United States at (317) 572-3993 or fax (317) 572-4002.

Wiley also publishes its books in a variety of electronic formats. Some content that appears
in print may not be available in electronic formats. For more information about Wiley
products, visit our Web site at www.wiley.com.

"America's Finest Companies®," "America's Money Coach®," "The Baker's Dozen
Guided Portfolio®," and "America's Smartest Companies®" are registered trademarks
of The Staton Institute® Inc., 2431 Hartmill Court, Charlotte, North Carolina 28226,
www.statoninstitute.com.

Library of Congress Cataloging-in-Publication Data:

Staton, Bill.
    Double your money in America's finest companies : the unbeatable power of rising
dividends / Bill Staton ; edited with a foreword by Jeffrey A. Hirsch.
        p. cm. — (Almanac investor series)
    Includes index.
    ISBN 978-0-470-33604-5 (cloth)
        1. Investments—United States.   2. Dividends—United States.   3. Finance,
    Personal—United States.   I. Hirsch, Jeffrey A.   II. Title.
HG4910.S633   2009
332.63'220973—dc22

                                                                2008026308

Printed in the United States of America.
10 9 8 7 6 5 4 3 2 1

What greater wealth could a man have than being blessed with a wonderful family? I can think of none. I dedicate this book to my lifelong best friend and partner in all that I do, Mary, and our four incredible children—Gracie, Tate, Whitney, and Will—and Austin, our grandson. You all have my heartfelt gratitude for enriching my life so often and in so many ways. You have given to me far more than I have given back. And for that, I will always be grateful.

CONTENTS

FOREWORD

Investment strategies come and go, but the results of Bill Staton's philosophy, investment methodology, and America's Finest Companies® (AFC) have not wavered. Bill has been through all types of markets over the last four decades. His system was forged at the depths of the stagflation, economic malaise, and market morass of the 1970s—and is rock-solid because of it.

After getting acquainted in the early 1990s, Bill wrote for a couple of our early newsletters on a regular basis. Working on this book has once again given me the pleasure of editing Bill's snappy, sometimes down-home, but as always entertaining style. He has taught me some new things, reminded me of and reinforced some old ones, provided me with some great new quotations and ideas for the *Almanac*, and made me laugh out loud.

Reading Bill's philosophy and techniques was also inspiring, prompting me to open accounts and start portfolios for my two young sons using AFCs, as well as for a portion of my own retirement plan, in addition to the market timing and other investing I do. Bill is right about getting young people started investing early. I was weaned on the market and finance, and my three-year-old is already asking to pay for things at stores and restaurants. Show them how their money grows exponentially with the power of compounding by investing wisely, and by the time they head off to college they'll have an incredible jump on their future with an impressive portfolio.

The AFC system fits right in with our mantra of profiting from history. There is no predicting or forecasting, but all the companies in AFC have a long *history* of consecutive years of rising dividends and/or earnings. These companies have not only stood the test of time; they have excelled.

Whether you've never traded a stock before or are a seasoned veteran, Bill Staton's *Double Your Money in America's Finest Companies*® fits easily into your investment and long-term financial needs. In this book, Staton unlocks the key to long-term capital building. Follow it step by step or tear right into picking a portfolio. It's amazingly simple and easy. Bill has whittled down the entire universe of over 20,000 stocks to just over 300 of the highest-quality firms proven to produce market-beating results with less risk.

For individual investors, AFC stocks have some of the best reward/risk ratios for long-term planning I know of. Savvy professionals will want to use AFC for making recommendations to, and creating portfolios for, their clients. America's Money Coach®, Bill Staton, provides the pep talk you need to get started and to do extremely well with ease.

And so it is with great honor and privilege that I introduce the first installment of our new Almanac Investor Series. This series would not exist without the diligent work and patience of our associate editor at Wiley, Jennifer MacDonald, and the vision of our editorial director, Pamela van Giessen. My compatriots at the Hirsch Organization, J. Taylor Brown and Christopher Mistal, have once again been invaluable to my efforts. And finally, without the towering shoulders of my illustrious father Yale Hirsch (founder of the Hirsch Organization) to stand on top of, the view would be rather obscured.

It is completely apropos that this inaugural edition be in collaboration with Bill Staton. Our firm has been steeped in history since Yale began his research for the first *Stock Trader's Almanac* in 1966. Bill Staton has been beating the market for the last four decades and has helped countless clients and readers achieve financial superiority and live the good life. Enjoy!

JEFFREY A. HIRSCH
Editor-in-Chief, *Stock Trader's Almanac*
Nyack, New York
September 2008

PREFACE

Depending on how it's used, [money] proves to be a blessing or a curse. Either the person becomes master of the money, or the money becomes the master of the person.
                          —David McConough, Money the Acid Test, 1918

In the 1990s I was fortunate to have three editions of the forerunner of this book published by Hyperion, at the time one of this country's largest and most accomplished publishers. The original title was *The America's Finest Companies*® *Investment Plan.* Some of the material was based on another book I self-published in 1990 under the title *60-Minute Investing,* whose subtitle was rather catchy, I thought then and still do: *The "It's-Not-Over-Your-Head, All-You-Really-Need-to-Know" Guide to Making Money with America's Best Companies.*

On page 9 I made a truly bold statement: "Since *60-Minute Investing* is so short and takes less than two hours to finish, I strongly suggest you read it to the end in one sitting. Once you complete the first reading, turn again to the 11 steps [for stock market success] and review them. Cement them in your mind. You might even fold the corner of the page for quick reference. At your leisure reread the book. After finishing it the second time, start the 11 steps to stock market success. Don't put it off another moment. Time is money! The sooner you start the road to stock market success, the happier you will be."

The America's Finest Companies® *(AFC) Investment Plan* was a more thorough and refined version of *60-Minute Investing.* And this book is an even more thorough and refined version of the three Hyperion printings. For example, there's up-to-date historical data on stock market and AFC performance. Also, and perhaps most important, there's new and additional data, coupled with increased emphasis, about how important dividends are to overall stock market performance whether you invest in stocks in general or in America's Finest in particular. I certainly hope that it's the latter.

> *"The present of dividends signifies more than management's generosity. It is a by-product of the firm's success."*
> — TIMOTHY VICK, AUTHOR OF WALL STREET ON SALE,
> FOUNDER TODAY'S VALUE INVESTOR AND
> SENIOR ANALYST WITH ARBOR CAPITAL MANAGEMENT

There's more than one reason I call them America's Finest Companies (AFCs), as you will come to understand as you read this book. But it's important for you to know that they don't make the headlines with phony accounting, jail-bound CEOs, shoddy balance sheets, and the like. In addition, in most years they outpace the stock market in general. The proof of that last statement will be clearly demonstrated.

I and Mary, my wife/business partner, owe a lot to John Wiley & Sons, Inc. for giving us the opportunity to come out with this book. (Mary was my strongest supporter in keeping the writing on schedule to meet a tight deadline. Jeff Hirsch of the *Stock Trader's Almanac* was a huge help as well, especially with his editorial critique.) Wiley is one of the oldest companies among America's Finest Companies® and celebrated its 201st year in business in 2008. They are fine people to work with and leaders in financial publishing. I am very grateful they allowed me to complete this project.

Bill Staton, MBA, CFA
America's Money Coach®
Charlotte, North Carolina
September 2008

Get all you can, without hurting your soul,
your body or your neighbor.
Save all you can, cutting off every needless expense.
Give all you can.
      —JOHN WESLEY, FOUNDER OF THE METHODIST CHURCH
    ("METHOD-IST," A DISCIPLINE, A LONG-RANGE STRATEGY)

DOUBLE YOUR MONEY
in America's Finest Companies®

CHAPTER

1

Invest Only in America's Finest Companies®

The fact that it's [value investing] so simple makes people reluctant to teach it. If you've gone and gotten a Ph.D. and spent years learning how to do all kinds of tough things mathematically, to have to come back to this is—it's like studying for the priesthood and finding out that the Ten Commandments were all you needed.

—WARREN BUFFETT

POINTS TO REMEMBER

- Stocks provide the finest long-term real returns.
- Doing it yourself is fast and easy.
- America's Finest Companies® (AFC) stocks have higher returns and a greater margin of safety.

Making your money work for you ought to be fun and easy, safe and sure. You don't have to be a professional or spend every waking moment to build funds for your future. You don't have to take a lot of time from your own career and personal life. And you don't have to hand your money over to one of the more than 8,000 mutual funds.

As a money manager, I don't like mutual funds. Never have. Never will. In general, I think they underperform and overcharge. Worse, most of the people who manage mutual funds don't have even

3

a penny of their money in their own funds. That number is 47 percent for U.S. stock funds and 61 percent for foreign stock funds. The numbers are even worse for bond funds: 66 percent for taxable, 71 percent for balanced and 80 percent for municipals. This is according to a 2008 study from Morningstar. MarketWatch commentator Chuck Jaffe observed, "Ouch. That's a lot of managers who are going out to eat, rather than eating their own cooking."

On the other hand, we invest the Staton family money in line with the way we invest for all of our managed accounts. We do eat our own cooking, and we believe that, given enough time, it produces tasty returns.

Investing isn't voodoo or hocus-pocus. The word "invest" comes from the Latin *investire*, to clothe. Merriam-Webster says to invest is "to commit (money) in order to earn a financial return . . . to make use of for future benefits." To invest means to put money to work today so that it will earn more money for the future. You invest your money into something to reap a profit.

Investing (as opposed to speculating and taking unnecessary risks) is a process—a series of actions leading to an end. By definition, then, investing is something you should start now, or should have already started, and plan to continue indefinitely. Stocks are the best—and the easiest—asset to invest in. They also can be highly profitable.

For the past 14 years, Thornburg Investment Management® has published "A Study of Real Real Returns." The Thornburg report covers several classes of U.S. and international stocks, taxable and tax-free bonds, commodities, and residential real estate. Garrett Thornburg, CEO, commented in the latest report, "It is no surprise that over the last 20 years common stocks and municipal bonds [surprise!] were able to provide the best 'real real returns'" after taking inflation, taxes, and fees (operating expenses) into account.

> *For all long-term investors, there is only one objective—maximum total return after taxes.*
> —SIR JOHN MARKS TEMPLETON

During my 38 years as a financial advisor and money manager, I've learned that most individuals can get the most from their money just by following a few simple guidelines. My investment program is built around America's Finest Companies, and shows you how to

Dear Bill,

I've been using your America's Finest Companies editions to build the core of my portfolio. The benefits of using your books have been substantial:

- By adhering to the selection criteria, one is forced into a discipline of maintaining a long-term view, helping the investor avoid fads.
- By retaining a stock over years, you learn how the company responds to crises and downturns. You invest in the company, rather than treating your investments like a casino gamble.
- It reduces the desire to market-time, one of the big mistakes I and other investors make. I don't look at my stocks daily, or sometimes even weekly.

I still have some stocks that I have picked out myself, but with few exceptions the AFC selections have performed better over the long term. I invested in a few "hares" over the AFC "turtles", and these were generally shown to be mistakes in the long run. I invested, unfortunately, in Enron, a company you never would have recommended. The AFC turtles have solidly plodded on, through various economic environments, while the fads have fallen by the wayside.

In sum, the AFC system has aided me in building a solid portfolio, and helped me avoid costly mistakes. I appreciate each edition I receive.

Best regards,

C.C.

New York, 2006

be your own money manager. There is no Wall Street jargon, no complicated rules, no complex formulas, nothing to buy except my annual America's Finest Companies directory published each July.

I'll explain in plain English how the stock market works—why certain principles apply and a lot of others don't. I'll show you that stocks have provided a higher return than any other asset class for more than a hundred years, except for perhaps timberland. Timberland, like stocks, is a natural hedge against inflation.

COMPOUND ANNUAL RETURNS

Professors Jack W. Wilson, PhD, and Charles P. Jones, PhD, at North Carolina State University examined the returns of $1.00 invested on the last day of 1919 through the end of 2006 (see Table 1.1). With inflation taken out (the cost of living rose nearly ninefold during that

TABLE 1.1   Returns as of 2006 on $1.00 Invested in 1919

	Small Stocks	Large Stocks	Corp. Bonds	Long-Term Government Bonds	Treasury Bills
$1 becomes	$550.08	$1,751.88	$18.30	$9.80	$3.28
Adjusted annual rate of return	7.52%	9.55%	3.40%	2.66%	1.38%

Source: Jack W. Wilson and Charles P. Jones, North Carolina State University, 2006.

period) and assuming no taxes or transaction costs, that $1.00 grew to the amounts shown on the first line of the table. Compound annual, inflation-adjusted rates of returns are shown on the bottom line.

The table clearly shows that stocks in general have kept investors well ahead of inflation for close to 90 years. That's been true not only in this country but also in various other countries as well. According to John Authers in *The Financial Times* (June 21, 2008): "In spite of long periods in the doldrums, stocks are a better long-term inflation hedge than anything else. From 1900 to 2007, their real return was more than double that on bonds in every country [academics at the London Business School] surveyed."

I will demonstrate that the stocks of America's Finest Companies ought to do even better. You'll learn what it takes for a firm to be among America's Finest Companies and why these companies have far outdistanced the stock market. You'll also learn the simple process of investing for maximum profits with the lowest risk.

My America's Finest Companies® investment directory is compiled once each year by The Staton Institute® Inc. (www.statoninstitute. com) and is eagerly awaited by investors all over the world and members of the financial media. That's because these companies are the elite of corporate America—the top 2 percent of all public companies—with at least 10 straight years of higher earnings and/ or dividends per share.

Most of America's Finest Companies (AFCs) are on the list because of their exemplary dividend records. Dividends are the cash rewards for owning stocks. Dividend-paying enterprises prove their investment mettle year after year after year.

Dividends allow any investor . . . to earn investment returns right from the source: corporate profits shared directly with stockholders. Too much time, energy, and even profits are wasted by the singular pursuit of capital gains [price appreciation]. Dividends offer a different, easier, and vastly superior way to collect returns from a portfolio of stocks.

—MORNINGSTAR.COM, DECEMBER 5, 2007

According to Ned Davis Research, for almost 35 years from January 31, 1972 through September 30, 2007, an initial $100,000 investment into nondividend-paying (some would label them growth) stocks would have grown to only $240,000. That's a compound annual return of 2.56 percent, less than you would have safely earned in a bank.

A well diversified portfolio (group) of dividend-paying stocks would have grown to slightly more than $3.2 million. That's a compound annual return of 10.55 percent, an annual return that would have kept you ahead of both inflation and taxes.

Even better, with a focus on companies featuring rising dividends (even if not every year), the original $100,000 would have grown to $4.1 million, an annual return of 11.29 percent (see Table 1.2. Companies in the AFC universe would have been among this group.).

The Standard & Poor's stock market index of 500 companies traces its roots back to the beginning of 1926 and represents roughly 75 percent of the total value of all publicly traded U.S. companies. For the period from January 1, 1988 through the end of 2007, the nondividend payers in the index rose 494 percent, or 9.32 percent per year. However, the dividend payers, with dividends reinvested, climbed at 11.81 percent per annum.

You wouldn't go to the racetrack and bet on the nags, would you? That would be a sure way to lose money. Doesn't it make sense, then, that your hard-earned dollars—the dollars you're accumulating

TABLE 1.2   Compound Annual Returns (January 31, 1972–September 30, 2007)

No Dividends	Dividends	Rising Dividends
2.56%	10.55%	11.29%

Source: Ned Davis Research, 2007.

for your children's college education, a larger home, a second home, another car, retirement, or whatever—should be invested in shares of the finest companies, companies that are proven winners?

MAKING MONEY WITH THE CREAM OF THE CROP

Building and managing your own mini fund picked from America's Finest Companies, takes very little time—one or two hours a year—and should allow you to outperform at least 75 percent of the pros 100 percent of the time. This is the best way I know to reach your financial goals. It's even better than investing in mutual funds because America's Finest Companies historically have delivered consistently superior returns.

Since the end of World War II, U.S. stocks have grown at more than 10+ percent compounded annually. (From 1930 to 2007, the average compound annual return was 9.8 percent, according to Wachovia Securities. From December 31, 1957 through December 31, 2007, the S&P 500 compounded at 10.97 percent per year, according to Standard & Poor's.)

Just by earning the stock market's return each year, you should regularly outperform 75 to 85 percent or more of all professional money managers who try to do that and fail. But you might be able to earn more than that—12 to 15 percent annually—with a diverse portfolio chosen from America's Finest Companies. Maybe that doesn't sound much better than 10 percent, but, assuming you invest as little as $2,000 per year for 30 years, the 20 to 50 percent improvement will be worth an additional $154,000 to $540,000.

I don't want to be a wet blanket, but outperforming a particular market index is not a financial goal and never should be. As one financial planner puts it, "An income you don't outlive in a three-decade retirement full of dignity and independence, now that's a financial goal." I heartily agree.

This book is an easy-to-read-and-understand guide to making money with the cream of American companies. Anyone can dramatically improve his or her financial health with my time-proven, powerful method, which is deceptively simple to implement. There are no gimmicks or tricks. A young person can begin to invest with as little as $300 and easily become a millionaire (even a multimillionaire) well before retirement.

BUYING HIGHEST-QUALITY SHARES

Florence Gray

Let me share with you the wonderful story of Florence Gray, the proverbial little old lady who amassed an estate worth $2.5 million. And she never earned more than $9,000 in any single year.

Florence Gray was a market researcher who passed away at age 89. She accumulated almost her entire fortune by using simple, sane principles of long-term investing, the same ones I emphasize over and over again in these pages. In 1924, Ms. Gray made $19.27 a week in her first job.

Remembered as a stickler for details, she was a numbers cruncher before computers were born. She had a talent for tracking down information on market and population trends. Her boss talked her into putting money into stocks, and she took the plunge with gusto by speculating (i.e., taking a huge risk) with borrowed money (or buying on margin) just before the Great Depression struck. Learning the hard way a great lesson in how to lose a lot of money, she switched to buying only the highest-quality companies and never again strayed from the course.

Florence Gray didn't go to college, and, unlike most Americans today, she knew exactly where her money went. She didn't spend it unless she had to, but she was fond of traveling to Europe and did so on several occasions. She favored companies with rising dividends, and after retiring she invested all the money from her Social Security and pension checks and lived off her dividends. The bulk of her portfolio at death, not surprisingly, was in America's Finest Companies, including ExxonMobil.

Her attorney, Ed Hack, summed up her winning philosophy very simply: "Over the course of time, she managed to invest in equities for the long haul and stuck with them and rode the winners. She was not supporting an extravagant lifestyle, and it just began to compound." Florence Gray, I wish we'd known you.

One cardinal principle holds true: By buying the shares only of the highest-quality companies, you'll become a successful investor. You'll be part owner of companies that are in sound financial condition, that won't go out of business, and whose earnings and dividends will continue to grow.

A company must earn money to remain in business. Otherwise it eventually goes bankrupt. Part of those earnings can be paid to investors in the form of cash dividends. The rest is plowed back for research and development to bring new products or services to market, to buy new, more productive equipment, to hire more employees. All earnings put back into the company enhance its value. As the value of the business rises, so does the price of the company's stock. It has to.

Wal-Mart Stores

An excellent example of a company that's done a superior job of enhancing the value of its business—and its share price—is Wal-Mart Stores, one of the brightest lights in America's Finest Companies. Wal-Mart is one of just two American companies with more than 40 consecutive years of increased earnings per share. Through the end of 2007 (January 2008 fiscal year), Wal-Mart had 46 straight years of rising earnings and 33 of higher cash dividends paid out to its stock owners. Since 1985, revenue skyrocketed from about $8.5 billion to more than $375 billion. The share price exploded more than twentyfold from $3 to $63.90 during that period.

Wal-Mart and its founder, the late Sam Walton, are practically household words, as are a lot of America's Finest Companies, such as Coca-Cola, Clorox, ExxonMobil, Hershey, Johnson & Johnson, PepsiCo. and Pfizer. But there are just as many that are totally unfamiliar to most people, investors or not. For example, there's the Washington Real Estate Investment Trust (Washington REIT). Ever heard of it? Probably not.

Washington REIT

Washington REIT—you guessed it—invests in real estate. It prides itself on being maverick, unorthodox, and conservative. The company mails some of the most interesting annual and quarterly reports to shareholders (which tell how the company is doing). One quarterly noted that the company moved out of its old headquarters (after selling it for a tenfold profit) into the basement of its new WRIT Building. I'd never seen a company press release about abandoning offices with windows for offices without them. But Washington REIT isn't your typical enterprise. When the company burned its last outstanding mortgage in the company stove, toasting a few marshmallows in the process, to be on the safe side they asked the building fire marshal to stand by with a fire extinguisher.

In an unusual move, they also mailed a press release about this extraordinary event.

Your Own Investment Program

If you want to begin your own investment program, you can quickly name 10 or 12 financially sound American companies whose earnings or dividends will continue to grow well into the future. General Electric is an example whose roots stretch back to Thomas Edison in the late 1800s.

How do I know that these companies are ongoing successes? Everywhere I have led a workshop on investing (including more than 20 years teaching high school students through Junior Achievement), I've asked the audience to choose a portfolio of five to eight companies. In every instance to date, they've picked highest-quality companies in a variety of industries. The majority of the companies they always pick are among America's Finest Companies. These are companies with at least 10 years in a row of increasing earnings or dividends per share, establishing them as the top 2 percent of all public companies.

Of course, you may be thinking: "Why should I be in stocks at all? They're too risky. Look how far they fell during the Crash of 1987—23 percent in one day. That was worse than any single day during the Great Depression. Or how about the Great Bear Market of 2000–2002, the worst stock market decline since the 1930s. [Bear markets fall, bull markets rise.] I wouldn't own any stocks. I couldn't sleep at night if I did."

If you're thinking like that, you're not alone. The most frequent comments I hear about stocks and the stock market are negative. (I use the terms "market," "stock market," and "market indexes" interchangeably. They mean the same thing in the investment world.) Here are a few I've heard in my seminars:

"High risk/high reward." (The emphasis is always on high risk.)

"Frothy." (Picture a rabid dog foaming at the mouth.)

"A bottomless pit."

"Extremely volatile."

"A loser's game."

"Only an expert should try it."

"Like walking down a dark alley in a crime-infested neighbor-
hood."

"I'd rather visit the dentist."

I do hear positives, too, but they're normally about as few as
friends in a cobra pit. It's been like this for the close to four decades I've been in the investment field.

Let's suppose you'd been in my office 30 years ago asking me
what you should do with your money in the eighties and nineties
and on into the current millennium. I would have said,

> You should invest all the money you can into stocks, but first
> there are a few things you ought to know.
>
> An actor will become president of the United States and
> will preside over the biggest budget deficits in the nation's his-
> tory. The deepest recession since the 1930s will occur in 1981–
> 1982. Nearly 20 percent of the workforce will be unemployed
> at some point during that period. There'll be another reces-
> sion in 1990–1991, in which that high percentage will again be
> without jobs.
>
> The biggest crash in stock market history will occur in fall
> 1987, followed by a "crashette" of huge proportions two years
> later. And oh, by the way, there'll be war in the Middle East
> with the United States leading the charge. A new plague—
> AIDS—will crop up around the world, plus there'll be record
> droughts and floods and some record-shattering hurricanes,
> too. There will also be a collapse of the dollar, scattered depres-
> sions in various states, a record number of personal, banking,
> and S&L bankruptcies, alongside numerous criminal convic-
> tions on Wall Street.
>
> Crime will appear virtually out of control in many major
> cities, and a riot in Los Angeles will turn out to be the most
> expensive in history. Some of the largest corporations in
> America will lay off employees ten thousand at a time. Various
> executives from companies like Enron and WorldCom Inc. will
> serve lengthy prison terms. Oil will soar to more than $140/
> barrel, and gold will climb past $1,000 per ounce, both new
> all-time highs, and both in 2008.
>
> Then in the early part of 2008, there will be a global financial
> panic with stocks in general performing worse in January than
> in any other January going back for decades and that stocks

will be down for five consecutive months (November–March) for first time since 1942. Citigroup, America's largest bank, will slash its dividend 41 percent and get a hefty cash infusion from a number of overseas investors. Because of the dividend cut, it will be eliminated from America's Finest Companies. Then later in 2008 the crisis will knock AFC behemoths Lehman Brothers and American International Group off the list. Lehman will be the first AFC company forced into bankruptcy and AIG barely survives by government bailout and takeover.

Now, do you still want to buy some stocks, America's Finest or otherwise?

Most likely, your answer would have been a resounding "No." Yet that would have been a bad answer. Stocks on the whole generally outperform all other investments when given enough time, preferably at least 10 years.

The May 19, 2008 *Barron's* had an article by Thomas Healey and Mark Oshida entitled "A Passion for Profit." The table on page 49 showed the annual total return (price appreciation plus reinvested dividends) from U.S. stocks was 11.0 percent between 1900 and the end of 2005. First-edition books were said to have earned 12.0 percent per year, but the period covered was only 20 years from 1982 to 2002. Next came fine violins at 10.0 percent (1980–2005), artwork at 8.5 percent (1990–2000), Bordeaux wines at 8.0 percent (1986–1996), and lastly collector's stamps at 7.0 percent (2002–2006).

Since these are all highly illiquid markets, I don't know how trustworthy the numbers are. What I do know is that stocks have a very long record of reliable inflation-beating results. There's no close second I'm aware of unless it's raw timberland, but few individuals can invest small amounts of money into timber.

If you picture investing in stocks as buying pieces of paper that go up and down in value every day like yo-yos—and a lot of people unfortunately do—I understand why you might be hesitant about owning shares of any companies. But you don't have to look at them that way. A better viewpoint is that you become part owner of one or more of the finest businesses in this country.

My guess is that if you had enough money, you wouldn't mind owning all of Coca-Cola or Wal-Mart or Tootsie Roll Industries or Colgate-Palmolive or Procter & Gamble or McDonald's. You know they're well established corporations with superior credentials. You also instinctively know that year after year their earnings and dividends should continue to grow, and you have no reason to suspect they won't remain viable enterprises for as long as you live and even for decades after that.

Although you don't have the billions of dollars it would take to buy a Wal-Mart or PepsiCo and make it your own, you do have enough money to buy a few shares of one, if not both, of these companies. Those shares, or pieces of the business, represent your proportionate ownership of Coca-Cola, McDonald's, or whatever else you buy. They're great businesses to own parts of, and they're bound to increase in value over the long term—the next 5, 10, 15, 20 years, or more—because the values of their businesses are growing every year. That hasn't been the case with companies like a Ford or a General Motors, which never qualified to be in America's Finest.

DOING THE MATH

By assembling a portfolio of at least five companies in America's Finest Companies, each in a different industry, and by adding to the portfolio on a regular basis with as much money as you can and as often as you can, you should consistently—and safely—double your money every five to seven years (approximately 12 to 15 percent compounded annually).

By investing only in corporate thoroughbreds, you can take a lot of worry out of your life. You can quit worrying about inflation, interest rates, government legislation, recessions, and the like, and

TABLE 1.3   Money Doubles Every 5 to 7 Years in AFC

Annual Rate of Return	Initial Investment	Year 1	Year 2	Year 3	Year 4	Year 5	Year 6	Year 7
10%	$1,000	$1,100	$1,210	$1,331	$1,464	$1,610	$1,771	$1,948
11%	$1,000	$1,110	$1,232	$1,368	$1,518	$1,685	$1,870	$2,076
12%	$1,000	$1,120	$1,254	$1,404	$1,572	$1,761	$1,972	$2,209
13%	$1,000	$1,130	$1,277	$1,443	$1,631	$1,843	$2,083	$2,354
14%	$1,000	$1,140	$1,300	$1,482	$1,689	$1,925	$2,195	$2,502
15%	$1,000	$1,150	$1,323	$1,521	$1,749	$2,011	$2,313	$2,660

Source: The Staton Institute® Inc.

about how they will affect your investments. Because you're going to invest only in the finest that American industry has to offer, you can let the companies do the worrying for you.

Think of yourself barreling down a fury of white water like the Gauley River in West Virginia, which has the meanest rapids east of the Mississippi. I've rafted the entire length of this beautiful river three times. You have to cross the world's largest earthen dam to get to the foot of the Gauley. It's extremely intimidating to look well over 100 feet down at the treacherous water gushing through the chutes at the bottom of the dam. The roar is so loud it's hard to hear anyone talk.

I was mildly terrified (all right, I was scared to death) the first time we put our raft into the water, despite the fact I knew we had a reliable guide to get us safely through the roughest parts. Contrary to what I thought, the most dangerous part of white water rafting isn't shuttling through the turbulent rapids. It's people clowning around with the paddles and hitting one another in the face. The next most dangerous thing is trying to stand up in the fast moving shallow water and getting a foot caught under a rock. That's an easy way to drown. Despite the threats, the Gauley River isn't menacing when you know what you're doing.

Buying shares of companies in America's Finest Companies isn't menacing either because these companies know what they're doing and have proven it for at least the past 10 years or longer. They know how to circumnavigate problems in business and the economy and how to take maximum advantage of the opportunities. Placing your money into a portfolio of them is about as sure a bet as you can make. Two hundred plus years of American investment history proves that.

LEARNING THE HARD WAY

As America's Money Coach®, I am a trainer, an instructor, and an investment guide. I am not a drill sergeant. I coach people to manage their money themselves, to take charge of their financial affairs, and to achieve financial security. I learned what I know the hard way. [I and Mary, my wife and partner, also manage money for individual investors and small businesses through Staton Financial Advisors LLC (www.statonfinancial.com)]. By financial security, I mean having enough money to enjoy life and not outliving your money.

Having graduated from the Wharton School (University of Pennsylvania in Philadelphia) with an MBA in finance in 1971, I toured Europe for 12 weeks with my roommate and then settled down as a freshman analyst with Interstate Securities (now part of Wachovia Corp.) in Charlotte, North Carolina. Interstate had a small equity (stock) research department with a CPA, a nice fellow, as its director. One of the early lessons I learned at Interstate was never to make a CPA the head of your research department. They may know their numbers, but they're usually not the greatest stock pickers.

Since I knew virtually nothing about stocks, the stock market, investing, or the economy, I was immediately assigned to review customer portfolios and make suggestions about what to buy and to sell. I'm glad our customers didn't know how little I knew. At the time, even I didn't realize how little I knew, but somehow I muddled through.

Early in my career, the stock market entered a protracted bear market that wouldn't finish killing investors until December 1974, two years after it began. This bear market was the most savage since the 1930s up to that time. It was my first but certainly not my last. The closing Dow Jones industrial average (the principal market index that major network news now report every night) peaked in early 1973 at 1,052 and finally troughed 20 months later at 578, a 45 percent plunge.

Most of the stocks that my department of analysts and I were recommending did far worse. Some fell 80 percent or more, and that was not particularly atypical. Brokerage houses across America were enduring similar fates. In addition to watching all my recommendations being pounded to the floor, I lost about 75 percent of my personal portfolio (approximately $300,000) in the carnage. After it was all over, but while I was still thinking the world might end any day, I decided it was time to take a different tack. By then I had been put in charge of the research efforts. Toward the end of 1975 I was officially named research director and an officer of the firm.

I set out on a quest to discover (1) how to keep from losing money and (2) how to make substantial profits investing in companies. I had just entered a three-year program to become a chartered financial analyst (CFA), considered to be The Gold Standard in securities analysis and money management. The most important thing I learned in the CFA program was about a book called *Security Analysis* by Benjamin Graham and David Dodd. Though this book was no longer used in the CFA program, I thought I needed to own it. So I purchased it and began the slog through more than 600 pages.

Followers of the Graham and Dodd method of investing, as it's called, don't mind down or bear markets because they bring a lot of solid companies formerly selling at so-called fair or even high prices down to a bargain level. You might say we are the Wal-Mart shoppers of Wall Street. We love low prices and will love them every day they're available.

Graham himself and his money management clients suffered greatly during the Great Depression. However, the market took off in 1933. Stocks on the whole rose 67 percent, the second best year ever. (The best was 1915, when stocks were up 82 percent following the July–December market closing at the outset of World War I.) As well as the market did, Graham did better. Even including the 1929–1932 period, between 1929 and 1956, Graham and his partner Gerald Newman produced a compound annual return of 17 percent, a phenomenal record even to this date. During the same period, the Dow Jones industrials eked out a measly 1.8 percent compounded annual return. Graham and his partner beat the Dow average by a 10-to-1 margin!

I uncovered some valuable lessons that Graham developed, particularly margin of safety, and took them to heart. There's more about this in Chapter 3, "Valuable Investing Lessons from Benjamin Graham." Warren Buffett, Graham's best and wealthiest student (he's worth more than $60 billion) at Columbia, likened margin of safety to building a bridge to accommodate 40 tons when nothing heavier than 10 tons ever crosses it. It's akin to building levees to withstand category 5 hurricanes or 100-year floods that rarely occur or that have a slim chance of happening.

Buffett has said about Ben Graham:

> I consider there to be three basic ideas, ideas that if they are really ground into your intellectual framework, I don't see how you could help but do reasonably well in stocks. None of them are complicated. None of them take mathematical talent or anything of the sort.

[Graham] said you should look at stocks as small pieces of the business. Said another way, "It's far better to own a portion of the Hope diamond than 100 percent of a rhinestone."

Look at [market] fluctuations as your friend rather than your enemy—profit from folly rather than participate in it.

And in the last chapter [of Graham's *The Intelligent Investor*], he said the three most important words of investing: "margin of safety."

I think those ideas, 100 years from now, will still be regarded as the three cornerstones of sound investing.

[Graham] wasn't about brilliant investments and he wasn't about fads or fashion. He was about sound investing, and I think sound investing can make you very wealthy if you're not in too big of a hurry. And it never makes you poor, which is better.

As Interstate's research director, I urged all the analysts to become students of Benjamin Graham and to adhere strictly to the margin of safety concept. In late 1974, unlike other firms in the industry then and still today, we began keeping records of all our recommendations and how they stacked up against the market indexes. We also told our brokers and customers that when we thought it was time to sell a stock we'd say so in writing. (That's a rarity on Wall Street and within the financial community.) Margin of safety worked. The research record, published annually, served as a check.

When I left Interstate at the end of 1985, our research department had compiled an 11-year performance record that was the envy of Wall Street. The annual *Stock Trader's Almanac* has encouraged this sort of diligent record keeping and performance tracking since the first 1968 edition and has provided the simple forms needed to do so. They are available in the printed edition and online at *www.stocktradersalmanac.com*. A few examples appear in Figure 1.1 on pages 19–22.

STOCKS: THE MOST PROFITABLE INVESTMENT

Stocks have always been, and will continue to be, the most profitable form of investment for most people. The historical evidence is overwhelming, so I'll show you only a little of it. After that, you'll learn the value of a simple investment program, and we'll examine what it takes for a company to become one of America's Finest.

PORTFOLIO PRICE RECORD 2009 (FIRST HALF)

Place purchase price above stock name and weekly closes below

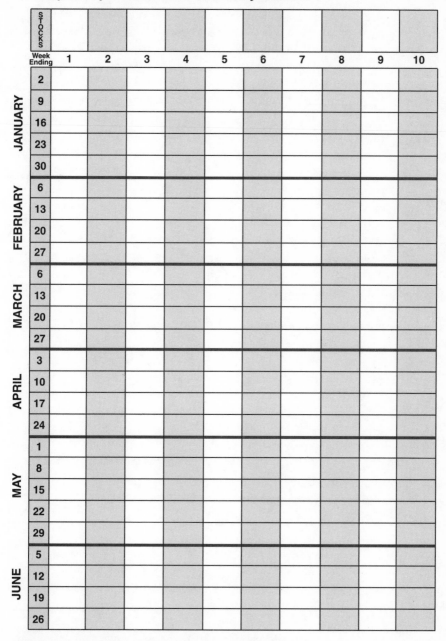

FIGURE 1.1   Stock Trader's Almanac Record Keeping Pages

Source: Yale Hirsch and Jeffrey Hirsch, Stock Trader's Almanac 2009 (Wiley, 2009).

PORTFOLIO PRICE RECORD 2009 (SECOND HALF)

Place purchase price above stock name and weekly closes below

STOCKS / Week Ending	1	2	3	4	5	6	7	8	9	10
JULY 3										
10										
17										
24										
31										
AUGUST 7										
14										
21										
28										
SEPTEMBER 4										
11										
18										
25										
OCTOBER 2										
9										
16										
23										
30										
NOVEMBER 6										
13										
20										
27										
DECEMBER 4										
11										
18										
25										

FIGURE 1.1   Continued

WEEKLY INDICATOR DATA 2009 (FIRST HALF)

Week Ending	Dow Jones Industrial Average	Net Change for Week	Net Change on Friday	Net Change Next Monday	S&P or NASDAQ	NYSE Ad-vances	NYSE De-clines	New Highs	New Lows	CBOE Put/Call Ratio	90-Day Treas. Rate	Moody's AAA Rate
JANUARY												
2												
9												
16												
23												
30												
FEBRUARY												
6												
13												
20												
27												
MARCH												
6												
13												
20												
27												
APRIL												
3												
10												
17												
24												
MAY												
1												
8												
15												
22												
29												
JUNE												
5												
12												
19												
26												

FIGURE 1.1   Continued

WEEKLY INDICATOR DATA 2009 (SECOND HALF)

	Week Ending	Dow Jones Industrial Average	Net Change for Week	Net Change on Friday	Net Change Next Monday	S&P or NASDAQ	NYSE Advances	NYSE Declines	New Highs	New Lows	CBOE Put/Call Ratio	90-Day Treas. Rate	Moody's AAA Rate
JULY	3												
	10												
	17												
	24												
	31												
AUGUST	7												
	14												
	21												
	28												
SEPTEMBER	4												
	11												
	18												
	25												
OCTOBER	2												
	9												
	16												
	23												
	30												
NOVEMBER	6												
	13												
	20												
	27												
DECEMBER	4												
	11												
	18												
	25												

FIGURE 1.1   Continued

Your own federal government and the state where you live will gladly help you make more money if you'd be interested in deferring taxes for years, if not decades, down the road. Most people don't know how to take advantage of this generosity, but I'll teach you how to make it work for you.

Being your own money manager sounds like a lot of hard work, but really it isn't. Is 60 minutes too much time to spend each year? That's about the length of time many Americans use for lunch each day. I'm asking for only about one hour annually. That's all it takes, and you can become a millionaire if you'll stick with this easy-to-start-and-maintain investment program.

If you don't need the annual cash dividends from your stocks for personal use, I'll show you how to make them make more money. I'll even show you how to buy shares directly and bypass the stockbroker. You can save hundreds if not thousands of dollars on transactions costs—and make tens of thousands from those savings—over a lifetime of investing.

Cannot people realize how large an income is thrift?
— Marcus Tullius Cicero (great Roman orator and
politician, 106–43 b.c.)

You have to open your investment account somewhere. The mechanics aren't difficult. I'll show you how to get started the easiest way.

Do you want to start your children on an investment program, as I did with my daughter Gracie in 1978 and son Will in 1989? The earlier they start, the more successful they'll be. What about giving money and securities to your children? We'll look at that option, too.

2

It Pays to Be Bullish

*It ain't so much the things we don't know that gets us into trouble.
It's the things we do know that just ain't so.*
—ARTEMUS WARD, AMERICAN HUMORIST,
PEN NAME OF CHARLES FARRAR BROWN (1834–1867)

POINTS TO REMEMBER
- Stocks rise most over the long term.
- Negativity keeps you out of stocks.
- Value stocks are number 1—the best risk/reward ratio.

Millions of Americans are afraid to buy shares of companies. They get goose bumps just thinking about putting money into stocks, even those of the top-rated companies, because they reason that one day prices might go over the cliff as they did between 1929 and 1932, between 1973 and 1974, in 1987, and from 2000 through 2002. Investing in stocks is as terrifying to them as skydiving would be to me. That's why I don't do it—skydiving that is.

Besides this large group of people who don't want to enter investment waters with stocks as the vehicle, a second large group consists of those who own shares of companies but are antsy during the day and don't sleep well at night either. They're always nervous about stocks.

When stocks go down, they worry they'll fall farther. When stocks go up, they worry they'll soon stop going up and then go down. Or, if they don't know which way stock prices are headed, they worry that they don't know and that the direction might not be the way they want to go. Not being nervous about the stock market makes them nervous. These people are worrywarts and don't need to be. They're like the person comedian George Burns described "who feels bad when he feels good for fear that he'll feel worse when he feels better."

If you fit into any of these categories, I want to convince you: Stocks are a great place to have your money—the safest, least risky place of all. Just for the moment, put aside any hesitation you may have and accept these words: You can always change your mind later. I believe that when you finish this chapter you'll know why stocks have always been, and will continue to be, the number one investment for almost everyone. I don't want you to feel about investing in stocks as Gertrude Stein, the American writer, did about life in general: "There ain't any answer. There ain't going to be any answer. There never has been an answer. That's the answer."

Picture this. It's January 1, 2005, and, after suffering through a lackluster 2004 in your stock portfolio, you suddenly have the 100 percent certain insight that the following is going to occur before the year is out:

1. Oil rises 66 percent.
2. Natural gas leaps 130 percent.
3. General Motors and Ford see their bonds downgraded to junk.
4. Two hurricanes, Katrina and Rita, followed by Wilma, will not only devastate one of America's greatest cities but also wreak record havoc in a number of states during the most active hurricane season on record.
5. Part of the Gulf Coast is wiped out, and nearly 30 percent of the United States' refining capacity is shut down.
6. Terrorists unload their bombs in London's tube system, not once but twice.
7. Numerous commodity prices explode on the upside.
8. America reports continuing record trade deficits.
9. A very large commodity/derivatives company (Refco) implodes.
10. President George W. Bush's popularity sinks to an all-time low.

What would you do? Liquidate your portfolio and head to cash? Take profits in your home? Leave the country and move to a safer place? Bury your head in the sand and hope to survive? All the above?

At the very least, you'd think the stock market would collapse. But it didn't, nor did the world come anywhere close to an end. Yet everything above occurred before Halloween of 2005.

What history clearly teaches anyone who has ears and chooses to listen is that there are always serious problems somewhere. There never has been smooth sailing, and I doubt there ever will be. Even so, well assembled portfolios, though they stumble once in awhile, continue to grow, given enough time and patience.

The August 13, 1979, cover of *BusinessWeek* featured a crumbled bunch of stock certificates beneath the headline in all caps, "THE DEATH OF EQUITIES: How Inflation Is Destroying the Stock Market." The inside article went to great lengths to show why "the age of equities may be over." They quoted such luminaries as Robert S. Salomon Jr., general partner in Salomon Brothers, who observed, "We are running the risk of immobilizing a substantial portion of the world's wealth in someone's stamp collection." Thomas Martin of American Asset Management chimed in that "we are coming down with the European disease." The article concluded with this gem of wisdom: "Today the old attitude of buying solid stocks as a cornerstone for one's life savings and retirement has simply disappeared." The Dow Jones industrial average stood at 875.

Shortly before the Great Market Crash of 1987 (when the Dow dropped 23 percent in one day), I wrote about "peace and the coming Super Boom," which in fact materialized. The Berlin Wall disappeared, the Cold War between Russia and the United States ended, various world economies went on a tear, and the Dow Jones Industrials rose for an unprecedented nine consecutive years (1991–1999). And all the time, there was doubt after doubt after doubt, negative headline after negative headline after negative headline about the markets, interest rates, the economy, and the state of the world in general.

According to the *Bull & Bear* newspaper from summer 1991:

> A historic economic summit on the future of Western Civilization and the U.S. economy recently took place the weekend of February 9, 1991, at Bally's Hotel in Las Vegas. At that meeting, John King, editor of *Future Economic Trends*, made the following incredible predictions: Interest Rates will soar; the Prime Rate will reach 35%. Gold will surpass $1,800 per oz. Silver will reach $120 per oz. Real Estate will fall still

lower, perhaps to 1 cent on the dollar. The price of oil will fall from $20 to $10 a barrel, then $9, then $5, then $3, and finally, to 25 cents a barrel. The Dow Jones Average will retrace its historic low of 41.

When that meeting was held, the Dow was at 2,831, triple the level of 12 years earlier. By the end of December 1991, the Dow had risen to an all-time high of 3,169 as *BusinessWeek*'s cover focused on "HIGH ANXIETY." Pessimism abounded.

At mid-December 1993, Robert Prechter of *The Elliott Wave Theorist* said that "the stock market has achieved its predicted peak of 3,710 and is now ready to fall. Bonds have begun a bear market that will last for years." Sorry, but Prechter was way off base about both stocks and bonds. *Investment Quality Trends* stated, "By every historic measure of investment value, the market is classically over-valued." The Dow was 3,700 with a 2.7 percent dividend yield.

On January 13, 1995, I published a lengthy special report enti-tled "The BIGGEST Boom in History Is Now Underway." In it I said, among other things:

> Despite all the negatives you're reading and hearing from the media and most other newsletters, it's important to stick with the information in this report and ignore anything and anyone that wants to throw you off the track.
>
> The majority of forecasters cannot and will not see a Super Boom, or anything close to it, or the huge profit gains that will also accrue. But economic forecasters, in this country or any-place else, have never been famous for their foresight. Just over 12 years ago, 365 British practitioners of the dismal science wrote *The Financial Times* bemoaning Margaret Thatcher's "ruin-ous policies." Their letter, exactly to the month, was printed as Britain kicked off its longest growth period since 1945.

As my report came out, the Dow was at 3,908.

Skipping forward to 1996, *Barron's* March 25 cover featured "Why This Market Looks So Dangerous." Two weeks earlier, *U.S. News & World Report* warned on its cover, "The Aging Bull Market: Investor Beware!" And *BusinessWeek*, not to be left out, headlined, "Economic Anxiety." The Dow was close to another record high around 5,600 and change.

Need I say more? Optimists are continual moneymakers. Pessimists, those who are lead by their emotions rather than by the facts and who can always tell you what's wrong or going to be wrong, are losers. They are losers at life. They are losers with their money. And, sad to say, unless they turn around their thinking, they always will be losers.

Before we get into why stocks are right for almost everyone, I'll share a little history about how stocks came to be and why they always go up given enough time.

THE HISTORY OF STOCKS

By the time Columbus and his crew set sail for what he thought were the East Indies (he landed in the Caribbean instead in 1492, lost, battered, and overcome with dysentery), shares of various commodities and what were then called joint stock companies were actively bought and sold in Antwerp, Belgium. The city of Antwerp claims that, of the world's 160-odd stock exchanges, its exchange is the oldest, having been founded in 1531. Amsterdam lays claim to the second with a start-up date of 1602.

Stock certificates of ownership were sold to investors in some European countries to finance powerhouse enterprises like the United East India Company, which came to life in 1602. This phenomenal company returned about 18 percent annually to investors for three decades ($1 grew to more than $143), an incredible performance, and it remained in business until 1799.

Stock trading on a limited basis existed well before the Christian era. The early Romans formed joint stock companies and sold pieces of them to the public. The word "company" is from the Latin *cum* (with) and *panis* (bread) because business, even in those days, was often conducted over a meal as it so frequently is today. Under the law, joint stock companies of that time could do just two things: government contracting and tax collecting. What fantastic businesses to invest in! Capital (money) was raised by selling *partes* (shares) to willing investors.

Securities markets in the United States can be traced to the late 1700s. In 1789, Congress authorized and issued $80 million of government bonds to pay down war debts and to inject money into this fledgling country's economy, thereby creating the first money market. According to *American Heritage* magazine, "The new

United States was desperately short of money in any reliable or secured form. Accounts were still kept in pounds, shillings, and pence."

Brokers (they were initially called stockjobbers) traded securities literally in the street. The word "broker" is derived from a term used by wine merchants, who broached (tapped) their wine kegs. "Broacher" was later shortened to "broker." Brokers primarily bought and sold government bonds, as well as any stocks offered by the infant First Bank of the United States. When the weather turned sour, they retreated to coffeehouses (presumably to warm up) and carried on their business.

The several dozen established brokers operated a highly risky market of a sort. James Madison was so concerned about the risk that he fired off a letter to Thomas Jefferson warning that "stock jobbing drowns every other subject. The coffeehouse is an eternal buzz with the gamblers." Since stock brokering, trading, or whatever you want to call it was so risky in the early days, the phrase "gambling in the stock market" still has deep meaning for most Americans.

In 1792, 24 brokers and merchants gathered at Corre's Hotel in New York City to sign the Buttonwood Agreement, which was written front and back on a sheet of paper:

> We, the Subscribers, Brokers for the Purchase and Sale of Public Stocks, do hereby solemnly pledge ourselves to each other that we will not buy or sell, from this day, for any person whatsoever, any kind of Public Stock at a less rate than one-quarter per cent Commission on the Special value, and that we will give preference to each other in our negotiations.

This unusual contract laid the foundation for the later New York Stock & Exchange Board (the Big Board, formed in 1817). The following winter the brokers built a home for themselves, the Tontine Coffee House, on the corner of Water and Wall Streets in New York, then the nation's capital. The famous street named Wall, one of the best-known in the world, is only four blocks long. It lies on the site of the original wall (a stockade) built at the tip of Manhattan Island.

The original inhabitants of the island, the Lenape Indians, called their island Mannahatta for thousands of years, long before Henry Hudson sailed up the river now named after him. Mannahatta was home to more than 50 ecosystems and heavily populated with wolves, mountain lions, turkeys, and white-tailed deer. The skies were often darkened by thousands of pigeons. Shorebirds were counted in the millions.

In 1644, Dutch settlers laid a brushwood barrier to keep Indians out and cattle in. Nine years later Governor Peter Stuyvesant replaced it with a nine-foot-high palisade. Wall Street is named for this barrier, not for the high buildings on both sides of the street that seem like walls.

"Wall Street" is the common name for the American financial institutions, markets, and mechanisms that formalized and democratized the capital-formation (money-raising) process to help companies thrive. Wall Street, with the New York Stock Exchange (NYSE) as its flagship, has allowed millions of Americans to participate in this country's unmatched growth through the ownership of common stocks. *Life* magazine, in its special Spring 1992 issue dedicated to the Big Board, observed:

> For two centuries, men (and much more recently women) have met at the convergence of Wall and Broad streets in lower Manhattan to buy, sell and haggle, all in the name of capitalism. They have not always done so politely . . . or fairly. But as Americans traded, so the country was built. Canals, Railroads, Automobiles, Electronics. Ideas may spring from laboratories, but the money that turns them into reality is raised here.

With capitalism rapidly spreading across the globe, new stock exchanges sprouted behind what used to be the Iron Curtain. Poland opened a stock market in early 1991 in the old Communist Party headquarters (ironic, isn't it?). The Polish market was funded by British money and modeled after France's Bourse (another name for stock exchange or place of meeting to conduct business). Initially, trading took place only once a week in five different companies, but there are hundreds today because the government long ago privatized more than 3,500 firms that had been under its control. Communist Party headquarters must be luxurious because St. Petersburg followed Poland by opening its exchange on the third floor of its own party building. (*The Wall Street Journal* calls a stock exchange the "icon of capitalism.")

What exactly is a common stock? It's a security (stock certificate) representing proportionate ownership (an investor's share) of a publicly traded company. It's estimated that there are as many as 20,000 public companies in America. You can buy shares in most of them through any stockbroker. These shares are traded (bought and sold) either on the New York Stock Exchange (NYSE), the American Stock Exchange (AMEX), NASDAQ (National Association of Securities Dealers Automated Quotation System), or on several regional and electronic exchanges. They range in price from a penny to well north of $100,000 for Warren Buffett's Berkshire Hathaway on the NYSE.

Where did the word "stock" come from? Here's my theory. William Bradford, governor of the Plymouth Colony, reported that under an agreement with the Pilgrims' sponsors in England, "all profit" (crops, fish, and trade goods) would "remain still in the common stock." All Pilgrims were allowed to obtain their food and goods from the common stock (to share), just as all investors can make their profits by investing (sharing) in the common stock of public companies.

Stocks originally were priced in points instead of dollars. One point equaled $1.00. One-half point equaled $0.50, one-quarter point $0.25, one-eighth point $0.125. Stocks traded in eighths rather than tenths like money. That may seem strange, but there's a practical reason. When stock trading began in colonial days, coins were in short supply. To make coinage go further, Spanish silver dollars were sliced into halves, then halved and halved again. The result was that the dollar could be divided into eight bits, and each bit was one-eighth of a dollar. Together, eight bits became a piece of eight. This is also the origin of the expression "two bits," which would be $0.25. Prices today are quoted to the penny and in some instances to the hundredth of a penny.

HOW STOCKS WORK

Here's how stocks work. In this example, MakeMoney Enterprises (MME), a fictitious company, has one million shares outstanding. Each share sells for 20 (note that stock prices are quoted without the dollar sign), so MME's total stock is worth $20 million. If you invest $4,000 in MME at its current price, you can purchase 200 shares.

When you purchase your shares, you own part of the company. Although it's a tiny part (1/5,000), it's all yours. What good is part ownership? Let's use this example to find out.

MME earns $2 million after taxes in 2008. Dividing earnings by the number of shares (one million), each share earned $2.00. MME pays shareholders money out of earnings, a cash dividend, as incentive for you to buy and hold its shares. (Not all companies pay dividends, but the bulk of America's Finest Companies do.) Out of the $2.00 per share of earnings, MME pays you half, $1.00. The dollar is your immediate reward for owning a piece of the company.

MME retains (keeps) the other half and plows it back into the business for much the same reason that humans eat daily to survive. Retained earnings go for research and product development, to build a new plant, to purchase new equipment, to hire more people—to grow.

By keeping $1.00, MME is now worth $1.00 more per share for each share outstanding than before. The company's total asset value increases by $1 million (one million shares times $1.00 per share retained). MME's business prospers. After five years, its earnings have risen 50 percent to $3.00 per share. And as further reward to you for holding the shares instead of selling them, the company boosts its dividend (as it has done every year since you bought your shares) to the newest annual rate of $1.50. Each year it keeps as much as it pays you, and the kept amount annually enhances MME's value.

Your annual income is increasing. Ten years after you buy the stock, earnings per share are $5.00. Your dividend is now $2.50 per share, up 150 percent from the year of purchase. The company keeps $2.50 per share that year, $2.5 million total, to further boost asset value by that amount.

Question: If the share price is 20 in the year you buy into MME, and the shares are not overpriced, do you think the price will be higher five years later? Is it likely to be even higher 10 years later? (See Table 2.1 on page 34.)

Answer: If the share price maintains the same relationship to its earnings and dividend, it will rise to 30 in five years and to 50 in another five years. Your original investment of 200 shares at 20 each will be worth $10,000 in 10 years. Your cost is $4,000, and your profit will be $6,000. In 10 years, your annual income from MME will jump from $200 to $500. Your yield on original

TABLE 2.1   Buying into MME

	2008	2013	2018
MME earnings per share	$2.00	$3.00	$5.00
MME dividend per share	$1.00	$1.50	$2.50
MME retains (keeps)	$1.00	$1.50	$2.50
MME share price	20	?	?

Source: The Staton Institute® Inc.

investment will rise to 12.5 percent ($500 divided by $4,000), a handsome return.

Over a period of years, the majority of publicly owned companies grow. (All the companies in the AFC universe are growing; otherwise they wouldn't be included.) Growing companies earn more money and pay out more cash as dividends. Growing companies plow back an increasing stream of earnings into their businesses, thus enhancing their value. This explains why stock prices always go up in the long run. The Dow Jones industrial average, the most famous measure of stock prices, rose from 28.45, its all-time low in 1896, to more than 14,000 before the end of 2007. That growth is from price appreciation alone and excludes cash dividends.

THE DOW JONES INDUSTRIAL AVERAGE

You need to know a little background about the Dow Jones industrial average because it is by far the most widely followed stock market index in the world. Around the time of what is sometimes known as "the other great depression" in 1893, stocks were for gamblers. Prudent, conservative investors purchased only bonds.

Charles Henry Dow (along with partners Edward Davis Jones and Charles Milford Bergstresser) founded Dow, Jones & Company in 1882 at 15 Wall Street in a tiny basement. They produced handwritten daily news bulletins known as flimsies, which were delivered to subscribers in New York City's financial district. Seven years later on July 8, 1889, Dow Jones' "Customers' Afternoon Letter" became the now famous *Wall Street Journal.* Advertising in *The Journal* was $0.20 a line. The four-page publication itself cost only two pennies.

The Dow Jones company wanted a gauge, a thermometer, for the growth of America; so the Dow Jones industrial average was born. Whereas there are more than 2,800 companies of all sorts listed on the New York Stock Exchange today, at that time about 20 percent were railroads. Most companies' stocks were illiquid, that is, they couldn't be readily bought or sold without markedly disturbing the price.

From 1884 to 1896 Dow Jones published several different stock averages before the industrial average was first published on May 26, 1896, with a dozen industrial companies and a beginning level of 40.94. It has since soared above 14,000 and changed considerably. General Electric (originally Edison General Electric Company) is the sole survivor from the original Dow 12 among the 30 current companies, though GE was removed and added twice, remaining on the list since 1907.

Quite some time ago, H. Bradlee Perry, then chairman of the David L. Babson investment counseling firm, neatly summed up investing in stocks this way:

> In the long run the price of just about every individual stock and market value of all stocks together are determined by the growth of earnings and dividends. This is so simple that many of the sophisticated people in our [investing] field seem to overlook it. That is too bad because it does provide the basis for a very sound and unworrisome investment approach.
>
> Over the span of many decades corporate profits and dividends have trended upward in all industrial nations because their economies have expanded, not without business cycle interruptions of course, but in an inexorable trend of long-term growth.[1]

In their book, *Investment Analysis and Portfolio Management,* Jerome B. Cohen and Edward D. Zinbarg, state that:

> It can be demonstrated by statistical analysis that stock price changes are often more closely related to dividend changes than to changes in reported earnings. One possible explanation for this fact is that since reported earnings do not necessarily represent "true" earnings, investors look to dividends for an indication of what management really thinks earnings are.[2]

[1] H. Bradlee Perry, *The Babson Staff Letter* (Cambridge, MA: David L. Babson and Company, Inc.).
[2] Jerome B. Cohen and Edward D. Zinbarg, *Investment Analysis and Portfolio Management* (Homewood, IL: Richard D. Irwin, 1967), p. 221.

You can participate in America's future growth by owning shares of common stock in a variety of businesses. But by investing in companies in America's Finest Companies, you're virtually assured that their businesses will continue to thrive and increase in value. As they do, so will the value of the stocks themselves and the cash dividends they pay. This is why you want to own your part of corporate America with America's Finest Companies.

The great patriot Patrick Henry, addressing the Virginia Convention on March 23, 1775 (in his famous "Give me liberty or give me death" speech), stated, "I have but one lamp by which my feet are guided, and that is the lamp of experience. I know of no way of judging of the future but by the past."

The past is important to investors because it gives us a glimpse of the potential future returns we can expect from our investments. The point I stress throughout this book is that stocks have always outperformed other investments for more than two hundred years, and America's Finest Companies have outperformed most other stocks. That being true, why would you want to invest your money in anything besides America's Finest Companies?

I was fortunate to receive my MBA in finance from the Wharton School of the University of Pennsylvania in 1971. The prestigious *Financial Times* newspaper named Wharton the number one global business school in February 2008. Today the MBA school's best-known teacher is Jeremy J. Siegel, Russell E. Palmer Professor of Finance, and widely known as the Wizard of Wharton. Siegel is known as a Wizard because he's collected probably more data about the history of various investments than any other person. His best-selling book, *Stocks for the Long Run*, came out in early 2008 in a fourth edition.

According to Siegel, the value of $1.00 invested in 1802 is shown in Table 2.2. Taking into account the loss of purchasing power due to inflation from 1801 to 2006, that same $1.00 grew to the values shown in Table 2.3. Note that the value of the U.S. dollar has plummeted to $0.06 because of inflation. All of that decline has occurred since the early 1930s. Until then, $1.00 was $1.00 was $1.00.

What's important to learn from Siegel's research is that, since the end of World War II, the return from stocks on the whole, with inflation taken out, generated a compound annual return of 6.9 percent. Siegel writes, "This means that purchasing power has, on average, doubled in the stock market about every 10 years."

TABLE 2.2   Following the Dollar

Stocks	Bonds	Treasury Bills	Gold	Inflation (CPI)
$12.7 million	$18,235	$5,061	$32.84	$16.84

Source: Jeremy J. Siegel, *Stocks for the Long Run, 4th ed.* (New York: McGraw-Hill, 2008).

TABLE 2.3   Following the Inflation-adjusted Dollar

Stocks	Bonds	Treasury Bills	Gold	U.S. Dollar
$755,163	$1,083	$301	$1.95	$0.06

Source: Jeremy J. Siegel, *Stocks for the Long Run, 4th ed.* (New York: McGraw-Hill, 2008).

Dividends accounted for a little more than half of that 6.9 percent return. And that fact tells us that dividends are highly important to generating strong returns from stocks.

Several pages later Siegel continues, "The superior performance of U.S. equities over the past two centuries is not a special case. Stocks have outperformed fixed-income assets in every country examined and often by an overwhelming margin. International studies have reinforced, not diminished, the case for equities."

Speaking of inflation, for every 30-year period from 1801 through 2006, there were only two when the annual total return from stocks wasn't at least 3.5 percentage points ahead of inflation. The highest real returns (i.e., after inflation is deducted) were in the 1990s and outdistanced inflation by more than 10 percentage points.

JUST HOW RISKY ARE STOCKS?

Some people argue that investing in general, as well as buying individual stocks in particular, is just too risky. So let's take a close look at risk. In our 2,129-page *Webster's Unabridged Dictionary*, the word "risk" means "the chance of injury, damage, or loss; a dangerous chance; a hazard." To run a risk is "to expose oneself to the chance of injury or loss; to endanger oneself; to take a chance." Let's talk first about risk in the Big Picture of life and then narrow it down to supposed investment risk.

There seems to be more interest today in risks of all types, including investment risks, than at any other time. Lightning-fast computers and bloated databases of all kinds beckon oddsmakers to spew out the probability of something bad happening. It's ironic, I think, that few of us rarely see the odds on anything good such as that cars are safer now than ever. In fact, your chances as an individual investor are actually better than when you turn your money over to most professionals (including mutual funds), particularly when you invest for 10 years or longer.

The point is that risks in investing, as in so many areas, are perceived to be much greater than they are. For example, such tragic events as a plane crashing and killing 350 people stand out in our minds. That many die every three days in auto accidents, yet nobody makes much of a stir about it. Likewise, the stock market Great Crash of 1987 was a spectacular, once-in-a-lifetime sell-off, but millions of investors sold their stocks, remained on the sidelines, and missed one of the greatest stock price rises in history through most of the 1990s.

In World War II President Franklin Roosevelt observed that the only thing we have to fear is fear itself. When it comes to managing your money, it is certainly wise to be prudent but to be unnecessarily fearful is counterproductive.

Time magazine's November 27, 2006 issue featured an intriguing article, "Why We Worry About the Things We Shouldn't." The article stated, "We pride ourselves on being the only species that understands the concept of risk, yet we have a confounding habit of worrying about mere possibilities while ignoring probabilities . . . ."

More than 500 times as many people die on U.S. roads every year compared to airline accidents, but far more people are afraid to fly than to drive. We think people would be far likelier to protest a nuclear power plant than to help shut down a tobacco company, yet smoking, not nukes, kills an average of 1,200 Americans per day, about 440,000 per year. In many instances, we as humans don't seem to be able to perceive risk accurately, whether it's about investing or any other subject.

THE PSYCHOLOGY OF INVESTING

Most people probably have never heard of Princeton psychologist Daniel Kahneman or his now deceased research partner Amos Tversky. Yet the two (especially Kahneman) have done more than anyone else to explain why we behave the way we do in various facets of life and particularly in investing. They've researched many areas on what drives entrepreneurs, automobile drivers, and basketball players on a hot shooting night.

In terms of every action that each of us takes, we're always making a choice. Should I do it or not? Each one of us makes this decision hundreds of times every day and seldom realize we're making it, and in virtually all instances we tend to think we know more than we do. We often act out of overconfidence, but emotion, fear, greed, hindsight, and clouded foresight also come into play. Our decisions are frequently based on what we believe and want rather than on what we know and need, especially in the area of money and finances. Our own psychology determines our decision making and personal and business performance.

In the realm of personal finances and investing, Kahneman and Tversky developed in 1979 a concept called prospect theory, which they later named loss aversion. In a nutshell, their research proves that the pain of a financial loss is several times greater than the satisfaction of a financial gain. Therefore, nonprofessionals and professionals alike generally go to greater lengths to avoid realizing a monetary loss than they do to lock in a monetary gain. That kind of avoidance sometimes involves even greater risk than the risk they are trying to avoid.

A simple example is the 1990s mania involving hundreds of dot-com stocks, most of which ultimately turned into dot-bombs. Companies with clever names, no solid business plan, no earnings, and paltry revenue would offer their shares to a greedy public (the pros were sucked in as well) who saw the stocks keep going up and up in price. Value didn't seem to matter.

All was well for a few years before March 2000, when the bubble burst and those same stocks began to slide in price. The farther they declined, the more people didn't want to actually sell their shares and realize a loss, even though they already had a loss.

Let's say Dot-Bomb.com reached $100 a share in March 2000, the month the NASDAQ index closed above 5,000 for the first time. By May 2000 Dot-Bomb could easily have dropped to $70 because, when these stocks went over the peak, it was like an avalanche on the downside. If investors kept their shares, they had a $30 unrealized loss because the stock had gone down that much in value. If they sold, there would still be a $30 loss, but it would have been captured for tax purposes (as a deduction). There would also have been the opportunity to shift into a high-quality company to start to recoup the loss.

The so-called paper, or unrealized, loss doesn't seem real to the majority of investors, whereas selling the shares, which is the same real dollar loss, is painful. What's the difference? There is none, really. A $30 realized loss is the same as a $30 unrealized loss. It's just that somehow selling the losing share feels a lot worse than holding on to it and hoping for a recovery. Realizing the loss is an admonition of failure, and investors are a prideful bunch. In the case of the dot-bombs, people held on far too long and lost the bulk or all of their money, as dozens and dozens of these companies went bankrupt.

The Kahneman-Tversky duo showed us that, if we recall something easily, we tend to think it happened more often than it did, particularly if it's bad, like a plane crash or a severe stock market decline. They also demonstrated that the most recent short-term information is typically the source of long-term money and investment decisions.

Other conclusions we can formulate from their work include:

1. Watching the stock market and the stocks in your portfolio all the time and noticing every blip in the economy is a bad idea.
2. Trying to time moves into and out of stocks (trading) produces mediocre results at best for most investors.
3. The future of stocks and stock returns becomes more and more certain as your time horizon moves farther out.
4. Chasing huge returns (such as buying last year's hottest stock or mutual fund) typically results in huge losses.
5. A corollary is that recent returns and performance say nothing about future returns or performance. Kahneman explained that, if eight people each have a coin flip chance to beat the market each year, then after three years there ought to be at least one who beats the market all three times based solely on the law of probabilities. That person would look supersmart, wouldn't he? But his superior performance would just be the result of chance.
6. Nobody can accurately forecast the economy or the stock market because there is no foreseeable future.

7. Investors are naturally disposed to hanging onto losing stocks and selling their winners early; study after study proves that. Gerald M. Loeb (1900–1974) of E. F. Hutton, who predicted the 1929 Crash, made this crystal clear in his famous book, *The Battle for Investment Survival.* As emphasized in the annual *Stock Trader's Almanac*'s "Strategy, Planning and Record Section," one of Mr. Loeb's main mantras was, "Do not sell solely because you think a stock is 'overvalued.' If you want to sell some of your stocks, in most cases, it is best to go against your emotional inclinations and sell first the issues with losses, the weakest, the most disappointing."

8. It doesn't matter that one of your friends may be making more money with his investments than you and your family; what counts is that you and your family do what's in line with your needs, wants, knowledge, and abilities.

When you look at the typical pyramid that shows up in so many financial planning books, stocks are near the top in risk, whereas government bonds and banking accounts reside at the bottom. We don't know who drew this pyramid, but it isn't exactly correct when you take into account the full definition of risk.

Putting your money into a bank account is also considered to be 100 percent safe because the banking system is backed by the Federal Deposit Insurance Corporation (FDIC). Buying the bonds of highest-quality companies like General Electric is thought to be practically 100 percent safe because the financial strength of these companies, and many more like them, is impeccable. But after taxes and inflation, you'll be behind the eight ball.

If you invest in U.S. government bonds, which are widely known as the world's safest and most liquid security, you're assured by Uncle Sam of getting 100 percent of your principal and interest. We think all but the most rabid doom-and-gloomers would agree with that statement. On the other hand, when you buy shares of companies, regardless of their quality, there's always a chance one or more might go under.

However, if you have a diversified portfolio of America's Finest Companies, the cream of American industry, the odds of the whole thing going bust are approximately zero. Many of these companies easily survived even the Great Depression and every disaster since.

I'm not nearly so concerned about the return on my capital as I am the return of my capital.

—WILL ROGERS, AMERICAN HUMORIST
AND SHOWMAN (1879–1935)

That brilliant investor, Will Rogers, opined that he didn't want to lose any of his original principal. Neither does anyone else we've ever met, yet that's exactly what millions of people do when they plop their hard-earned dollars into a bank, buy corporate or government bonds, or buy investment products from an insurance company. In all these cases they are loaning their money to the bank, to the corporation, to the government, and to the insurance company. These entities take the lenders' (aka investors') money, use it for their own purposes, and pay a fixed rate of return. (Some insurance products do pay a variable return, and some allow you to participate in the stock market's gains.)

If you have money in a bank account earning 3 percent interest each year, the bank assumes (and it's almost always right) that it can earn more than what it's paying you on your money. Ditto for corporations who issue bonds and the insurance companies too. They keep the so-called spread between what they can earn and what they have to pay you comfortably wide. Their goal is to pay you the least you'll take and to earn as much as they can with your money. The more they're able to do this, the wider their spread; hence the more profits they make.

There is nothing wrong with this. You make money, and they make money too. The problem is that you're a lender, and lenders don't make nearly as much as owners. Lenders have far more difficulty keeping ahead of inflation and taxes than owners.

WHY STOCKS ARE THE RIGHT CHOICE

Let's say you earn as much as 5 percent interest (this is well above the historic norm and rates today) annually in your bank account for each of the next 20 years. Also assume that inflation is 4.0 percent a year, roughly the same as it's been since 1945, and that you're in the 25 percent combined tax bracket (which could be low). Table 2.4. shows what your bank account earnings will look like after taxes and inflation take their bites. You'll actually lose ground to the tune of –0.25 percent a year.

TABLE 2.4   Bank Interest Earnings

Interest	5.00%
Less: Taxes	1.25% (25% × 5%)
Less: Inflation	4.00%
Net Return	−0.25%

Source: The Staton Institute® Inc.

Now look at the same example using America's Finest Companies' assuming a 12 to 15 percent annual return. Your net return would be 5.0 to 7.25 percent after taxes and inflation are deducted. That's quite a difference compared with –0.25 percent, a positive difference you can "bank" on for your secure financial future.

Will stocks do as well in the future as they have in the past? Will they remain the number one investment? History resoundingly says the answer is yes. Every long-term study I've ever seen says that, given enough time, stocks will be the finest investment.

Since stocks offer such superior returns on investment, why are certificates of deposit (CDs) and money market funds so popular, especially in tax-deferred retirement plans? I think the answer must be because the principal is considered safe. With a CD, people know exactly what their rate of return is going to be. A money market fund doesn't earn a guaranteed rate, but it is easy to get into and out of, and the return can be closely estimated in three- and six-month periods. Unfortunately, the vast majority of people mistakenly perceive that returns from stocks are wildly uncertain. That is not true except over very short periods of time.

George F. Baker, founder of First National Bank of New York (the forerunner of Citigroup), said that patience is one of three prerequisites for making a fortune in stocks. He knew time is on the side of the investor. He also knew that the longer you invest, the better your results will be. History proves him correct.

No one knows what the future return from common stocks will be, or the inflation rate. If I were to guess, I would say that stocks in general—over the next 30, 40, 50, or 60 years—will grow at their historic rates. The same is true of America's Finest Companies and inflation too. This is important to know for two reasons:

• If stocks and inflation continue to increase at their historic rates, you can project what a given amount of money today will be worth (with inflation taken out) in the future.

TABLE 2.5 The Awesome Power of Compounded Returns

$1000 A Year Compounded at Various Interest Rates of Return for Different Periods (years)

Rate	5	10	15	20	25	30	35	40	45	50
1%	$5,152	$10,567	$16,258	$22,239	$28,526	$35,133	$42,077	$49,375	$57,046	$65,108
2%	5,308	11,169	17,639	24,783	32,671	41,379	50,994	61,610	73,331	86,271
3%	5,468	11,808	19,157	27,676	37,553	49,003	62,276	77,663	95,501	116,181
4%	5,633	12,486	20,825	30,969	43,312	58,328	76,598	98,827	125,871	158,774
5%	5,802	13,207	22,657	34,719	50,113	69,761	94,836	126,840	167,685	219,815
6%	5,975	13,972	24,673	38,993	58,156	83,802	118,121	164,048	225,508	307,756
7%	6,153	14,784	26,888	43,865	67,676	101,073	147,913	213,610	305,752	434,986
8%	6,336	15,645	29,324	49,423	78,954	122,346	186,102	279,781	417,426	619,672
9%	6,523	16,560	32,003	55,765	92,324	148,575	235,125	368,292	573,186	888,441
10%	6,716	17,531	34,950	63,002	108,182	180,943	298,127	486,852	790,795	1,280,299
11%	6,913	18,561	38,190	71,265	126,999	220,913	379,164	645,827	1,095,169	1,852,336
12%	7,115	19,655	41,753	80,699	149,334	270,293	483,463	859,142	1,521,218	2,688,020
13%	7,323	20,814	45,672	91,470	175,850	331,315	617,749	1,145,486	2,117,806	3,909,243
14%	7,536	22,045	49,980	103,768	207,333	406,737	790,673	1,529,909	2,953,244	5,693,754
15%	7,754	23,349	54,717	117,810	244,712	499,957	1,013,346	2,045,954	4,122,898	8,300,374
16%	7,977	24,733	59,925	133,841	289,088	615,162	1,300,027	2,738,478	5,759,718	12,105,353
17%	8,207	26,200	65,649	152,139	341,763	757,504	1,668,994	3,667,391	8,048,770	17,654,717
18%	8,442	27,755	71,939	173,021	404,272	933,319	2,143,649	4,912,591	11,247,261	25,739,451
19%	8,683	29,404	78,850	196,847	478,431	1,150,387	2,753,914	6,580,496	15,712,075	37,503,250
20%	8,930	31,150	86,442	224,026	566,377	1,418,258	3,538,009	8,812,629	21,937,572	54,596,629

Source: Hirsch Organization.

- You can also see what the miracle of compound interest does, especially when you invest in America's Finest Companies and possibly produce 5.0 to 7.25 percent total returns annually after inflation.

In Chapter 6 I'll show you the reality of saving money easily and simply. For now, to illustrate the awesome power of compounding, look at Table 2.5. and see what happens to an annual $1,000 investment at various rates of return over the years. Saving $1,000 each year may seem daunting, but it's less than $3 a day; skip the latte or one beer and secure your financial future.

The Power of Compounding

Compounding can be traced back to the Babylonians. They were the original mathematicians, scientists, engineers, and financiers. Babylon is perhaps most famous for its hanging gardens, protected by a huge wall completely surrounding the city. Thousands of Babylonian writings on clay tablets have been discovered, including tables of compound growth, a law as secure as gravity.

Einstein considered compound interest to be humanity's greatest invention because it allows for the systematic, reliable increase of wealth. Baron de Rothschild, when asked to name the seven wonders of the world, remarked, "I cannot. But I know that the eighth wonder is compound interest."

Sidney Homer, formerly with the investment-banking firm of Salomon Brothers, described the awesome benefits of compound interest this way: "One thousand dollars left to earn interest at 8 percent a year will be worth twenty-three quadrillion dollars [$23,000,000,000,000,000] in four hundred years, but the first hundred years are the hardest."

With the knowledge that stocks produce the best long-term returns, you can maintain a healthy positive attitude toward saving and investing for your future. Sticking with America's Finest Companies increases your returns and reduces your risk because of their longevity and track record of consistently rising earnings and dividends. Now you can let the power of compounding returns take the wheel.

CHAPTER 3

Valuable Investing Lessons from Benjamin Graham

To achieve satisfactory investment results is easier than most people realize. The typical individual investor has a great advantage over the large institutions.

—BENJAMIN GRAHAM

POINTS TO REMEMBER

- Have a simple, sound investing method.
- Stick to it consistently over the long haul.
- Use as little effort as possible and maintain an even temperament.

As stock prices fell relentlessly, day after day, week after week (I was so depressed it often seemed second after second) in the savage bear market of 1973–1974, I was beginning to think I'd entered the wrong profession. What good was it being a Wharton-trained securities analyst when all my stock recommendations were getting clobbered?

When the Great Bear finally went into hibernation in fall 1974, I'd been in the securities profession exactly three years and three months. By that time, I'd been named coordinator of my firm's research efforts. I thought "coordinator" was a strange title, but it was better than nothing and at least it meant I was in charge. Shortly after being appointed to that role, I was made an officer and director of research.

Between January 1973 and December 1974, the Dow Jones industrial average, the most widely followed stock index, plunged

45 percent. The few stock recommendations I'd made up to that time had collapsed in value, along with everything else my fellow analysts had on the buy list.

Looking back at the carnage was as painful to me as it must have been to all the Gulf Coast residents who saw what Hurricane Katrina did to the land they used to live in. My personal portfolio shed nearly 75 percent of its value, and I kept wondering how many millions, if not hundreds of millions, of dollars my company's customers had lost.

I tend to bounce back quickly. Rather than dwell on what had gone wrong, as research chief I began to search for a method—any method—that would prevent the devastating losses of 1973–1974 from ever afflicting me or any of my clients again. I was working on my chartered financial analyst (CFA®) certification. (It normally takes three years to complete, but I took four because I really enjoyed giving up a beautiful Saturday each June to endure a six-hour marathon exam.)

I discovered that some years earlier the CFA program had used a different book from the one I'd been studying: *Security Analysis* by Benjamin Graham and David Dodd. (They were using the fourth edition from 1962 with a third author, Sydney Cottle.) This bible of security analysts was originally published in 1934, shortly after the worst stock collapse in U.S. history ended.

The third edition, which I own, was essentially a rewrite, not a revision, of the original. When it came out in 1951, Benjamin Graham was president of the Graham-Newman Corporation, a money management operation, and guest professor at Columbia University's graduate school of business. His collaborator and colleague, David L. Dodd, was a professor of finance there.

What struck me about this edition was that it was dedicated to what the authors termed the "New Generation of Security Analysts." I'll never be able to ask either Graham or Dodd what they meant, but I suppose they were thinking that World War II had ushered in a new era, both for the economy and for analyzing stocks and other securities. Their revised version was meant to educate a new breed of analysts and start them off on the right foot.

BENJAMIN GRAHAM

Benjamin Graham is called the principal author of the five editions of *Security Analysis*. When he died in Aix-en-Provence in 1976 at age 82, he was a multimillionaire This "dean of security analysts" had sold more than 100,000 copies of his book before his passing. That's quite a large total for any book, especially a textbook.

Graham, born in London in 1894, grew up in New York, where he received his Bachelor of Science degree from Columbia in 1914 and was second in his class. Upon graduating Phi Beta Kappa, Graham went to work on Wall Street. His first job was chalking up stock and bond prices on a board. From that lowly position he became a runner who delivered securities and checks, then on to assistant of a two-man bond department where he wrote concise descriptions of the bonds in inventory to be sold. He also began writing a daily market letter.

Ben Graham was so proficient and got along so well with people that he soon became what they called a customers' man and personally visited customers as a bond salesperson. A salesperson he wasn't but a quick study he was. Young Graham soon realized how little his firm's customers really knew about the bonds they were buying and selling. He was later named a partner in the Wall Street firm of Newburger, Henderson & Loeb.

During the roaring bull market of the 1920s, Graham and Jerome Newman formed the Graham-Newman Corporation and an investment partnership, Newman & Graham. Even though they were pummeled in the 1929–1932 stock freefall, their partnership churned out impressive returns (17.4 percent annually) before they dissolved it in 1956. Ten thousand dollars invested in Graham-Newman in 1936 threw off about $2,100 per year in income for the next 20 years (roughly $42,000), and the original principal was repaid when the firm was liquidated.

Security Analysis isn't called the "Bible of the trade" for nothing. It's thick, it's not easy or fun reading, and far too many of the professionals who have read it ignore many of its basic principles, just as have most readers of the Bible, the world's best-selling book.

I studied the fourth edition, which had further refinements over the previous three, but the guts of it were the same. I bought a copy and began to trudge through it on my own time. "Trudge" is the right word because, as in medical textbooks, there was much to learn on each page. I absorbed many lessons from Benjamin Graham, including his famous margin of safety concept: Buy when stock prices overall are undervalued or pick out specific issues with promising prospects that sell well below their intrinsic worth.

When Graham started on Wall Street, a formal method for establishing the true value of stocks and bonds was all but nonexistent. There were various theories about how to speculate successfully in stocks, but not much attention was paid to investing. Speculating was a game of sorts. Graham knew investing to be the opposite—that it could and should be scientific. He believed in basic principles that would enable students of the trade to learn how to buy $1.00 of assets at far less than their true worth. If they could do so, he reasoned, they could earn handsome profits because few, if any, others were approaching securities analysis from such a solid quantitative base.

Because he was a teacher by nature and profession, Graham wanted to make his scientific investing principles available to others. That strong desire led him to write the epic on how to analyze securities. Unfortunately, *Security Analysis* is so unwieldy it has never engaged a widespread audience of individual investors, as Graham so fervently desired, and it has managed to bypass more than its fair share of Wall Street's best. Although the tools for investment success are within its pages, Graham's techniques are so cumbersome that the vast majority of people whom he wanted to benefit didn't have the time to, and could never, put them to work (even if they were interested).

Even so, Benjamin Graham's works and his various interviews and research papers were tremendously interesting to me. Everything I could learn from and about this investment master absorbed me. I was especially fascinated to discover that Graham's primary reason for continually perfecting his craft was to show how to invest safely and with as little effort as possible.

Why? He knew, even back then, that individuals are often their own worst enemy when it comes to personal money management. It's been proved over and over. They like to buy stocks when prices are highest, and they either panic and sell out at or near lows and/ or refuse to buy more of what they already own when prices are cheap, as they were in late 2007 and on into 2008.

The most recent study I saw covered the 20 years prior to 2008. Stocks in general (as measured by the two most popular market indices, the Dow Jones Industrials and Standard & Poor's 500) churned out an annual compound total return (price appreciation with dividends reinvested) in excess of 11 percent. During that same span, the typical individual investor earned about 4.5 percent a year in stock mutual funds, or roughly seven percentage points less than the market (according to Dalbar, Inc.).

Graham's passion to share the gospel of investing with anyone who would listen led him to write *The Intelligent Investor* in 1949. In the introduction of a later edition of this book, Graham made certain the reader knew he wasn't writing for those who liked high risk or spending lots of time on their portfolios. Instead, *The Intelligent Investor* was dedicated to the defensive (or passive) investor who wanted to avoid large losses and the hassle of worrying about his investment strategy. Right away he had my attention. Graham observed that the investor's worst enemy is himself or herself:[1]

> We have seen much more money made and kept by "ordinary people" who were temperamentally well suited for the investment process than by those who lacked this quality, even though they had an extensive knowledge of finance, accounting, and stock market lore.

He made another astute observation: "Sound investment principles produce generally sound results."

ANCIENT WISDOM

By the time Graham was in his eighties, still as sharp as ever, financial institutions—brokerage firms, banks, insurance companies, and the like—were spending millions of dollars a year and grinding out thousands of pages of research on this or that security. Nothing like this had been going on when Ben Graham stepped onto Wall Street some 60 years earlier. Little time or effort was exerted on practical securities research. The kind of in-depth analysis Graham pioneered paid off handsomely for him and for anyone who listened to him because there was virtually no competition.

As he grew older, Graham realized that hordes of others were attempting to follow in his giant footsteps—so many, in fact, that they were bumping into one another trying to pick undervalued securities—especially stocks—that would rise in value. He thought that, because Wall Street was pouring such vast resources into stock research, the elaborate techniques he devised were rapidly losing their value. It seemed to be a case of what everybody else knows isn't worth knowing.

---

[1] Benjamin Graham, *The Intelligent Investor*, 4th rev. ed. (New York: HarperCollins, 1973).

Graham communicated this view shortly before his death in 1976 in a final interview, which appeared in the September–October 1976 *Financial Analysts Journal* (FAJ). Customarily, only one person in the United States is introduced with no introduction: the president. Benjamin Graham was introduced, almost as reverently, as one "who needs no introduction to the readers of this magazine."

What's all this got to do with you? The answer is quite a lot. Graham possessed what many would call "ancient wisdom."

Excerpts from that last interview appear here:[2]

FAJ: *In the light of your sixty-odd years of experience in Wall Street, what is your overall view of common stocks?*
BG: Common stocks have one important investment characteristic and one important speculative characteristic. Their investment value and average market price tend to increase irregularly but persistently over the decades as their net worth builds up through the reinvestment of undistributed earnings. However, most of the time common stocks are subject to irrational and excessive price fluctuations in both directions, as the consequence of the ingrained tendency of most people to speculate or gamble—i.e., to give way to hope, fear and greed.

FAJ: *What is your view of the financial community as a whole?*
BG: Most of the stockbrokers, financial analysts, investment advisers, etc., are above average in intelligence, business honesty and sincerity. But they lack adequate experience with all types of security markets and an overall understanding of common stocks—of what I call "the nature of the beast." They tend to take the market and themselves too seriously. They spend a large part of their time trying, valiantly and ineffectively, to do things they can't do well.

FAJ: *What sort of things, for example?*
BG: To forecast short- or long-term changes in the economy, and in the price level of common stocks, to select the most promising industry groups and individual issues—generally for the near-term future.

---

[2] "Conversation with Benjamin Graham," adapted with permission from *Financial Analysts Journal*, September–October 1976. Copyright 1976, CFA Institute. Reproduced and republished from *Financial Analysts Journal* with permission from CFA Institute. All rights reserved.

FAJ: *Can the average manager of institutional funds obtain better results than the Dow Jones industrial average or the Standard & Poor's [500] index over the years?*
BG: No. In effect, that would mean that the stock market experts as a whole, could best themselves—a logical contradiction.

FAJ: *Turning now to individual investors, do you think that they are at a disadvantage compared with the institutions because of the latter's huge resources, superior facilities for obtaining information, etc.?*
BG: On the contrary, the typical individual investor has a great advantage over the large institutions.

FAJ: *What general rules would you offer the individual investor for his investment policy over the years?*
BG: Let me suggest three such rules:

(1) The individual investor should act consistently as an investor and not as a speculator.
(2) The investor should have a definite selling policy for all his common stock commitments, corresponding to his buying techniques.
(3) Finally, the investor should always have a [decent] percentage of his total portfolio in common stocks and a minimum percentage in bond equivalents.

FAJ: *In selecting the common stock portfolio, do you advise careful study of and selectivity among individual issues?*
BG: In general, no. I am no longer an advocate of elaborate techniques of security analysis in order to find superior value opportunities. This was rewarding activity, say, forty years ago when our textbook "Graham and Dodd" was first published; but the situation has changed a good deal since then. In the old days any well-trained security analyst could do a good professional job of selecting undervalued issues through detailed studies; but in the light of the enormous amount of research now being carried on, I doubt whether in most cases such extensive efforts will generate sufficiently superior selections to justify their cost.

In addressing the question about how individuals should create and manage their common stock portfolios, Graham wrote "to enjoy a reasonable chance for continued better-than-average results, the investor must follow policies which are (1) inherently sound and promising, and (2) are not popular in Wall Street." Further, "Investment is most intelligent when it is most businesslike."

I believe that investing exclusively in America's Finest Companies adheres to both these policies.

WHAT TO TAKE AWAY FROM GRAHAM

In addition to margin of safety, the cornerstone of the Benjamin Graham philosophy of investing, these are the other valuable lessons I learned from him:

- Stock prices rise "irregularly but persistently" over time because the value of the underlying businesses continues to increase as retained earnings are plowed back into those businesses.
- Financial professionals, on the whole, are well educated, honest, and sincere but have a shallow understanding of common stocks.
- Professionals spend far too much time trying to do what can't be done: predicting the future of the economy, the level of stock prices, and which industries and individual stocks will perform best.
- The average professional money manager cannot beat the market, as measured by the Dow Jones industrials, Standard & Poor's 500, or any other major index. Professionals are the average, and it's a "logical contradiction" that they can "best themselves."
- Individuals have tremendous advantages over the professionals.
- To be the most successful, individual investors (a) must invest rather than speculate, (b) have a rule of thumb for the appropriate time to sell, and (c) always have at least a decent portion of their investment holdings in stocks.
- Complicated techniques of security analysis aren't necessary to unearth superior opportunities.
- The stock-picking method an investor uses should be rational and easy to apply and have "an excellent supporting record." Investment that is most "businesslike" will generate the best returns, especially as it goes against the grain of Wall Street.

By investing in America's Finest Companies in the way I'll detail, you'll be aligning yourself with the investment wisdom and success of Benjamin Graham, the father of security analysis and a multimillionaire when he died. I can't say for certain that Ben Graham would endorse my techniques, but I strongly believe he would. They meet all the criteria outlined in his farewell interview. They are time-proven and they work. What else could an investor want?

CHAPTER 4

Hit the Easy Button for Above-Average Profits

The simpler your investment plan, the more likely it will work.
— *U.S. News & World Report*

POINTS TO REMEMBER

- Do it yourself with America's Finest Companies (AFC).
- The method is simple, easy, fast, and fun.
- The effects are reduced expense, improved results, and little hassle.

A SIMPLE STRATEGY

A simple investment program—one that is uncomplicated, readily understood, and easily implemented—is best because it's efficient. Simple investing will work exceptionally well for you, as it does for me and for other knowledgeable investors. In the 1950s, Garfield Drew, a noted and wealthy stock market technician (someone who analyzes market and individual stock patterns as a guide to future direction), stated, "Simplicity or singleness of approach is a greatly underestimated factor of market success."

When people think of investing, simplicity is the last thought they usually have. Everyone knows that investing (setting aside money today for the future) is a complex chore and not any fun either, right? Fun is not mentioned in investment books, in courses in securities analysis, or in investment materials (except mine).

But it should be. Having fun while you invest is critical to success. My strong belief is that if investing in stocks isn't fun for you, it won't be nearly as profitable as it can be.

Even if investing is profitable but you're not having fun, you just might want to try a new strategy. This applies if you constantly worry about day-to-day fluctuations in stock prices or about what you heard on CNBC, what you read on the Internet, or what the Federal Reserve did with the money supply, or if you fret about the direction of the economy, which way inflation and interest rates will go, or what ABC News says about whether we're on the brink of recession—or some of the above or all of the above.

The method I'm unfurling here is a good one. It's simple. It's rational. It generally produces superior results. It's fun. And it will beat the results of most professional money managers year in and year out. My method is too simple for most of Wall Street to adopt; so they ignore it.

In the previous chapter, I related that Benjamin Graham was asked in 1976 (the year he died) whether he recommended "careful study of and selectivity among individual issues." Even though Graham was a detailed and thorough securities analyst, he responded, "In general, no. I am no longer an advocate of elaborate techniques of security analysis in order to find superior value opportunities." In the end, his was a vote for simplicity.

For me, my own studies of market history dating back to the early 1920s confirm exactly what Graham said: The more complicated your stock market strategy is, the more difficult it is to implement and to monitor. What's worse, it almost always leads to mediocre performance. Simple is far better. The pros tend to make investing complicated, but it doesn't have to be.

If you think about it for 15 seconds, you can readily see why investment counselors, financial advisors, stockbrokers, and money managers at banks, insurance companies, and mutual funds especially rarely beat the market indices. Even the professionals who try to replicate the market's results almost always fail. Here's why:

A Las Vegas tourism billboard on the I-15 freeway in California proclaimed "Seven Deadly Sins; One Convenient Location." This sums up our feeling about most mutual funds, which are a repository for bad investing habits.

Paul Orfalea, *The Entrepreneurial Investor*

The Dow Jones industrials and Standard & Poor's 500 have no operating expenses. They go up and down without transaction costs because they're indexes charted on paper. Money managers, trying to make their portfolios match one or another market index, have to make frequent buys and sells to keep the portfolios in proportion with the stocks making up the index they're supposed to match. Stocks cost money to buy, and they cost money to sell. The cost of trading, by itself, makes attempts to equal a market index impossible.

If they're trying to beat the market instead of just equal it, money managers have another dilemma. They usually cannot adopt a fun, businesslike, simple approach to investing like the one in this book. Why? They might not have to work a 40-hour week. They'd be taking so much time off, while beating the indexes consistently, their bosses would fire them. How could a company justify paying money managers a full year's salary when they didn't have to work every day to profitably execute their investment plans?

The prudent money manager and/or securities analyst—that is, one who wishes to remain employed—must create activities to fill his or her time. These include scouring the Internet, reading voluminous industry and company reports, meeting and perhaps dining with the managements of prospective companies, attending numerous presentations to financial professionals, talking with friends in the business, sitting through an untold number of investment committee meetings, scanning in-depth and ultrathick computer runs, and listening to the latest Wall Street gossip, which drolls on nonstop.

By doing all these things and more, the typical money manager's day is out of control. Money managers drown in wasteful short-term activities, which history shows don't produce above-average results. Yet they generally cannot quit because they can't afford to lose their salary. If you were in their shoes, would you be any different?

Fortunately, you don't have to get sucked into the rut of the typical money professional. You can go your own independent profitable way, and you'll start by buying only the shares of highest-quality companies: America's Finest. You won't learn to do that in other investment books, which dwell on this or that method for picking the next Wal-Mart, Home Depot, or other company that is sure to make a million dollars for you from a small amount of seed money. The reason these books generally aren't worth much (besides being hard to understand) is that they focus on the wrong things. Choosing just the "right" stocks for your portfolio is not nearly as important as many people think.

Of course, you do have to pick companies for your portfolio. But doing so yourself can be quick, easy, and hassle free, and it can incur less expense and produce better results than what you will expect from most professionals. There are two basic characteristics to look for when you invest in shares of companies:

1. The companies are in sound financial condition and won't go out of business.
2. Earnings and dividends continue to grow.

WHERE ARE THESE COMPANIES?

Seventeen of the 30 Dow Jones industrials are included in America's Finest Companies. Coca-Cola is one. Another is Procter & Gamble, one of the world's premier consumer products companies. Pfizer is the planet's largest pharmaceutical firm, and McDonald's sells more hamburgers (and owns more commercial real estate) than any other company in America.

The others are American International Group (cut from AFC list and Dow in 2008), AT&T, Bank of America, Caterpillar, Chevron, ExxonMobil, General Electric, Home Depot, IBM (International Business Machines), Johnson & Johnson, 3M (Minnesota Mining & Manufacturing), United Technologies, and Wal-Mart Stores. That's a fine list of highest-quality companies, isn't it?

Table 4.1 shows how well the 17 Dow stocks that make the AFC cut perform, especially in the most recent difficult market environment.

When you buy shares of America's Finest Companies, you are 99.9 percent guaranteed that they'll remain in business as long as they remain within the AFC universe. By investing in them exclusively, you know you will own shares of companies that will stay afloat through the worst economic storms.

Benjamin Graham believed in buying quality. In *The Intelligent Investor* he noted, "The risk of paying too high a price for good-quality stocks—while a real one—is not the chief hazard confronting the average buyer of securities. Observations over many years has taught us that the chief losses to investors come from the purchase of low-quality securities at times of favorable business conditions."

TABLE 4.1   Annualized Return of Dow Stocks 12/31/07

	Annualized Total Return		
	5-Year	10-Year	20-Year
17 America's Finest Companies in DJIA	12.1%	7.7%	13.4%
13 remaining Dow Jones industrial average (DJIA) components	10.6%	4.6%	12.3%

Source: Hirsch Organization.

Dozens and dozens of U.S. companies have been around for well over a hundred years. Quite a few are among the corporations in America's Finest Companies. They've survived panics, financial crises, depressions, earthquakes, droughts, floods, political scandals, wars, and any other disaster you can name. Among these are some of the so-called blue-chip companies such as Colgate-Palmolive and John Wiley & Sons, Inc. They've been through just about everything, yet they are still healthy and growing.

The phrase "blue chip" describes highly regarded enterprises that generally make up the Dow Jones industrial average and a good part of the S&P 500. Blue chips have long earnings and dividend histories, and they are assumed to be able to withstand the most adverse economic circumstances. The name "blue chip" came about because in the game of poker blue chips have the highest value.

Although not all the companies included in America's Finest Companies are blue chips by the widely accepted definition, they are all highly regarded and have exceptional records: at least 10 consecutive years of higher dividends and/or earnings per share. As a group, they are well above average in financial strength. They are the thoroughbreds of corporate America and should be on the shopping list for assembling your personal market-beating portfolio.

America's Finest Companies comprise the top 1 to 2 percent of the estimated 20,000 or so U.S. public companies. How have they been able to string together at least 10 years in a row of higher earnings or dividends per share when the other 98 percent of public companies have not? Have they gotten into industries that are so good it would be hard not to superachieve? Have most of them just been lucky? Or are there other factors? Do some common threads unite this elite group of companies?

Having studied and analyzed hundreds of the enterprises in America's Finest Companies over nearly 20 years, I learned that they share the following traits:

1. The finest companies serve customers and employees with a passion.
2. Their managements are strong and decisive.
3. Each company knows where it wants to go.
4. They carve out their own paths for growth.
5. The companies are creative and innovative.
6. They carefully control expenses.
7. They respond to problems rather than react to them.

If you invest exclusively in the companies in America's Finest Companies, you'll be putting these seven traits to work for you in your own portfolio(s). If the historic performance of their stocks continues, you'll do far better than most professional money managers. To make it even easier to narrow down the companies to choose for your portfolio, here are two of my favorite subgroups of AFC stocks. These lists are straight from my 2009 18th Annual Investment Directory of *America's Finest Companies* (which is published every July, www.statoninstitute.com). The entire list of 306 top-quality stocks appears for your convenience in the appendix of this book.

AMERICA'S SMARTEST COMPANIES®

These select 20 companies (versus 22 last year) recorded at least 10 straight years of higher dividends per share through calendar 2007 and higher earnings per share by the fiscal year ended May 31, 2008.

Only 6.5 percent of the companies in America's Finest Companies qualify to be in this elite group. Out of all publicly traded companies in America, these are in the top 0.1 percent. This is an amazing feat, to say the least. Because of their elite status, these gems are trademarked as America's Smartest Companies® (see Table 4.2).

THE SUPER 50 TEAM

Only 20 American companies have a combined total of at least 50 years of higher earnings and dividends per share, an extraordinarily remarkable accomplishment.

TABLE 4.2   America's Smartest Companies®

	Consecutive Years Higher	
	Earnings per Share	Dividends
Brown & Brown, Inc.	15	14
Cintas Corp.	38	25
CLARCOR Inc.	15	24
Commerce Bancshares Inc.	23	38
Compass Bancshares Inc.	19	25
Donaldson Co.	18	14
Energen Corp.	12	25
Expeditors International	14	14
General Electric Co.	32	32
Glacier Bancorp	11	21
Johnson & Johnson	24	45
Kimco Realty Corp.	16	16
National Penn Bancshares	30	29
Paychex Inc.	18	19
Realty Income Corp.	13	13
SEI Investments	15	16
Tompkins Financial	35	19
Walgreen Co.	32	30
Wal-Mart Stores Inc.	46	33
Weingarten Realty Investors	18	23

Source: The Staton Institute® Inc.

Qualifying to be on The Super 50 Team is a mammoth achievement because just a microscopic 0.1 percent of all U.S. public companies make it. Once a company makes the team, it's even harder to stay on it because maintaining higher earnings and dividends year after year is getting more and more difficult.

The Super 50 Team members are ranked in descending order based on their composite score (combined years of higher earnings and dividends; see Table 4.3). The Super 50 companies will generally outperform the stock market over long periods of time.

TABLE 4.3   Super 50

Super 50 Team Member	Total Score	Rank	Consecutive Years Higher Earnings per Share or EPS	Consecutive Years Higher Dividends or Divds.
Wal-Mart Stores Inc.	79	1	46	33
Johnson & Johnson	69	2	24	45
Comerica Inc.	64	3	0	64
General Electric Co.	64	3	32	32
Walgreen Co.	64	3	33	31
Cintas Corp.	64	3	39	25
Commerce Bancshares Inc.	61	4	23	38
National Penn Bancshares Inc.	59	5	30	29
Procter & Gamble Co.	59	5	7	52
NW Natural Gas Co.	57	6	5	52
American States Water Co.	56	7	1	55
Dover Corp.	56	7	5	51
Genuine Parts Co.	56	7	5	51
3M Co.	55	8	6	49
Bank of Granite Corp.	54	9	0	54
Diebold Inc.	54	9	0	54
Tompkins Financial	54	9	35	19
Emerson Electric Co.	51	10	0	51
Coca-Cola Co.	50	11	5	45
Illinois Tool Works Inc.	50	11	5	45

62

Owning shares of America's Finest Companies not only allows you to generally outpace the market and professional managers with ease, it also allows you to keep more of your hard-earned cash and investment returns. In Chapter 5 you'll find out how the pros live fat and happy whether you make money or not. Through the rest of this book you learn how simple and easy it is to be your own money manager and how to create long-term wealth for your entire family.

CHAPTER 5

Where Are the Customers' Yachts?

The whole investment management business together gives no value added to all buyers combined.

—CHARLES T. MUNGER, VICE CHAIRMAN
OF BERKSHIRE HATHAWAY AND CEO OF
WESCO FINANCIAL, ONE OF AMERICA'S FINEST COMPANIES

POINTS TO REMEMBER

- Avoid exorbitant fees.
- Assemble your own mini fund.
- Don't pay advisors for substandard results.

William R. Travers was a well-known nineteenth-century lawyer who regularly visited swank Newport, Rhode Island. That was where J. P. Morgan, John D. Rockefeller, and other notable Wall Street financiers and millionaire industrialists built what they called cottages (we call them mansions today) for weekend and summer retreats. Yacht racing was the sport of that day, and Travers was present at all the best events. One Sunday he was in a small group at the finish line watching yacht after yacht glide across. As the names of the owners were announced, Travers noticed each one was a wealthy stockbroker. While staring at the fancy flotilla, Travers, a stutterer, shouted, "And w-w-where are the c-c-customers' yachts?"[1]

Fred Schwed, Jr., wrote the best-selling *Wacky, the Small Boy* in 1939. In that book, Schwed is said to have "attended Lawrenceville and Princeton and has spent the last ten years in Wall Street. As a result he knows everything there is to know about children." That doesn't say much about Schwed's forte in the financial arena, but it gives you a good idea of his high sense of humor.

Schwed, an early skeptic of Wall Street, decided to write *Where Are the Customers' Yachts? Or a Good Hard Look at Wall Street* to share his witty wisdom, and he got Simon & Schuster to publish it in 1940. The book has been successful enough to have been reprinted several times since (and is now available through Wiley, published in paperback in 2005 as part of their Wiley Investment Classics series).

Schwed opens his book by reminding the reader that Wall Street has a river at one end and a graveyard at the other. Schwed said that he viewed Wall Street's daily activities from a trading table with every conceivable form of communication except the heliograph. In such an enviable position, he was "constantly exchanging quotations, orders, bluffs, fibs, lies and nonsense." Having observed all this for at least a decade, Schwed decided to dedicate his book to examining the nonsense, "a commodity which keeps sluicing in through the weeks and years with the irresistible constancy of the waters of the rolling Mississippi."

I particularly enjoyed his discussion of investment trusts, the forerunners of modern-day mutual funds. They were formed under the assumptions that the average individual is incapable of handling his or her own financial destiny and that, worse, the individual investor cannot, unless very rich, purchase the best financial advice.

"So a lot of us, who clearly are not magicians, pool our money and hire a set of professional experts to do the guessing. They may not quite be magicians, but they have everything that should be necessary: experience, reputation, trained staffs, inside information, and unlimited resources for research. Since the amount we pool today is often hundreds of million dollars, if not billions, we can afford to pay them fortunes for their ability. Paying them fortunes is a great bargain, as long as they deliver results. Many would think they could

---

[1] Fred Schwed, Jr., *Where Are the Customers' Yachts?* (Hoboken, NJ: Wiley, 2005; New York: Simon & Schuster, copyright 1940 by Fred Schwed, Jr.; renewed 1967 by Harriet Wolf Schwed).

do so, or at least do so better than we could. If in actuality mutual funds would only function anywhere nearly as well as they do in theory, they would be a tremendous asset to the general welfare."

Schwed believed most investment professionals aren't dishonest. They're simply inept. He wrote, "This book has chiefly tried to paint a picture of thousands of erring humans, of varying degrees of good will, solemnly engaged in the business of predicting the unpredictable. To this effort most of them bring a certain cockeyed sincerity." I agree with Schwed.

THE MUTUAL FUND MISTAKE

Since I started my newsletter *Staton's Investment Advisory* in 1986 (now available as *Staton's E-Money Digest* at www.statoninstitute.com), I've continually written about why the large majority of professional money managers—the experts millions of people rely on to help their money grow—consistently underperform the stock market. At one time I had a file more than two inches thick, but it was taking up too much space in my cabinet and I chucked most of it out. It was jam-packed with articles from all sorts of places, but for the most part they were straight from everyday business and financial journals, including *The Wall Street Journal, Forbes, Fortune, BusinessWeek,* and *Financial World.* I didn't go out of my way to obtain the evidence, yet even today more and more keeps coming my way.

For more than 20 years I've advocated avoiding stock mutual funds and assembling your own portfolio comprised solely of America's Finest Companies. One of the key reasons is to save the onerous fees the fund industry charges. According to Morningstar, a mutual fund tracker, funds expenses as a percentage of assets under management equate to 1.4 percent annually, and those fees come out of an investor's money. *BusinessWeek* (February 4, 2008) observed that the percentage may not seem like a lot, but "with mutual fund assets surpassing the $3 trillion mark, plenty of critics wonder why that figure has stayed the same for years." If fund expenses were shown as a percentage of reported profits, the magazine goes on, "That puts mutual fund overhead in a whole new light—and it's not pretty."

On top of that, Warren Buffett and his sidekick Charles Munger have made fun of so-called professional money management for years, arguing that there's no use paying someone to do something you can easily do yourself, likely with superior results.

Multibillionaire John Bogle, founder of the enormous Vanguard family of funds, has been on the warpath against rising fund costs a very long time (and still is). He states, "The fees keep going up—going up like you're in an elevator." The expense ratio of the average stock fund (money that comes out of the investor's pocket) continues to rise, and it appears to remain in the same relentless upward trend that it's been in for more than two decades.

The new kids on the block, exchange-traded funds (ETFs), in general have much lower expense fees than mutual funds, and they trade throughout the day like stocks. However, the ETF explosion over the last several years, from about 50 in 2001 to 650 and counting today, has created some sketchy and way-out funds.

Much of the noise, confusion, and fees of all manner of funds can be eliminated by investing in a handful or a dozen or so of America's Finest Companies, using an online discount broker for a few dollars a trade.

MANAGING YOUR MONEY

Before I explain why most professionals cannot beat the market on a regular basis, let's look at some evidence of the poor job they're doing:

Way back in 1989 in the respected *Financial Analysts Journal,* the president of Martingale Asset Management, Arnold S. Wood, summed up my belief quite nicely: "One might expect that our investment judgments, given our training and experience, would prove sound and profitable for our clients. But this is, strikingly, not true." Four years later, *BusinessWeek* chimed in: "By and large, professional investors do a mediocre job of stock picking. That, along with their expenses and fees, causes them to lag well behind the market." One year later on Halloween in 1994, *Fortune* magazine observed, "Overall, money managers have done a dismal job."

You can easily see that this knowledge has been around for many a moon, yet stock mutual funds remain the most popular way for individuals to invest. According to the Investment Company Institute, there are now in excess of 8,000 different mutual funds in the United States, with about $12 trillion in assets at the end of 2007. About 4,800 of them invest in stocks.

With so much money on the line and still pouring into equity funds at a record clip, you'd think investors would be more careful about where they put their money. But they are often lured by the creative advertising of mutual funds, which seem to offer so much and in reality frequently produce so little. Thumb through any of dozens of investment publications, and you'll see ads for this fund or that. Note how they tout their outstanding records. One of my money manager friends wryly noted, "Every money manager in the country says he's in the top 25 percent." But we all know that's impossible.

Warren Buffett and Charlie Munger have used a similar investing mantra as I have year in and year out to fashion Berkshire Hathaway into the amazingly successful investing icon that it is today. *Poor Charlie's Almanack: The Wit and Wisdom of Charles T. Munger*[2] is loaded with salient investing knowledge. Here are few zingers:

- "We're partial to putting out large amounts of money where we won't have to make another decision. If you can buy a few great companies, then you can sit on your ass. That's a good thing. We just look for no-brainer decisions. As Buffett and I say over and over again, we don't leap seven-foot fences."
- "Our investment style has been given a name—focus investing—which implies ten holdings, not one hundred or four hundred."
- "Beta and modern portfolio theory and the like—none of it makes any sense to me. We're trying to buy businesses with sustainable competitive advantages."
- "How can professors spread this [nonsense that a stock's volatility is a measure of risk]? I've been waiting for this craziness to end for decades. It's been dented, but it's still out there."
- "Warren [Buffett] once said to me, 'I'm probably misjudging academia generally [in thinking so poorly of it] because the people that interact with me have bonkers theories."
- "Over many decades, our usual practice is that if [the stock of] something we like goes down, we buy more and more."
- "The general systems of money management [today] require people to pretend to do something they can't do and like something they don't. It's a terrible way to spend your life, but it's very well

---

[2]*Poor Charlie's Almanack: The Wit and Wisdom of Charles T. Munger* (The Donning Company Publishers. © 2005, 2006, 2008).

paid. It's a funny business because on a net basis, the whole investment management business together gives no value added to all buyers combined."

- "Mutual funds charge two percent per year and then brokers switch people between funds, costing another three to four percentage points. The poor guy in the general public is getting a terrible product from the professionals. I think it's disgusting. It's much better to be part of a system that delivers value to the people who buy the product."
- "I think a select few—a small percentage of the investment managers—can deliver value added."
- *Question:* "All kinds of people ask me for some foolproof system for achieving financial security or saving for their retirement." *Answer:* "Spend less than you make; always be saving something. Put it into a tax-deferred account. Over time, it will begin to amount to something. *This is such a no-brainer.*"

ADVANTAGE: THE INDIVIDUAL INVESTOR

Because so few professionals, whether they are investment counselors, pension fund managers, or mutual fund managers, beat the market, investors need to understand why so that they don't make the same mistakes the pros make.

Financial institutions control 80 percent or more of all trading volume on the New York Stock Exchange. On an average day some three to four billion shares are bought and sold. Individuals account for 20 percent of that.

Vilfredo Pareto was an Italian sociologist and economist for whom the famous Pareto principle is named. After observing thousands of workers in hundreds of businesses from the late nineteenth through the early twentieth centuries, he concluded that 80 percent of results come from 20 percent of effort. For example, 20 percent of a day's work produces 80 percent of the benefits of that work, or 20 percent of an advertising budget results in 80 percent of the incremental revenue, or 20 percent of the workers in an organization typically produce at least 80 percent of sales and earnings.

Although no results break down exactly into 20/80, the principle is an excellent rule of thumb. And it's interesting to me that NYSE volume is now almost exactly 20 percent by individuals and 80 percent by financial institutions. As you've already seen, the 80 percent produces subpar results, which implies that the 20 percent—individual investors—produces superior results.

In Chapter 3, we heard Benjamin Graham, in just ten sentences, rip apart the fantasy that the financial community can accurately predict short-term changes in the economy and stock prices. He also reasoned that the stock market experts can't continuously beat the market because they *are* the market. You can't beat the average when you are the average.

On the other hand, "The typical individual investor," Graham said later in the interview, "has a great advantage over the large institutions." As I'll demonstrate, that advantage can lead you to above-average profits if you create and manage your own portfolio made up of America's Finest Companies.

This sounds as though I'm bashing all professional money managers and advisors. For the record, I am not against professional advice or money management because I am a professional advisor. But I am against paying a so-called expert for subpar performance and advice, something far too many individuals are doing. In fairness to the pros, though, their customers help create these inferior results. Here's how.

For whatever reasons—lack of time, no investment background, personal finance seeming too complicated—many people believe they can't manage their own money well. Because they lack confidence in their own ability, they turn to experts to take care of their money for them.

Investors must pay annual fees for services from trust departments, investment counselors, and mutual funds. If they use brokers, the brokers charge a commission (or fee in lieu of commissions) for all transactions. If they use financial planners, they pay fees and/or sales loads on the various financial products and mutual funds that the planners recommend. Anywhere investors turn, there's a charge for advice and management unless they choose to do it themselves. There's certainly nothing wrong with this. What professionals in their right minds would manage money or give financial advice for free?

Paying someone to manage relatively smaller amounts of money can be quite expensive. Here's an example from one of the country's largest stock brokerages. The minimum annual fee is $1,000 plus a percentage of assets under management. And, the money manager's fee is on top of that.

Total Assets	Broker Fee
First $500,000	$1,000 + 2.0%
Second $500,000	$1,000 + 1.5%
Next $1.5 million	$1,000 + 1.0%

For a $250,000 managed account through this broker whose figures we're using, it could cost $6,000. The manager's fee on top of that could easily add another 0.5 percent to 1.0 percent, making the total cost $7,250 to $8,500. Respectively, these numbers would eat up 2.9 percent to 3.4 percent of total assets each year.

When investors pay to have their money managed, they expect the professionals they're paying to earn their keep by studying the economy and stock market, by buying and selling when the time is ripe, and by going into cash in case the market should go down. Isn't that right? Would you pay an expert to spend only a little of his time taking care of your money? Of course not. You want that expert to be working—and working hard—on your behalf. You want that expert to spend as much time with your money as possible, and, because you want that, the expert typically does what you expect.

> *Those who have knowledge don't predict.*
> *Those who predict don't have knowledge.*
> —LAO TZU, SIXTH-CENTURY BC CHINESE PHILOSOPHER

Professionals rely heavily on forecasts of expected performance of the economy, the stock market, and individual companies. That's not too surprising because forecasting, especially of the economy, has been in existence for centuries. People from all walks of life are attracted to it. Everyone wants that special peek ahead.

When Marco Polo returned to his homeland from the Orient, he told of kites used as economic forecasting devices. Before a merchant ship embarked on a trading voyage, a drunk (you had to be drunk to do this) was tied to a kite and launched from the ship's deck. If—and it was a big if—the drunk actually made it into the air, the voyage was expected to be successful. But if he crashed, the trip was postponed if not canceled.

Despite the awesome academic evidence that forecasts are usually wrong (because no one can see into the future), many money managers continue to defy logic and rationality. It's not really mysterious, though, when you consider that millions of people still smoke and chew tobacco, although they know that tobacco is a killer. Or they continue to gamble at the racetrack, in lotteries, or in Las Vegas, although the house wins 99 percent of the time. Or they abuse drugs or drive without seatbelts fastened. Far too many money managers/financial advisers believe they have found the forecast (or system) that affords a profitable gaze into the future, even though they most likely believe that their counterparts haven't.

Let me take you on a brief journey through history to show you some of the most widely heralded predictions about the economy and the stock market, made by acclaimed experts:

Stocks have reached what looks like a permanently high plateau. [Irving Fisher, professor of economics at Yale, October 17, 1929.]
Eleven days later, on October 28, panic struck Wall Street and stock values plummeted.

The end of the decline of the Stock Market ...will probably not be long, only a few more days at most. [Irving Fisher, trying to regain some of his lost luster, November 14, 1929.]
Nice try, Irving.

Financial storm definitely passed. [Cablegram to Winston Churchill from Bernard Baruch, November 15, 1929.]
Security prices had just begun their freefall into 1932.

Gentlemen, you have come sixty days too late. The Depression is over. [Herbert Hoover responding to a delegation requesting a public works program to help speed the recovery, June 1930.]
What recovery? The economy hadn't come close to bottoming.

During the next four years . . . unless drastic steps are taken by Congress, the U.S. will have nearly 8,000,000 unemployed and will stand on the brink of a deep depression. [Henry C. Wallace, U.S. Secretary of Commerce, November 1945.]
Between 1945 and 1950, the U.S. GDP rose nearly 50 percent.

With over 50 foreign cars already on sale here, the Japanese auto industry isn't likely to carve out a big slice of the U.S. market. The Japanese don't make anything the people in the U.S. would want. [John Foster Dulles, 1954.]
Dulles's misplaced forecast needs no further explanation.

Nineteen sixty promises to be the most prosperous [year] in our history. [Robert A. Anderson, U.S. Secretary of the Treasury, April 14, 1960.] . . . Business conditions will stay good for some time to come. We are not about to enter any sharp recession. [Henry C. Alexander, chairman of the Morgan Guaranty Trust Company, April 22, 1960.]

The recession of 1960 began that same month.

There ain't going to be no recession. I guarantee it. [Pierre Rinfret, popular economist and investment counselor, April, 1969.]

The 1969–1971 recession started the following summer.

There will be no recession in the United States of America. [Richard Nixon, president, State of the Union Address, 1974.]

The GDP dropped 5.8 percent the first quarter of 1974, and by July the economy was (you guessed it) in the deepest recession since the 1930s.

A drastic reduction in the deficit ... will take place in the fiscal year '82. [Ronald Reagan, president, March 1981.]

In fiscal 1982, the government had a record deficit up to that time— $110.7 billion.

New Coca-Cola will be "the most significant soft drink development in the company's history, the surest move ever made. [Robert Goizueta, chairman of Coca-Cola, 1985.]

New Coke was significant, that's for sure. It turned out to be the biggest bomb in the company's corporate history.

A grim first quarter is projected for stocks. [*Wall Street Journal* headline, January 3, 1995.]

Not only was the first quarter one of the strongest for stocks in history, so was all of 1995 and, for that matter, the rest of the 1990s.

"[A major bank] analyst says U.S. stocks may fall for a 4th year" and "the reasons to be cautious are smacking me in the face every day." [*Bloomberg News*, October 2002 and January 2003.]

The stock market surged 29 percent in 2003.

Uses the word "Armageddon" in talking about the economy. [Stephen Roach, chief economist at Morgan Stanley, early 2004.]

Roach has been bearish about the U.S. economy for many years, which was strong in 2004, 2005, 2006, and again in 2007.

Clearly, Will Rogers was on target when he once said, "An economist's guess is liable to be as good as anyone else's." In spring 1990 the National Association of Business Economists (whose main function seems to be polling itself) "guessed" that the remainder of the year and the several beyond it would be good. Specifically, 80 percent of the members predicted no recession for 1990, while 67 percent said there wouldn't be one of these nasty little events for at least three more years.

In response to their poll, supercolumnist Alan Abelson of *Barron's* wrote, "Near-unanimity in this case breeds contempt. Anyone with even a taint of contrarian blood can only pray that, please, Lord, just this once, let 68 economists be right." Despite Abelson's plea, the economists were dead wrong. The recession of 1990–1991 began shortly after the NABE poll was released.

These are only a few examples of predictions that were way wide of the mark. David Dreman, author of *The New Contrarian Investment Strategy*, said, "Expert opinion—which investors naturally rely on—is very often wrong and not infrequently dramatically so." He devotes page after page to detailing the poor performance of experts who try in vain to predict accurately.

If the evidence is so overwhelming that economic and stock market forecasting is a fool's game, why do people rely on it so heavily? Eric Hoffer, author of *The True Believer* in 1951, believed society is addicted to pollsters and forecasters. "Even when the forecasts prove wrong, we still go on asking for them. We watch our experts read the entrails of statistical tables and graphs the way the ancients watched the soothsayers read the entrails of a chicken."

If bad trends do not turn out to be self-limiting, society intervenes to reverse or eradicate them.

—RICHARD TOMKINS, *FINANCIAL TIMES*,
FEBRUARY 13, 2007

WHY FORECASTING GOES AWRY

The Futurist magazine long ago (January–February 1990) explained why so much forecasting so often goes awry:[3]

> Forecasts that a current trend will continue indefinitely are generally wrong, since most trends eventually reach a constraint.
>
> Forecasts that describe ominous doom are frequently wrong, since society usually addresses a problem once it has been identified as being critical.
>
> Forecasts that describe a traditional solution to a critical problem are usually wrong. Society seems to find creative and innovative solutions.

The Futurist wasn't completely negative on forecasting then and still isn't. (I'm an ardent subscriber.) They believe forecasting can be much improved if it's based on analogy. The forecaster looks at past developments and sees how a similar sequence of events might happen in the future. That's the technique I've successfully used for close to 40 years as an economic historian and stock picker.

It's easy for professional money managers to attempt to make a perfect science of forecasting and investing. If they put A into a computer, they expect B to come out. However, although B always follows A in the alphabet, it doesn't always follow A out of a computer. Thinking and acting this way creates frequent mistakes.

No one knows where the Dow or the S&P 500 will be a year from now. No one knows how much money any company will earn this year, next year, or any year beyond that. No one knows how strong the economy will be in any given year. Yet some if not much of the typical professional's time is involved in trying to find these answers, all for naught.

Bennett W. Goodspeed, who, in his words, "overcame the handicaps of having an MBA and working for several prominent Wall Street firms," wrote *The Tao Jones Averages: A Guide to Whole-Brained Investing* in 1983. It's a fascinating little book (154 pages).

---

[3]John Center, "Where America Was a Century Ago: History as a Guide to the Future," *The Futurist* (1990). Reproduced with permission from *The Futurist*, published by the World Future Society, 7901 Woodmont Avenue, Suite 450, Bethesda, Maryland 20814. Copyright 1990.

Goodspeed said analysts and portfolio managers "create an over-load of information in their frenzied activity." I call it Paralysis from Overanalysis. Overload is harmful. In the words of the Chinese philosopher Lao-tzu, "The more stuffed the mind is with knowledge, the less able one can see what's in front of him."

Even if their forecasts for the economy and direction of the stock market were always on the money, most professional money managers would still rarely beat the market. The chief reason is the market has no operating expenses, but the professional does. Expenses, even if kept relatively low, can eat sharply into returns.

THE DISADVANTAGES OF PROFESSIONAL MONEY MANAGEMENT

Most professionals can't match the market for other excellent reasons. One is cash. Mutual funds have to keep cash available for customers who wish to redeem (sell) shares. The cash amount usually ranges between 5 percent when they're optimistic on stock prices and 10 to 15 percent when they're negative. On any given day, funds must have reserves in case more of their customers want to redeem shares than buy them. But the fund manager wants to dip into the cash reserve, not be forced to sell part of the portfolio, to pay for redeemed shares. For the long term, stocks earn three to four times as much as cash. The higher the fund's cash reserve, therefore, the more its return is penalized. Every fund has such a reserve, and every fund is damaged by it in varying degrees. Because individuals don't have to have a reserve cash kitty, their results aren't affected.

Still another problem for money managers, including mutual fund managers, is forced panic selling. During the Great Crash of 1987, the shortest and most brutal ever, mutual funds were bombarded with so many redemptions that they had to sell even though they may not have wanted to. Fortunately their phone lines were jammed with panicked callers. Otherwise they would have had to sell even more of their portfolios. This unplanned selling occurred—you guessed it—at or near the bottom. Once the chaos subsided, they had to reinvest at higher prices. The prudent individual, on the other hand, simply rode through the storm.

On Black Monday, October 19, 1987, the day of the crash, I mailed a one-page memo to all my clients urging them to stand pat because there was blood in the streets and you never sell when the blood is running. This is one Wall Street maxim that's true. I also told them to wait a few days for orderly trading to resume and then add to their portfolios. Those who heeded my advice not only recovered all their paper losses but also added greatly to their coffers. Mutual funds, on the other hand, were forced to react. Savvy individuals responded and took advantage of what looked like a horrible situation but what was in reality one of the premier buying opportunities in history. In fact as Baron Nathan Rothschild, the renowned eighteenth- and nineteenth-century London financier said, "The time to buy is when blood is running in the streets."

When a financial institution (including mutual funds) buys or sells shares of a company, it normally does so at various prices. Their buying and selling power is so enormous it can affect their own transactions. As an example, let's say you and a money manager hear an analyst on CNBC talking about a great idea that sparks new interest in an underfollowed New York Stock Exchange (NYSE) company that doesn't trade in big volume. The following Monday you call your broker to buy 100 shares, and the price is 28 (remember that stock prices don't need the dollar sign). For $2,800 plus commission you own the stock. At the same time, the money manager calls his broker and wants to buy 10,000 shares. He gets the first 2,000 at 28, the next 3,000 at 29, 3,000 more at 29½, and the final 2,000 at 30.

Three years later the same analyst who recommended that stock is on the same money show saying, "Sell it." Coincidentally, you and the money manager are watching the show and both decide to sell on Monday. You call your broker and get out of your 100 shares at 42 less commission. The manager calls his broker and sells 3,000 at 42. Because stock prices happen to be very weak that day, the specialist handling the order on the NYSE takes the stock down a point on the next 3,000. Then he knocks it another 1½ points and clears the remaining 4,000 shares.

In both of these situations, which aren't unusual, the fund's average cost to buy is higher than the individual's. The fund's proceeds from selling are lower too. Financial institutions deal in thousands and tens of thousands of shares and more. Their buying and selling can drive stocks up or down before they complete their orders. It can take days, if not weeks, to accumulate or unload a position, whereas the individual can get in or out with one phone call with the price usually confirmed before he hangs up or with a few clicks online. This is another reason professionals have a tough time equaling or beating the market.

The Cost of Giving Up Control

The Wall Street Journal asks, "How much does it really cost to have someone manage your money?"

Money managers and investment advisers all quote rates that seem straightforward enough. But the prices that they give for their handholding may not include certain other charges investors typically end up paying. These include brokerage firm trading costs to buy and sell stocks or management and administrative fees levied by mutual fund companies. There could also be the cost of setting up a new portfolio in the first place.

The differences in total costs can be huge. Depending on the adviser's investment style, the total annual costs can range from a low of about 1 percent of assets under management to perhaps 4 percent or more.

The rest of this chapter is limited solely to mutual fund costs because this book is about creating your own minifund and outpacing most existing ones.

The first cost is the load. That's the charge you may incur to buy or redeem a fund's shares. No-load mutual funds don't charge anything, and they make up about half the equity funds.

The other half of the funds charge loads; they are so-called load funds. Their load goes up to 8.5 percent, although that's extreme. The industry average is 3–4 percent. Most loads are front-end; that is, they're deducted before you invest into the fund. A few funds have back-end loads that are taken out only when you sell your shares.

Services rating mutual fund total returns—capital appreciation with dividends reinvested—don't take loads into account. That makes comparing load funds to no-loads a more difficult chore, but there's one thing for certain. If a load fund and a no-load fund have exactly the same rates of return, the no-load always puts more money into your pocket. These rating services do list loads and rate them, but deciphering what's included is rarely clear or easy.

Taxes are another bugaboo. Performance rating services often don't consider them either. If your mutual funds are in a retirement account, taxes are no problem. But since the bulk of mutual funds are in taxable accounts, taxes are a sad reality. They can cripple returns, particularly if you're in a high tax bracket.

If taxes and loads aren't enough heavy yokes on the investor's shoulders, there are also annual administrative expenses and the management fee to consider. Mutual fund administrative expenses range from ½ percent to 1½ percent of assets. Yearly management fees are in the same range. Together, they cost the investor between 1 and 3 percent of total assets under management, and over the years they've been rising, not falling.

Finally, there are trading costs, and these are higher than you might think. A round-trip trade (a sell and a buy) executed on one of the stock exchanges probably costs a fund at least 0.35 percent of the transaction amount; for small, illiquid NASDAQ stocks, the cost is closer to 1 percent. That's an annual cost of 1 to 3 percent for a fund reporting a 300 percent turnover.

The Rodney L. White Center for Financial Research at the Wharton School (one of the oldest financial research centers in the country) published a paper titled "Mutual Fund Trading Costs." Its conclusion: "We estimate trading costs for a sample of equity mutual funds and find that these costs average 0.78% of fund assets per year." Their next sentence deserves special emphasis: "Trading costs are negatively related to fund returns."

Even the best of funds have high turnover rates. That is, they literally sell and rebuy the equivalent value of the entire portfolio one or more times every year. Each time they buy and sell, two commissions—no matter how small—are paid. And those commissions eat into the investor's return.

It's estimated that some two-thirds of all funds charge the notorious 12b-1 fee, which can range up to 1 percent of assets each year even in so-called no-load mutual funds. Frequently part of this fee is directed to stockbrokers and money managers as an incentive to sell a particular fund. The downside is that the portion paid to brokers may encourage them to keep you in a fund even if it's doing poorly. Another portion of the fee can pay for advertising and marketing a fund.

Morningstar rating service has said that the average fund loses 0.3 percent of its annual value to commissions but, depending on the activity in the fund, might surrender up to 1 percent of asset value every year. This loss comes out of the investor's pocket, not the fund's.

DO YOU REALLY WANT TO OWN A STOCK MUTUAL FUND?

You must be joking. We don't get it. The financial services industry continues serving up stock mutual funds as the end-all-and-be-all for top-of-the-line investing. Surely they jest. The returns to investors from almost any stock mutual fund you care to name are mediocre at best. But please don't take our word for it.

The February 6, 2006 *Wall Street Journal* observed:

> Stock-mutual-fund investors will probably remember the 2000s as fondly as farmers look back on the Dust Bowl [that was during the Great Depression for all you young bloods out there]. With four years left in this decade, the Standard & Poor's 500 stock index is underwater. [And remained so as this book went to press] At this rate, the decade is shaping up to be the worst in at least a generation and perhaps longer.
>
> Consider: Even if the index rings up 10% annualized gains during the next four years (the historical average), stocks will finish this decade with only a 4% average annual gain. That would make it the worst since the 1970s.
>
> Given that most mutual funds lag the index over time, the math is even nastier for many fund investors, who came to expect returns three times that amount during the bull market from 1982 through 2000.

In a separate article from that same issue, *The Journal* wrote:

> Fund buyers believe today's hot portfolios are likely to keep trouncing their peers in the future. Money comes out of the poorly performing categories each year and goes into the ones that delivered last year's knockout results.
>
> During the past 20 years, Morningstar studies repeatedly have shown that the stock fund categories that investors pulled out of tended to beat the popular fund categories and the Standard & Poor's 500 stock index during the next three years. The research firm found that funds from "unloved" categories had beaten the three most-popular fund categories more than 90% of the time.

Investors in general are their own worst enemies because they let their emotions run their money. In addition, so many are absolutely clueless about how much money they actually have made (or lost) year in and year out, net of commissions, fees, and taxes. Totally clueless. Golfers who invest often know more about their golf scores than their money.

Almost all investors have a lower return in their investment accounts than the average annual return of the investments they bought on their own. If you doubt this assertion, visit www.dalbar.com and read their studies. The proof is in the pudding.

Alongside the many deficits of dumping your money into stock mutual funds come such questions as:

- Who manages my money?
- What is their investment style?

Getting the answer to either question is hard. Unless you're worth a ton of money, you'll never meet your funds' managers, and you probably won't even then. Thus, you are handing over your hard-earned dollars to a person or group you'll never know face-to-face.

Is that how you would purchase a new home—sight unseen? Do you know your attorney, CPA, minister, hair stylist, and other professionals like them face-to-face? Of course you do. Yet you'd turn over your money to a faceless investment advisor in a heartbeat? Think about it: How much of your money is managed and controlled by people you don't know—and whom almost certainly you will never meet.

My mission is to help you become a better steward of your money. I am not faceless. I respond to all phone calls and e-mails, and—take my word for it—I get a lot of them.

INVESTING OVER THE LONG TERM

I once attended a wonderful dinner at the Four Seasons restaurant in New York, hosted by Marty Edelston, the talented publisher of *Boardroom Reports* and *Bottom Line Personal*, in both of which I've been fortunate to have been profiled. Noted Beat generation poet Allen Ginsberg sat across the table from me. (My son Will, attending Tisch School of the Arts at NYU, still can't believe his old man met Ginsberg.)

On my immediate left sat Jonathan Clements, the thoughtful and widely read columnist for *The Wall Street Journal* who unfortunately left that post in early 2008.

Clements wrote a column called "A Harsh Truth: Most of Your Investments Won't Make Money, Even in the Long Term," with which I strongly disagreed then and still do. Here's his case: Look for long-run stock returns of 8 percent annually (the historical post–World War II average has been 10+ percent). Take away 2.5 percent for inflation, 2.0 percent for investment costs, and 1.5 percent for taxes (for a 6.0 percent total). After that, you realize a net 2 percent a year. At 2 percent a year, your real, or net, investment doubles in 36 years. [For any of you who crave the so-called safety of bonds, certificates of deposit (CDs), and other fixed-income investments, beware: They aren't going to come anywhere close to delivering an 8 percent annual return yet you'll still have to contend with investment expenses, inflation, and taxes.]

Now let's break this argument down. First, let's assume Clements is right about 8 percent for stocks for, say, the next 10 years. With that I would not necessarily disagree, but only if you're talking about the Dow or S&P 500 or some other broad stock index. With America's Finest Companies, we are not in the same universe. They will almost assuredly do better because they always have. They are the crème de la crème of America's companies, the top 2 percent, the thoroughbreds.

Second, Clements assumed 2 percent would be paid for investment costs. Who is he kidding? You don't have to pay 2 percent a year, either to have your accounts managed, to do it yourself, or to do it any other way. In the accounts that my wife and I manage, the total annual cost runs about 1.6 to 1.8 percent depending on size, which is 0.2 to 0.4 percent less than what Clements is referring to. When he assumes 2 percent, I believe he is referring to stock mutual funds.

Third, his inflation number seems awfully low to me, given that, for decades, it's averaged about 4 percent. Finally, there's that bane of all of us: taxes. Let's assume his 1.5 percent for taxes is correct. (I think it's higher based on about two dozen studies I've seen just over the past few years. Also, 1.5 percent for taxes is only 19 percent of the total 8 percent return. Vanguard funds founder John Bogle argues it may be as much half of the total return, compared to 19 percent in this example.). But let's stick with 1.5 percent taken out of the 8 percent total return.

The typical stock fund generally sells the equivalent of some 80 to 100 percent of the portfolio—or more—each year and then replaces some 80 to 100 percent or more of it. That, in turn, results in lots of commissions, which come out of your pocket, and in taxes on stocks with capital gains, which also come out of your pocket, not the fund's.

If you own stock funds, as many of my clients did before I took over their accounts (I sell all the funds immediately), you could have had losses during some of the last several years but still had to pay taxes on gains. How did that happen? The fund managers sold stock positions that they'd owned before you bought in and that, despite a bad market, had profits. You paid your pro rata share of those profits even though some or none of the benefits came your way.

Clements says:

Stocks return 8 percent annually.

   Deduct 2.5 percent for inflation. (I think this is too low.)

   Deduct 2.0 percent for investment costs. (I think this is too high.)

   Deduct 1.5 percent for taxes (for 6.0 percent of total expenses)

Net return is 2 percent a year.

Bill Staton says:

America's Finest Companies return an estimated 11 percent annually.

   Deduct 4.0 percent for inflation.

   Deduct a maximum 1.2 percent for investment costs, maybe less, because you're your own manager.

   Deduct 1.0 percent for taxes due to lower turnover and client tax planning (6.2 percent total expenses).

Net return is 4.80 percent a year.

In summary, if your AFC total return bumps up to 12 percent, the net return is 5.80 percent a year.

Vive la différence!

Letter from Bill and Mary Staton to the Editors of *The Wall Street Journal* in response to Mr. Clements article (March 2003)

Dear Editors,

We always enjoy reading Jonathan Clements' columns for their incisiveness and information, but the one he wrote about mutual funds (1/28/03) is way off the mark.

He asserts they are still the best way for "most investors to be in stocks," which is patently wrong. He is also incorrect when he says they offer "low cost, low risk and a low investment minimum." Warren Buffett, among other successful managers, clearly shows that you don't "need to own hundreds of stocks and bonds" for "proper diversification" as Clements believes.

First, the overwhelming majority of stock mutual funds fail to equal, much less, beat a benchmark index. That has been true since well before World War II and is still true today. This knowledge can easily lead investors to plop their money into index funds, which have never and can never beat the indices because of management fees and other expenses. My friend Larry Carroll, a nationally-recognized financial planner, likens investing in an index fund to waking up each morning and saying, "I look forward to another mediocre day."

Second, a typical stock fund requires $1,000–3,000 or more for a beginning investment whereas there are well over 1,000 companies which anyone can invest in directly with the companies themselves for far less money (as little as $20 to start), not to mention avoiding fees and commissions and also not having to deal with either a broker or a fund company.

Third, regardless of how much research anyone performs, it's almost impossible to determine what a fund owns at any given time or how much buying and selling they've been doing. History shows stock fund turnover approaches 100% a year. High turnover results in short-term capital gains (assuming there are any) and a ridiculous amount of trading commissions, all of which eat into the investor's pocketbook.

Stock mutual funds are okay if you have no other choice such as in a 401(k) or similar retirement plan. But investing in individual quality stocks with rising dividends makes a lot more sense. At the very least, an individual knows what he or she owns.

If you want to really understand why stock-mutual funds don't make sense, read Fred Schwed Jr.'s classic, *Where Are the Customers' Yachts?*, published in 1940. Even then a few of us knew the real truth about stock mutual funds.

Live Healthy & Wealthy!
Bill and Mary Staton

CHAPTER 6

Uncle Sam Is Your Greatest Retirement Planning Asset

The reward of energy, enterprise and thrift—is taxes.
—WILLIAM A. FEATHER, AMERICAN PUBLISHER AND AUTHOR
(1889–1981)

POINTS TO REMEMBER

- Invest as early as you can, with as much as you can, as often as you can.
- Take full advantage of the individual retirement account (IRA).
- Harness the power of compounding returns.

For most families, the top three financial goals are:

- Educating children.
- Having enough money to live comfortably in retirement.
- Long-term care.

A better phrase for retirement is, I think, "life after work" because retiring has connotations of being old and inactive, when the opposite is more and more true. If a married couple makes it to 60 in good health, the odds are close to 100 percent that at least one of them will make it to 90. One of the biggest problems older people in this country face is living a long, healthy life but not having enough money to travel and do whatever else they want to do in their later years.

If "senior" inflation continues to run well ahead of general inflation, it could raise . . . problems, even for those who are a long way from retirement.

—BRETT ARENDS, MARKETWATCH.COM,
FEBRUARY 27, 2008

WHERE YOUR MONEY GOES

Having enough money for life after work is easily achievable when you start early enough and invest your money wisely and on a regular basis. If you've already started, that's great. If not, it's still not too late, and you have plenty of company.

It's easy to see why so many people aren't prepared for life after work. If you're in your twenties or thirties, you're still some thirty to forty years away from life after work. Somehow 20, 30, or 40 years seems so far away that we feel that there's still plenty of time to get ready. So why worry about it now? All those who haven't begun planning think that way. If they don't think that way, then why haven't they started?

Only put off until tomorrow what you are willing to die having left undone.

—PABLO PICASSO

Another reason people don't get ready for life after work is that they don't save any money. All their income is spent to pay the grocer, the mortgage company, the auto dealer, the department store, the phone company, the local utility, the doctor, the electronics store, and all the other bills that come up month after month. The list goes on and on. These people spend every dollar they make.

Sometimes they spend more than they make and borrow to make up the difference. That's been particularly true in the new millennium as financial institutions of all sorts have allowed people to actually borrow more money than their underlying assets (usually their home or other real estate) is worth. The borrowers reason that one day they'll start to save some money as soon as they quit spending so much. But few really ever do it. It's a fantasy.

Economy does not lie in spending money but in spending it wisely.

—T. H. HUXLEY (1825–1895)

To be able to invest, you've got to be able to save, and the first place you ought to invest your savings is into a retirement plan. The only way you'll surely be able to invest is to budget for it, using my simple budgeting formula (detailed a little later in this chapter). Also, I strongly believe in giving away money, time, and your personal expertise, regardless of what field they may lie in.

Giving to Others

No man can tell whether he is rich or poor by turning to his ledger.
It is the heart that makes a man rich. He is rich according to what
he is, not according to what he has.
      —HENRY WARD BEECHER, ABOLITIONIST (1813–1887)

As a teenager I read the wonderful story in Norman Vincent Peale's *Guideposts* magazine about Joseph Colgate, founder of the forerunner of Colgate-Palmolive and Colgate University. Mr. Colgate's business was so successful he quickly turned into a multimillionaire and decided he had far more money than he needed. So he started giving it away.

Happiness pursued eludes. Happiness given returns.
      —SIR JOHN MARKS TEMPLETON, FOUNDER OF TEMPLETON
FUNDS AND ONCE ONE OF THE WORLD'S WEALTHIEST PEOPLE
BEFORE HE GAVE AWAY MOST OF HIS FORTUNE, MADE FROM
MANAGING MONEY, TO HIS OWN TEMPLETON FOUNDATION

Colgate first gave away 10 percent of each year's income, but, after he started giving, his income multiplied. He then upped the percentage to 15 percent, and the same thing happened. Next he gave away 20 percent of his income, but money poured into his coffers like water through a broken dam. After studying his "problem," Mr. Colgate finally turned his money over to a foundation and let others figure out what to do with it. Giving away his money created a giant hole, which was then refilled with even more money than before.

More modern-day examples are Bill Gates, founder of Microsoft, and the world's wealthiest investor, Warren Buffett of Berkshire Hathaway. At the time of writing, these two gentlemen were two of the three wealthiest on earth. Years ago Gates set up the Gates Foundation to contribute money to all sorts of things, ranging from bringing the poor out of poverty to preventing and curing malaria in various parts of the world, thus helping save the lives of millions who die from this awful disease each year. Buffett has pledged the bulk of his fortune to the Gates Foundation because he believes it is so thoroughly well run and with the same types of financial disciplines he looks for in the companies in which he invests.

Besides these living examples, Deepak Chopra's seminars and books have been a strong inspiration in my life. Of all his books on the best-seller list, my favorite is a short one at just 111 pages: *The Seven Spiritual Laws of Success.* Chopra's Second Law is The Law of Giving: "Giving and receiving are different aspects of the flow of energy in the universe. And in our willingness to give that which we seek, we keep the abundance of the universe circulating in our lives."

Chopra notes that the word "affluence" derives from the Latin root word *affluere*, which means "to flow to or toward." The full meaning, according to my dictionary, includes "abundance of money, property, and other material goods; riches; wealth." It's important to know that the expanded definition includes "an abundant supply, as of thoughts or words; profusion." He points out that the synonym for money is "currency." This word stems from the Latin *currere*, which means "to run" or "to flow."

Dr. Wayne W. Dyer, like Deepak Chopra, has been another significant inspiration in my life. (It happens that the two are best friends.) Dyer's book, *The Power of Intention,* has an interesting slant on giving under the broader perspective of generosity. He writes, "If asked, 'Why do you give us light and warmth?' I believe that the sun would answer, 'It's my nature to do so.' We must be like the sun, and locate and dispense our giving nature. The more you give of yourself, no matter how little, the more you open the door for life to pour in."

Dyer then goes on to share an incredible poem from Swami Sivananda, one of the great yoga masters of the previous century, noting that "everything that he suggests, you own in infinite amounts" and it discusses how best to give it away.

Each of us needs to keep the circle of giving intact, especially the money part. As Chopra says, "If our only intention is to hold on to our money and hoard it—since it is life energy, we will stop its circulation back into our lives. Like a river, money must keep flowing." Stated another way, in the crass words of Texas oil man Clint Murchison, Jr., "Money is like manure. If you spread it around, it does a lot of good. But if you pile it up in one place, it stinks like hell."

My wife Mary and I tithe a minimum 10 percent of our annual income each year to causes and organizations in which we strongly believe. When we file our tax return, we use the amount of income on which we pay taxes to be the blueprint for how much we'll give away during the ensuing 12 months.

Many years ago I heard about the reclusive Charles Feeney (his close friends call him Chuck). Feeney, now age 78, is chairman and founder of Atlantic Philanthropies, an international foundation (set up in Bermuda and kept secret for 15 years), which is 100 percent committed to giving its entire $4 billion away by the year 2020.

Feeney, who made his fortune with the DFS Group chain of airport stores, loves to build universities and hospitals and most recently became very interested in health care for the aging. Feeney is a most unusual giver in that he doesn't own either a home or car, travels tourist class, and avoids publicity like the plague. He told *BusinessWeek* in a rare 2003 interview, "It has always been hard for me to rationalize a 32,000-square-foot house or someone driving me around in a six-door Cadillac. The seats are the same in a cab. And you may live longer if you walk."

> *When you're 80 years old and about to kick it, anybody can give away money. It's important to give away a piece when it really matters. I'd suggest people try that.*
> —BILL GROSS, BILLIONAIRE AND THE WORLD'S
> LARGEST BOND MANAGER

Giving to Yourself

In our business and personal lives, we operate under an amazingly simple budgeting formula:

100 percent of income:
  Less: Income into retirement plans and other investments
  Less: Income given to others
  Less: Income for fun, like vacation
  Spend: Paying all your bills

In this formula, first, you give to yourself for your future. Second, you give what you will to others less fortunate than yourself. Third, you reserve some for yourself and your family to enjoy in the present. And, of course, reserve enough to pay your current living expenses.

Americans who don't do well with their money use a different formula. When money comes in, they spend it on everybody they can think of, and if—and this is a big *if*—there's any money left, they use it for their financial future. The dilemma is that there's rarely anything left because they don't plan for any to be.

> *It takes as much energy to wish as it does to plan.*
> —ELEANOR ROOSEVELT

If somebody says, "I'll try to do it," what are the odds that he or she will do it? This does not compare to the level of commitment with, say, "I *will* do it." You can't try to do anything. Either you do it or you don't. You can't try to save money for your future. Either you do it or you don't. There is no in-between about saving money. If people don't save money, they get trapped. Without actually paying themselves first, people rarely have any money left over to save and invest.

Any couple can easily save $600 a year by putting pocket change into a jar at the end of a day and taking it to the bank at the end of the month. Six hundred dollars a year, put into a handful of America's Finest Companies (and reinvesting all dividends), can grow to more than $1.5 million at the end of 50 years, even though the total invested was just $30,000 scattered evenly over five decades (see Table 6.1).

I believe not only in paying myself first, but also in paying others first who need it. When I set aside pretax income for myself, I also set aside the same for the charities, churches, organizations, and causes I believe in. Joseph Colgate proved that this works. Many others have proved it too.

I'm reminded of the story about a deep well with the purest, best tasting water that anyone for miles around had ever tasted. For generations the old well served all the descendants of a farming family and anyone else who wanted to partake of its goodness. Through drought after drought, the well always provided all the water the farmer, his family, and their animals ever needed. Not once did it ever run low.

During the Great Depression hard times hit, and the farmer had to sell his farm and move. The property stayed empty and the

TABLE 6.1 Awesome Power of Compounded Returns with Just $600 A Year Collected from Pocket Change

Annual rate (%)	Compounded at Various Interest Rates of Return for Different Periods (years)									
	5	10	15	20	25	30	35	40	45	50
	$3,000	$6,000	$9,000	$12,000	$15,000	$18,000	$21,000	$24,000	$27,000	$30,000
1	$3,091	$6,340	$9,755	$13,344	$17,115	$21,080	$25,246	$29,625	$34,228	$39,065
2	3,185	6,701	10,584	14,870	19,603	24,828	30,597	36,966	43,998	51,763
3	3,281	7,085	11,494	16,606	22,532	29,402	37,366	46,598	57,301	69,708
4	3,380	7,492	12,495	18,582	25,987	34,997	45,959	59,296	75,522	95,264
5	3,481	7,924	13,594	20,832	30,068	41,856	56,902	76,104	100,611	131,889
6	3,585	8,383	14,804	23,396	34,894	50,281	70,873	98,429	135,305	184,654
7	3,692	8,870	16,133	26,319	40,606	60,644	88,748	128,166	183,451	260,992
8	3,802	9,387	17,595	29,654	47,373	73,408	111,661	167,869	250,456	371,803
9	3,914	9,936	19,202	33,459	55,394	89,145	141,075	220,975	343,912	533,065
10	4,029	10,519	20,970	37,801	64,909	108,566	178,876	292,111	474,477	768,180
11	4,148	11,137	22,914	42,759	76,199	132,548	227,499	387,496	657,101	1,111,402
12	4,269	11,793	25,052	48,419	89,600	162,176	290,078	515,485	912,731	1,612,812
13	4,394	12,489	27,403	54,882	105,510	198,789	370,650	687,291	1,270,684	2,345,546
14	4,521	13,227	29,988	62,261	124,400	244,042	474,404	917,945	1,771,946	3,416,253
15	4,652	14,010	32,830	70,686	146,827	299,974	608,007	1,227,572	2,473,739	4,980,224
16	4,786	14,840	35,955	80,304	173,453	369,097	780,016	1,643,087	3,455,831	7,263,212
17	4,924	15,720	39,389	91,283	205,058	454,502	1,001,397	2,200,434	4,829,262	10,592,830
18	5,065	16,653	43,163	103,813	242,563	559,991	1,286,189	2,947,555	6,748,357	15,443,670
19	5,210	17,642	47,310	118,108	287,058	690,232	1,652,349	3,948,298	9,427,245	22,501,950
20	5,358	18,690	51,865	134,415	339,826	850,955	2,122,806	5,287,578	13,162,543	32,757,977

Source: The Staton Institute® Inc.

well unused for many years until finally a new family bought it. Even though they came from another county, they knew the reputation of the old well and its water.

When the family moved in and rushed to the well to sample its contents, they were shocked to find it completely dry. In great disbelief, they stared at each other and realized the terrible mistake they'd made buying a farm with a dry well. What they hadn't realized was that a well needs to be used to keep the water flowing. The thousands of tiny rivulets that flow into the well's cavern will stop up, just as blood will not circulate if veins and arteries become clogged.

And so it is with money. To do the most good, to help the most people, money must flow and must not be hoarded, as Hetty Green hoarded it. Hetty could read the financial pages at age 6. At age 30 she inherited her father's fortune and began trading on Wall Street with "bold audacity." It wasn't her looks but her fierce style that earned her the name: the Witch of Wall Street.

The Witch was so tightfisted she wore only a black dress (maybe because she had just one). To save soap, she seldom washed it. Working alone on the first floor of a bank, from which she coerced free space (probably because she owned the building), Green lived the life of a pauper. She bought *The Wall Street Journal*, read it, and then resold it each day.

Despite her intense nature, she managed to marry and bear two children. Her son, Ned, hurt himself sledding, and Hetty took him to a charity ward, where she was recognized as a multimillionaire who could easily afford a hospital. But Hetty refused to pay for treatment, the wound became infected, and Ned's leg was amputated. She left her children $50 million each when she died of a stroke in 1916 after arguing over the price of milk.

I have what I call a firm knowing that good things—often unexpectedly great things—happen when people with a giving attitude empty their glass. Only a completely empty glass can be totally replenished. One of Jesus' most famous parables is about the poor woman who gave her last two coins to help others. She trusted that, even though she had no money, her needs would be met, and we must assume they were. It's no secret that giving is good and what goes around comes around. All modern society, religious and secular, thrives on the goodwill of the well-off toward the less fortunate.

In polar contrast to Hetty Green is a divorced physician who has two children living with their father. I recently conducted a tailored financial coaching session via phone with this physician, Linda Z., who is in her mid-fifties and full of energy and zest. Simply talking with her is uplifting for me.

In 2007 she earned $225,000, about four times the median family income in America, but she gave away $100,000 of it. Few people in our country give away that much every year, especially when it amounts to nearly half their income. But she assures me the satisfaction of giving away such a lofty percentage brings much joy into her life. She'd like to earn more so she can give more away. So do Mary and I.

I'm reminded of the story Vanguard founder John Bogle likes to share about life and how money fits in. At a party on Shelter Island in New York, "the late Kurt Vonnegut informs his pal, author Joseph Heller that their host, a hedge-fund manager, had made more money in a single day than Heller earned from his wildly popular *Catch 22*. Heller responds, 'Yes, but I have something he will never have—Enough!'"

If you realize that you have enough, you are truly rich.
—Lao Tzu, Chinese philosopher, sixth century b.c.

The Gospel of Investing Money

My mission is to reach everyone who will listen to the gospel ("gospel" means truth) of investing money to earn the highest return possible in the least time with the least risk. I gladly give away my expertise to people who can't afford it without asking anything in return. The more I give, the more I am rewarded, frequently in ways never anticipated.

For example, I visited a federal penitentiary outside St. Louis to teach the inmates how to profitably invest even small amounts of money so that, when they got out, they'd be good stewards of whatever money they were able to earn. I aided Tony Robbins with a group of underprivileged youths in Houston, to each of whom he gave $250. I taught them how to easily put it to work for their financial futures and helped a number of them get started.

Mary and I have sent our investing materials to various churches, charities, and prisons across America at no charge, all in the hope that they will make even one life financially better off. We've gotten enough e-mails and letters back to know that we perhaps have helped more people than we thought we might and in more ways than we thought. I cherish this statement a former student recently sent: "I am confident that I will be able to use the tools that you have taught me to construct a very successful, long-term portfolio."

Share your knowledge. It's a way to achieve immortality.
—DALAI LAMA

"What goes around comes around" is really true. We are all part of a giant circle, 6.5 billion of us, and each one has a part to play. Every person has a way to serve, and serving is what being human is all about. To serve is to give: The more you give, the more you get because the hand that gives gathers. Mary and I are both Rotarians, and the Rotary motto is, "Service above self."

Before spending all your income, first allocate a certain percentage for investment, for your financial future. The amount can be 1 percent, 2 percent, 5 percent, 10 percent, or more of pretax income. The percentage is up to you. However, you need to start with some percentage, regardless of how small, and then gradually increase it as fast as you can. Once you decide on a percentage to invest, allocate that same percentage for giving to others. Logically, the larger your income, the larger the percentage you'll set aside to invest and to give.

While you're at it, make sure there's money set aside to have some fun during the year. After all, what good is money if you can't have fun with it?

Andrew Carnegie, the steel magnate who was at one time the richest man in the world, said, "You want to know if you will be rich? The answer is 'Can you save money?'" I might add, "rich" in the broadest sense means having abundant supply. Money is only part of that abundance, a tool to use and to use wisely. Giving, to me, is part of using money wisely by sharing our abundance with others.

Because I see so many adults failing to prepare for their financial futures, I have a strong sense of mission about teaching young people how to manage their money so that they'll end up where they want to be financially. Of course, the earlier they start, the easier it will be for them and the more likely they are to make it. Saving, investing, and giving are habits, some of the finest habits there are. Once a person adopts the saving-investing-giving habit, it's as hard to quit as smoking.

We are what we repeatedly do. Excellence, then, is not an act, but a habit.

—ARISTOTLE

WHAT YOU SHOULD BE PUTTING AWAY

Each year I have the privilege of teaching Junior Achievement's superb Applied Economics course to juniors and seniors at Charlotte Country Day School, right around the corner from where I live. Our oldest child Gracie (now 30) is a graduate. I insisted she be in my class. She was.

In the class, I always spend a lot of time on investing because that's the subject I know the most about. I've completed more than 20 years of service at Country Day, and I sometimes think I learn more than the students do. These eager juniors and seniors tell me they "waste" between $15 and $25 per week. This is money that slips through their hands—"crack" money in the sense that it falls through the cracks. They don't know where it goes. They just know it disappears.

The lesson I try to get across is that, if they invest that wasted money into a retirement plan at 12 percent per year, they'll easily end up with $1 million or more. Even minors can have retirement plans, as I'll show later. And it is very possible to invest in a well diversified portfolio of stocks with that small amount of money. I'll demonstrate how easy that is, too. You don't have to go the customary mutual fund route and end up with potentially inferior results. Besides, more and more mutual funds today require $2,000 and up just to get started.

The IRA (individual retirement account) has been available since the late 1970s. It's a brokerage account that is simple to open and use. Any individual, including a minor, with earned income from a salary, commissions, or bonuses (interest and dividend income don't count) can set aside up to $5,000 each year ($6,000 at age 50 or older) into a tax-deductible IRA or Roth IRA, funded with after-tax dollars.

By simply beginning to invest $50 per month at 12 percent per annum into an IRA—and never increasing the amount—a 16-year-old will have $1,440,011 by the age of 65. If he waits until 18, the amount will be $1,146,954. By waiting two more years until age 20, he will have only $913,331. That's still almost a million dollars, but

TABLE 6.2   Investing $600 a Year Compounded at
12% Per Year Starting at Different Ages

Starting Age	Total Invested	Value at Age 65
16	$30,000	$1,440,011
18	$28,800	$1,146,954
20	$27,600	$913,331

Source: The Staton Institute® Inc.

it's $526,860 less than the one who started at 16. The 16-year-old, who makes 48 more payments of $50 per month (a total of $2,400 extra) than the 20-year-old, will wind up with 58 percent more money at age 65. Clearly, the earlier you start investing, the more money you'll have when you need it (see Table 6.2).

Two young people, aged 19, graduate from high school. Both begin to work and have annual incomes. Investor Smart (a graduate of one of my Junior Achievement classes) opens a tax-deductible IRA through a stockbroker and begins to salt away $2,000, roughly $5.50 a day. (The maximum annual contribution starting in 2008 was $5,000, plus an additional $1,000 for those 50 and over.) She makes her contributions at the beginning of each year. Investor Not As Smart (who wasn't in my class) decides to wait a few years to open her IRA.

Investor Smart contributes $2,000 annually from age 19 through age 26 and quits. After contributing a total of $16,000, she decides (wrongly, in my opinion) to make no more contributions until beginning to withdraw funds from her IRA at age 65.

Investor Not As Smart, at age 27, wakes up to the realization she needs to begin preparing for retirement. She opens an IRA through her stockbroker and contributes $2,000 per year from age 27 through age 65, all the while earning 12 percent annually on her money just like Investor Smart.

For brevity, I've not shown every year, but Investor Not As Smart contributes $78,000 over the 39 years she contributes to her plan. Thus, she puts nearly five times more into her IRA than Investor Smart. But when both are 65, Investor Smart has $675,727 more than Investor Not As Smart. Even if Investor Not As Smart continues to invest $2,000 per year forever, she will never catch up with Investor Smart, who committed just $16,000 (see Table 6.3). This

TABLE 6.3   Investor Smart Starts At 19 Stops At 26;
Investor Not As Smart Starts At 27

Start Age	Total Invested	Value at Age 65
19	$16,000	$2,043,747
27	$78,000	$1,368,020

Source: The Staton Institute® Inc.

is the best example I know to demonstrate the power of investing early for a new home, vacation, college education, life after work, or whatever.

These numbers assume 12 percent annual returns. Even using 10 percent, the numbers remain impressive – $1,019,160 (65-fold return) and $805,185 (11-fold return) respectively.

You can certainly start with less than $2,000 per year—or thousands of dollars more. *The key point, of course, is to start as early as you can.* Then add to your investments, as often as you can, with as much as you can. Don't get caught up in magical numbers or formulas about how much you might need at some point down the road.

To paraphrase the title of a popular book many years back, "If all you invest is all you can invest, then all you're investing is enough." But in the words of Robert Redford, "If you can do more, do it."

Life After Work

The idea is to die young as late as possible.

—ASHLEY MONTAGU

Life after work requires a lot more money for some than for others. What might it take for you? When I launched my financial advisory and money management career, the accepted rule of thumb was that, if you were living comfortably on what you made when you were close to retiring, it would cost about 60 percent of that amount once you quit work.

The theory sounded plausible for a number of reasons. Your children were grown and gone. Because you were likely in your sixties, you weren't as active as when you worked. You didn't eat out as frequently, didn't travel as often, and didn't make as many purchases as before. I guess the so-called experts who came up with the 60 percent figure assumed that everyone who retired sat around and played cards or that, if they were really active, played rousing games of shuffleboard between naps.

One of my inspirations was fellow Rotarian Powell Majors, who passed away at 100 the day after Thanksgiving 2007. In the final year of his life, Powell was still married, driving a car, working out at the YMCA several days a week, and planning vacations for both 2008 and 2009. He came to all our Tuesday meetings, dressed sharply, and paid close attention to the speaker that day. Powell always ate a lot of food even though he wasn't even close to being overweight.

Another inspiration is alive and well and in the investment arena like me. Most people have never heard of Walter Schloss, now in his 92 year, but there was a three-page profile about him in the February 11, 2008 *Forbes*. None other than Warren Buffett labeled this "bushy-eyebrowed" "avuncular" man a "superinvestor" who uses a "laid-back approach" (like me) that "fast-money traders couldn't comprehend."

Today we know the truth. People are living longer. They are more physically active and mentally alert. As Eubie Blake, the famous jazz pianist, put it on his 100th birthday: "If I'd known I was going to live this long, I'd have taken better care of myself." He died at 104.

> *Someone born today would be expected to live to the age of 100 years.*
>
> —*THE FINANCIAL TIMES*, FEBRUARY 23, 2008

Various studies show that people spend between 80 and 90 percent of their final working year's income in the first few years of life after work. The erroneous 60 percent figure of yesteryear wasn't ever in the ballpark, or even close to being in it. These same studies also show that people emphatically do not want to reduce their lifestyles unless they're forced to do so.

A young person who begins a career around age 25 will probably work for 35 to 40 years. During that period, money has to be set aside for the 20 to 30 years, possibly more, of life after work. Social Security won't support more than a pauper lifestyle at best, fewer and fewer companies have pension plans to which employees don't have to contribute, and the chance of winning the lottery is one in many millions. Providing for the future is up to each individual, or else the future won't be secure unless a substantial inheritance appears out of the blue.

Inflation is a fact of life, and I want to take that into account. Let's assume it will increase at 4 percent per year in the future (the approximate rate for the past five decades). In recent years I believe it's been considerably higher than that, despite official government numbers to the contrary. But that's a subject for another book on another day.

Under even a 4 percent inflation rate, the cost of living will slightly more than double every two decades. How many decades have you got to live? Once you make a stab at that figure, it's easy to zero in on how much the next 20, 30, 40, 50, 60, or more years will cost.

Life after work will use up a lot more money than most people think, especially given they don't like to reduce their lifestyles and will probably live longer than expected. Wouldn't it be terrible to have plenty of good years left and a zest for life but no money for anything more than the bare necessities?

Besides an IRA, another simple way to invest for life after work is to participate in your company's contributory 401(k) retirement plan or its equivalent, the 403(b), if you work for a government agency or nonprofit institution. Under the typical 401(k) arrangement, you can contribute $15,500 in 2008 and $20,500 if age 50 or older (this amount is adjusted upward for inflation each year), and you can invest your money in a variety of mutual funds.

The most elite of 401(k)s allow you to invest in individual stocks other than the stock of the company offering the plan and assorted mutual funds. If your company or organization allows this, you have several legs up by following the America's Finest Companies strategy. Your returns will almost assuredly be higher and operating expenses far lower. This could mean an extra 1 to 3 percent (perhaps even more) per year of additional return to you.

If the place where you work offers only mutual funds as an investment choice, ask if they will allow you to open a self-directed IRA, roll the money out of the plan into the IRA, and purchase individual equities. If they do allow this, you can keep the 401(k) or 403(b) open to get the corporate dollar match yet still invest in America's Finest Companies®.

With a 401(k) or any other retirement plan (SEP, Keogh, solo 401(k), defined-benefit, profit-sharing, and the like) to which you can (and hopefully do) make annual (if not more frequent) contributions, the amount is excluded from your gross income for federal and state income tax purposes.

Contributory Retirement Plans

Let's say you earn $50,000 pretax in 2009 and invest $4,000 into your tax-deductible IRA. (A Roth IRA is funded with after-tax dollars.) Your reported gross income will be reduced to $46,000. The taxes you would have paid on the $4,000 in your IRA are now invested for your future. This is how Uncle Sam becomes your partner when you invest through any retirement plan. He doesn't tax you on dollars you put into it, and neither does the state where you live. Those unpaid tax dollars work for you tax free until you begin withdrawals (which are then taxed many years down the road at ordinary income tax rates).

> *The avoidance of taxes is the only intellectual pursuit that carries any reward.*
>
> —JOHN MAYNARD KEYNES

Uncle Sam will help you another way, too. He has made it expensive to voluntarily withdraw your retirement plan. Short of a loan, financial hardship, and a few other special considerations, once you invest money into any retirement plan you're not allowed to get it out before age 59 and one-half without a 10 percent penalty on the amount removed. Plus you have to pay taxes. Although you can move your retirement funds from one plan to another, you cannot spend it unless you want to pay a high price. Because Uncle Sam, our own federal government, doesn't want you to squander your retirement funds, he becomes an excellent financial friend.

So the advantages of contributory retirement plans are clear:

1. The money added each year reduces your gross income and hence your tax liability.
2. Your money grows with no tax consequences until it's taken out.
3. Because the federal government frowns on early withdrawals by penalizing them, it pays for you to stick with your plan.
4. You may have the tremendous opportunity to create your own minifund of stocks culled from America's Finest Companies within your retirement plan. By doing that, your money ought to grow steadily at an above-average rate.

As you near or enter retirement, many financial gurus suggest you sell a bunch of your stocks and go into bonds and cash because that's a far less risky strategy. Although this advice may appear sound, it's often way off the track—and can easily leave you financially impaired!

The reason has to do with the term "risk." The first thing most people associate with risk is buying something that goes down in price. Stocks, for example, are supposed to be much riskier than other assets because they decline in a bear (down) market.

The biggest risk of all is shortfall risk. This is the risk that you'll outlive your savings. And it is quite real.
    —ALEXANDER GREEN, INVESTMENT DIRECTOR,
                                THE OXFORD CLUB

But there's another, more ominous, side to risk. Cash doesn't suffer in a bear market, but it still goes down because of two things—inflation and taxes. Since the end of World War II, the total return from Treasury bills was 5.5 percent a year. Inflation was 4.0 percent, so the net real return was 1.5 percent a year (5.5 percent less 4.0 percent = 1.5 percent), not great, but at least was a tad or two ahead of inflation if taxes are excluded.

With taxes it's a different story. In life after work, your tax bracket frequently drops, but, when state taxes are taken into account, the combined tax rate including federal can easily be at least 25 percent, perhaps more. What does a 25 percent tax rate do to a Treasury bill return? Here's the answer:

Return:	5.5 percent annual return
Less 25 percent in taxes:	4.13 percent
Less 4.0 percent inflation:	0.13 percent

You gain so little ground after taxes and inflation that your net return is almost immeasurable.

Let's look at this another way. You and your wife are both 70 and in good health. Your life expectancy can easily be as much as 15 to 20 more years. Based on the historic rate of inflation, the cost of living will increase 80 percent to 120 percent during that relatively short period of time.

Inflation is the biggest financial threat to all Americans regardless of age. For a baby born today with a normal life expectancy within the plausible range of 85 to 100, the cost of living at 4 percent will rise 28 times before he dies age 85. If the baby lives to 90, inflation will multiply 34 times. By 100, 51 times. That's horrible any way you look at it.

What costs $1,000 today will cost between $28,000 and $51,000 then unless inflation breaks out of the twentieth-century pattern on the downside. I believe—and there's plenty of evidence to support me—that our own federal government purposefully understates inflation, as measured by the CPI (consumer price index).

Lendership versus Ownership

Other than spending your money or giving it away, there are only two options: lendership and ownership. You can loan money in a number of ways:

- To a bank through an interest-bearing checking or savings account.
- In a fixed-rate CD.
- To a corporation by buying its bonds.
- To the federal government or the state/municipality where you reside by purchasing their bonds.
- To an insurance company by buying any number of fixed-rate investments.

And all these borrowers will be eager to sell their products to you. The borrowers take the money you loan them, earn a higher rate of return than they pay you, and pocket the difference. Sure, you can make money by lending it, but not nearly as much as by owning real estate, your own business, or shares of companies that appreciate in value, especially when taxes are considered.

Ownerhip, on the other hand, can keep you ahead of the game. Quality real estate, particularly timberland, has generally provided the second highest return after dividend-paying stocks for the majority of the populace. For more than a century, dividend-paying stocks have outpaced inflation by nearly 7 percentage points a year. Real estate has outpaced inflation by 4 to 5 percentage points each year, depending on the period of time examined, certainly not the past three years. No other investment assets that I know have come close to these two; so they are where your retirement plan money should be if you're to stay well ahead of rising prices and the tax collector, too. However, investing in real estate through a retirement plan is difficult. Investing in companies is not.

Even when you're older, you can't afford to be too conservative with your money because inflation and taxes will assuredly chew up your purchasing power. But you also don't want to run the risk of being hurt too much in a severe bear market. So what's your option?

Inside your retirement plan, where taxes don't matter, you can shift into the higher-yielding America's Finest Companies, those with rising dividends like the REITs (real estate investment trusts), some banks, and utilities. Throughout the decades, these companies usually have provided greater dividend yields than the typical common stock. And, during a market decline, these stocks sometimes (not always) don't fall as far as the typical stock. Their dividends continue to increase year in and year out, providing you with a growing stream of income, something you won't get from cash or bonds.

Cash is certainly not the place to be. Following the Crash of 1987, someone asked what it was like to lose a lot of my money in one day. It was his less than subtle way of bragging that he was 100 percent in money market funds and hadn't lost a penny. I replied, "It feels terrible, but within two or three years, if not sooner, all that money and more will be recouped. You'll be way behind me." And, as it turned out, he was way, way behind me.

I coached a couple with more real estate than I felt was necessary, and they didn't owe a dime on it. They had a substantial six-figure amount of cash that they wanted to invest in stocks that could generate, from dividend income alone, enough to live on. They were concerned about falling stock prices at some future date; so I explained one thing some of my clients can do to take advantage of such a situation when, and only when, it occurs: lightly leveraging their real estate.

Let's say you have a $300,000 home in a neighborhood with at least stable, if not rising, prices. Also assume that stock prices fall again à la 1987 (a swift decline of more than 30 percent in four days, the second shortest bear market in history) or agonizingly as in the grueling great bear market from March 2000 through

October 2002. In a February 11, 2008 article about one of the world's wealthiest money managers, *The New Yorker* described that period aptly: "The severe decline ..., during which the S&P 500 dropped forty-nine percent and the technology-heavy NASDAQ composite an astounding seventy-eight percent, was devastating."

Periods like these create an extraordinary array of solid values, and they are the times to really get excited about owning America's Finest Companies. You could secure a fixed 30-year mortgage around, say, 6 percent, borrow $100,000, and reinvest in AFCs that should provide at least 12 percent a year total return, given enough time. If you're in a 25 percent tax bracket, the after-tax interest cost on the mortgage will be only 4.50 percent. So the America's Finest you bought, even after taxes, would easily beat that. Plus, you can construct an AFC portfolio with a dividend yield 4.50 percent and higher.

Unless you absolutely cannot risk any loss of principal, I can't think of one good reason why you shouldn't own stocks when you're older. I know that in a down market virtually all stocks fall. But if they're the stocks of America's Finest Companies or at least high quality, they'll come back—and then shoot to higher prices than before.

> *Lack of money is the root of all evil.*
> —GEORGE BERNARD SHAW, IRISH DRAMATIST, 1856–1950

AN EASY WAY TO KNOW HOW MUCH YOU NEED TO RETIRE

Inflation is a fact of life, and you want to take that into account when planning for life after work. With a 4 percent inflation rate, the cost of living will double approximately every 18 years. At 5 percent, it doubles in 15. At 6 percent, roughly 12.

How many decades have you got to live? Once you make a stab at that figure, it's easy to zero in on how much the next 20, 30, 40, 50, 60, or more years will cost using various inflation rate assumptions.

With that said, Table 6.4 will be useful for you. It shows you how long a given amount of money earning a certain rate of return will last under whatever withdrawal rate you pick. As an example, let's say you have $100,000 returning 12 percent a year in America's Finest Companies, and you're going to withdraw $14,000

TABLE 6.4   How Many Years Before Your Money Runs Out?

Annual Withdrawal Rate (%)	Annual Interest or Growth Rate (%)									
	5	6	7	8	9	10	11	12	13	14
6		36								
7		25	33							
8		20	23	30						
9		16	18	22	28					
10	14	15	17	20	26					
11	12	13	14	16	19	25				
12	11	11	12	14	15	18	23			
13	9	10	11	12	13	15	17	21		
14	9	9	10	11	11	13	14	17	21	
15	8	8	9	9	10	11	12	14	16	20

Source: The Staton Institute® Inc.

(14 percent of the beginning principal) each year. Go down the column for Annual Withdrawal Rate to 14 and then across the Annual Interest or Growth Rate row under the number 12. At that intersection is the number 17. That's how many years your money will last.

Large IRAs Not Fully Protected from Bankruptcy or Lawsuit Seizure[1]

A recent U.S. Supreme Court ruling and new federal law have extended bankruptcy and lawsuit protection over most assets in individual retirement accounts. But the protection may not be complete for owners of large IRAs, caution financial planners.

---

[1]The following columns were produced by the Financial Planning Association, membership organization for the financial planning community, and were provided by Bill Staton, MBA, CFA, a local FPA member.

Under federal ERISA law, assets held in most employer-based retirement plans such as 401(k)s, pension plans, 403(b)s, and profit-sharing plans have generally been beyond the reach of creditors. But IRAs were not protected on the federal level. Some states protected IRAs, but many provided no protection or only limited protection.

Also unprotected, unless by a particular state, were SIMPLE IRAs, used by small employers; plans established by the self-employed with no employees other than the owner and spouse, such as a simplified employee pension (SEP) plan or individual 401(k)s; and annuities not held inside a protected employer plan.

Consequently, workers retiring or changing jobs, or those most vulnerable to possible lawsuits, such as doctors, have often been reluctant to roll assets from protected employer-based plans into IRAs—even though that might have been the best strategy from an investment and estate planning standpoint. Then, in the time span of a little over two weeks in April 2005, all that changed.

First, the U.S. Supreme Court unanimously ruled that assets held in IRAs, both traditional and Roth, generally are protected from creditors. The case concerned a couple who had rolled their $55,000 in company pension and 401(k) assets into an IRA, only later to have creditors try to seize the IRA after they filed for bankruptcy protection due to hard times.

But the Supreme Court ruling left an important issue unresolved. It said that assets in IRAs were protected only to the extent of what might be considered "reasonably necessary" to support the IRA owner and his or her dependents. Anything above that value could be seized by creditors (depending on the laws of the state of residence). But it didn't define what constitutes "reasonably necessary."

Slightly over two weeks later, Congress passed and President Bush signed the Bankruptcy Abuse Prevention and Consumer Protection Act of 2005. Among its many provisions, the law resolved some questions left after the Supreme Court ruling and further strengthened protection of IRAs as well as plans for the self-employed.

Especially important to participants in employer-based retirement plans is that the bankruptcy act says that all assets rolled over from these plans into an IRA, and all subsequent earnings made inside the account attributable to the rollover, are protected from creditors, regardless of the amount of the rollover. That should remove much of the reluctance among investors to move most retirement plan assets into IRAs if they decide that's the best financial strategy.

While IRAs have unlimited protection for certain rollover amounts, such is not the case for original (non-rollover) contributions by the owner to traditional and Roth IRAs. The bankruptcy act put a price tag on the "reasonably necessary" amount that might be protected in these IRAs—$1 million. That is, if the aggregated value of your original contributions and their earnings to traditional and Roth IRAs exceed $1 million, the amount above $1 million (excluding any protected rollover amounts) could be vulnerable to creditors. That $1 million amount is indexed annually to inflation.

Most investors building an IRA from scratch won't exceed the $1 million limit, since annual contribution limits to traditional and Roth IRAs have been relatively low for the past two decades. And the bankruptcy act allows bankruptcy courts to permit the IRA owner to keep more than $1 million if it is in the "interest of justice" (though the act did not spell out what constitutes an interest in justice).

All of this emphasizes the importance of making sure you roll any money from employer-sponsored retirement plans and pensions into separate "rollover" IRAs designed specifically for such rollovers. Try to avoid mixing rollover dollars inside a traditional or Roth IRA you've been funding from scratch because it makes bookkeeping complicated. Keep accurate records to document rollovers, too.

Nonqualified annuities—annuities not held within qualified retirement plans—do not fall under federal creditor protections established by the Supreme Court and Congress. Depending on state law, those assets may remain vulnerable to creditors.

Eight Ways to Protect Your IRA Plans

Individual retirement accounts are one of the most popular ways Americans save for retirement. Yet many IRA owners make critical mistakes that can needlessly cost them or their heirs money or thwart the owners' plans. Here are eight ways you can ensure that your IRA works as you designed it.

1. *Begin your required minimum distributions on time.* Regardless of whether you are still working, you must begin taking an annual minimum required distribution from your traditional IRAs (not Roth IRAs) no later than April 1 following the year you turn 70½. If you don't withdraw enough or you don't withdraw it on time, the IRS will penalize you 50 percent of the difference between the amount you took out and the amount you should have taken out. The IRS has simplified the calculation of the minimum distribution. Furthermore, the law now requires all IRA custodians and qualified plan administrators (such as 401(k) plans) to inform the owner of the upcoming required distribution and to offer to calculate the minimum distribution amount (for only their account). But it's still up to you to take out the money, which you can draw from any or all accounts you own, as long as the total minimum amount is distributed.

2. *Don't wait until the last moment.* Some IRA owners wait until the April 1 deadline to take out their initial minimum withdrawal. But remember, you'll have to make another withdrawal by December 31 of the same year. Two minimum withdrawals in the same year could bump you into a higher tax bracket and increase your tax liability.

Also, owners of large accounts may actually reduce their tax bite by taking some withdrawals during lower-income tax years well before they turn 70½.

3. *Name a human beneficiary.* Failure to name a natural (human) beneficiary usually means the assets go to your estate and that will cost your heirs money. That's because if you hadn't already started taking distributions yourself by the time of your death, the IRA assets must be distributed to your estate's heirs within five years of death. Or if you had started, distributions must be paid out to the heirs over what would have been your remaining life expectancy. Either way, this deprives the heirs from "stretching out" the tax-deferred assets over their own lives and creates a bigger tax bite.

4. *Name a contingent beneficiary.* This allows the primary beneficiary to "disclaim" (reject) the IRA inheritance if he or she doesn't need the money so that it automatically passes to the contingent, who typically is younger and can stretch out the inheritance longer.

5. *Name the right beneficiary.* Your spouse isn't always the best choice to name as the primary IRA beneficiary. An adult child might be a better choice but usually not a minor child. Or a trust might be the best choice (such as for a minor child), though that's a complicated decision requiring professional guidance. Don't throw in a charity as a beneficiary to an IRA with human beneficiaries, because it forces accelerated distributions to the named heirs.

6. *Changing your beneficiary.* Don't forget to change, in writing, your beneficiary in the event of a marriage, divorce, birth of a child, death of a beneficiary or similar circumstances.

7. *Have the right number of IRAs.* For example, if you have a single large IRA but want to bequeath its assets to multiple heirs and a charity or two, consider separate IRAs for the charities and perhaps for each heir (especially if their ages are significantly different). Lumping them into a single IRA accelerates the required minimum distribution rate the heir(s) are required to take each year. On the other hand, if you have multiple IRAs but not multiple heirs or charities, consolidating them can reduce paperwork and custodial fees, and make it easier to track investments and calculate minimum distributions.

8. *Check to see what your IRA custodian allows.* Just because federal law allows you to choose certain options with your IRA doesn't mean the IRA custodian does. The custodian might not allow you to stretch out the payments with your children or grandchildren, for example, or allow the descendants of a deceased beneficiary to receive that heir's share if the IRA has other named heirs. The options are spelled out in the custody agreement.

Should You Stay in Your Old 401(k) or Roll It Over into an IRA?

Every year millions of workers who are either retiring or changing jobs struggle with a difficult decision regarding their old employer's 401(k) or similar defined-contribution retirement plan.

They know they don't want to cash in their account because of the income taxes, potential penalties, and loss of tax-deferred growth. Yet they're unsure whether to leave their money in the old plan, roll it into a new employer's defined-contribution plan if available, or roll it over into an individual retirement account. Each option has its benefits and disadvantages, depending on their personal situation.

Advantages of Staying with Old Employer's Plan or Joining a New Plan

Roughly one-in-three workers leave their money behind in old employers' 401(k) plans, according to the Employee Benefits Research Institute. Often it is because they don't want to fuss with the rollover paperwork or they're afraid of making a costly mistake. Nonetheless, staying put in the old employer's plan or rolling it into a new employer's plan does offer some advantages.

One is creditor protection. Federal law prohibits creditors from invading 401(k) accounts. The law no longer protects IRAs over $1 million, though some states shield IRAs from creditors.

If you leave work due to termination or retirement, you usually can begin withdrawing from a 401(k) as early as age 55 without the ten-percent early withdrawal penalty. With rare exceptions, you have to wait to age 59½ for penalty-free withdrawals from an IRA.

Two-thirds of 401(k) plans offer stable-value mutual funds, which are less commonly offered in IRAs. These funds appeal to conservative investors because they tend to offer healthier yields than money markets but with the same stable principal.

Investment choices are more limited in a 401(k). Why might this be an advantage? Some studies show that investors who trade a lot hurt their personal returns more than those who don't trade as much. IRAs typically offer a much bigger universe of investment choices than 401(k) plans. Thus, investors tempted to trade, or who are so overwhelmed by too many investment choices they do nothing, may actually be better off sticking with their 401(k). But the option to stay will depend in part on the quality of the investment options your particular 401(k) offers compared with an IRA.

You can borrow from a 401(k) if you're working for that employer, but you can't from an IRA. Financial planners generally discourage borrowing from a 401(k)—the borrowed money no longer grows tax deferred and there's a risk you won't be able to repay it in time, resulting in heavy taxes and penalties. Still, it is an option that often beats borrowing from a credit card.

If you want to leave your money in the 401(k), be sure it will stay there. Currently, employers can cash out defined-contribution accounts valued at $1,000 or less if the employee fails to take action. For accounts valued from $1,000 to $5,000 the employer must automatically roll the money into a default IRA unless the employee wants the cash or requests a rollover.

Advantages of rolling into an IRA

For prudent investors, one of the biggest attractions of IRAs is their wider universe of investment choices, particularly if the choices are superior to those available in their old or new employer's plan. And you don't have to worry about future investment options changing, as they often do in employers' plans.

Workers who change jobs frequently may find themselves accumulating a lot of employer retirement accounts and may risk losing track of some accounts. Also, it's easier to manage a single IRA than multiple employer plans accounts. Or you might consolidate into your current employer's plan if it's good quality.

Another major benefit for the IRA option is the potential for significant tax savings. With an IRA, you can designate a younger nonspousal beneficiary and "stretch out" the minimum withdrawals over that person's lifetime. A 401(k) plan probably will insist that the account be immediately cashed out if the heir is not a spouse, resulting in a much larger tax bite and loss of further tax deferral.

With a rollover IRA, you may also be in position to convert to a Roth IRA if that conversation makes financial sense for you.

CHAPTER

7

Be Your Own Money Manager: Right!

All there is to investing is picking good stocks at good times and staying with them as long as they remain good companies.

—WARREN BUFFETT

POINTS TO REMEMBER

- Know what to buy, when to buy, and when to sell.
- Beat the market and most pros by owning only top-quality stocks.
- Withstand market and economic storms of all proportions.

One nice thing about being your own money manager and investing exclusively in companies in America's Finest Companies is that you'll most likely only have to spend an hour or two each year (the equivalent of a long lunch) on your investment portfolio(s). Then you're finished for another 365 days.

Investing can be that easy and take that little time. This is my message wherever I give a keynote address or lead a workshop. I continually butt heads with the skeptics (mainly other professionals) who say investing can't be that easy; otherwise everyone would be doing it. But again, it surely can be.

If you follow the steps outlined in this chapter, you can ignore daily, weekly, and even monthly gyrations in stock prices. In fact,

113

you can forget about what the Dow Jones industrials, the S&P 500, or other market indexes are doing. Wouldn't that be a big relief? You can also safely ignore all forecasts about the direction of the economy and interest rates. Which way they head won't matter to you.

The only function of economic forecasting is to make astrology respectable.

—EZRA SOLOMON, ECONOMIST

For the moment, picture yourself as the biblical character Noah. God just told you that the worst storm ever was going to occur in a few months and that you need to build a boat to withstand the coming 40-day flood. How would you prepare for such an unprecedented event? Noah knew. He built the craft to the strict proportions written in the Bible and survived the most horrible storm in history. Replicas have been tested in laboratories under hurricane conditions. Even in storms of that magnitude, the ark remained upright at all times. It never came close to capsizing.

Just as Noah closely followed the blueprint to construct his ark, you can use certain simple principles to guide your portfolio through future economic and stock market storms. Whatever happens, you will survive and prosper because you'll know what to do and what not to do. Your success will not be tied to how much time and effort you spend keeping up with the economy, interest rates, and the anticipated direction of stock prices.

Perhaps, if you love reading about business and investing, you'll want to continue subscribing to financial publications. However, you're probably heavily involved in your family, in your business or profession, and in your community, and you have little time to track stocks actively or follow the economy—plus, you might not want to either.

What you'll learn in this chapter will allow you to feel good about everything you're *not* reading. If you subscribe to newspapers, magazines, and newsletters you don't want to read, cancel them. You can save dozens if not hundreds of dollars every year, and those savings can go right into your portfolio.

STEP 1: BE PATIENT

Like Warren Buffett and his mentor Benjamin Graham, my philosophy of investing is anchored in patience. George F. Baker, founder of First National Bank of New York (the forerunner of what is now

Citigroup), said that patience is one of three prerequisites for making a fortune in stocks. He knew that time is on the side of the investor. He also knew that the longer anyone invests, the better the results will be. History proves it.

Since stock trading began in America in the late 1700s, the long-term trend has been relentlessly upward. On a 100-year or longer-term chart of stock prices, only the Great Depression of the 1930s looks like more than a blip. Naturally there are frequent, wide, day-to-day, month-to-month, and even year-to-year swings (see Figure 7.1). But, given enough time, stocks on the whole go only one way: up!

Benjamin Franklin counseled, "He that can have patience can have what he will." This advice is certainly on the money for stock investors. It happens to be right for investors in every other field, too. If you're patient and give your stock investments time to work for you, you'll be uncommonly successful.

John Bogle, founder of the popular Vanguard Group of funds, gave a speech on October 11, 2007 in which he noted that the Standard & Poor's 500 Index had risen from 17 in 1950 to 1,554 then, more than 57 years later. That was a total of 14,528 trading days. Bogle said that if an investor had missed the 40 (0.3 percent) best up days out of the 14,528, the final return would have been equivalent to 276, which is only 17.8 percent of 1,554 (dividends excluded in both cases).

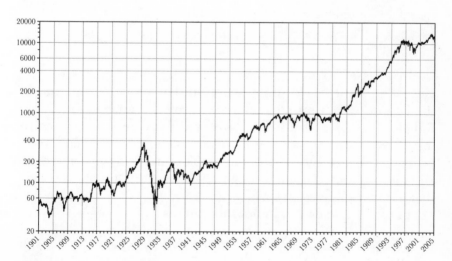

FIGURE 7.1   Long-Term Dow

Source: Hirsch Organization.

Benjamin Franklin's Wisdom for a Richer Life

Order—"Let all things have their places and let each part of your business have its time."

1. Keep a journal.
2. Make lists.
3. Avoid clutter.

Alertness

4. Plan, prepare, anticipate.
5. Have a positive outlook.
6. Relax.

Friendship

7. Be a giver, not a taker.
8. See people for their virtues.
9. Stay in touch.

Resolution—"Resolve to perform what you ought. Perform without fail what you resolve."

10. Stay on course.
11. Seek advice.
12. Be open to improvements.

Source: Dr. Mark Skousen, investment advisory panelist and Franklin descendant.

In a letter to the *Financial Times* (January 31, 2008), Javier Estrada of the IESE Business School in Barcelona, Spain, made a similar point. He wrote that, between 1969 and 2006 in the United Kingdom, an investor who simply stayed the course and never got out of stocks saw the money grow from £100 to £1,854, again without taking dividends into consideration. The investor who missed the 10 best days ended up with only £979. By missing the 20 best days, that number plunged to £596.

Estrada made two very important points:

1. Investors are highly unlikely to be in and out of stocks successfully.
2. Trying to time the market, like going to Las Vegas, may be exciting, but it's not a proven way to make money.

*If timing the market is such a great strategy, why haven't
we seen the names of any market timers at the top of the
Forbes list of richest Americans?*

—PETER LYNCH

Perhaps the most patient investor in the world, and without question the most successful, is Warren Buffett, chairman of Berkshire Hathaway. Buffett was one of Benjamin Graham's brightest students at Columbia University, and he learned his lessons well. Berkshire Hathaway is the most expensive stock in America and has traded for more than 150,000 per share. Buffett is the planet's wealthiest person with an estimated net worth in excess of $60 billion.

Warren Buffett has long been known for his investment prowess, but in recent years he's been made into a virtual investment god even though he'd be the first to admit that's not one of his goals. A couple dozen or more books have been written about him and his investing style. Buffett has never bothered to write one about himself and probably won't. He's appeared in countless articles in all sorts of publications. The 2008 annual meeting of his investment company, Berkshire Hathaway (held in Omaha, Nebraska), was attended by more than 23,000 loyalists from across the globe.

I was in Omaha in 2004 for his annual meeting. I met a twosome who had been to every annual meeting for the past 25 years; I guess they had nothing better to do. Omaha is a very nice city, but it isn't great enough to come back to that many times, at least in my opinion. And neither is what you learn from actually attending the annual meeting because so much of it is picked up in the press. However, it really is worth going at least once. After all, Buffett is 77 and Munger's past 80. No one can say how much longer they'll be around, but they're both so irascible it might be one to two decades, if not more.

Actually the annual meeting, which is held the first Saturday of every May, is boring; at least this one was because I didn't learn anything I didn't already know. After official business closed around 9:55 A.M. (wherein a shareholder wanted to reform the board because it's "too insulated"), the floor was open to questions from shareholders for the rest of the day until around 3:30, with a lunch break about halfway. Meanwhile, the Qwest convention center next door was open the entire day with booths from all the Berkshire companies, including Ginzu knives. (I never knew Buffett owned that company.)

Nevertheless, I was glad I went. It wasn't to see Buffett, although I got within six feet of The Master. He looked somewhat older than I thought and walked a little slower too. Perhaps his slowed stride was because he was surrounded by Jocko, Rocco, other body-guards, and assorted hangers-on. They looked like Secret Service agents guarding the president and didn't appear to have any sense of humor whatsoever. Charlie Rose (a fellow Tar Heel from North Carolina) was walking backward with a microphone in Buffett's face, while two camera operators tried to take it all in. This was in preparation for an excellent three-part series about Buffett that was broadcast in 2006 over public television.

The reason I'm glad I attended is that Buffett and Munger reinforced my own ideas that have worked over the years and that should continue to work in the future. Over and over again, I heard the words "simple" and "patient." In other words, the world's finest investing team was saying to all of us, "Find a simple strategy that works through thick and thin. Be patient and give it time to work. And most importantly, stay the course, regardless of what others may say or do."

They also advised that asset allocation is basically for the birds and that successful investors must wait for opportunities to come, not try to create them. I happen to believe that, at any given moment, there are always outstanding opportunities within my AFC universe.

Buffett said that, if the market closed for two years or so and his companies were doing well, it wouldn't bother him one iota. Munger commented that many investors focus on very short-term returns and don't bother to position themselves for extraordinary long-term profits.

Did I change anything about my investing style based on what I learned? Absolutely not. My way is not the only way to investment success, but it surely does work. Why mess with a great thing?

Buffett gives away valuable investment advice in each Berkshire Hathaway annual report. Anyone, even nonshareholders, can obtain a copy for any year for free at www.berkshirehathaway.com under Annual & Interim Reports on the home page.

What Buffett knows is well worth knowing, and simple enough to understand. But I'm not sure anyone can replicate his extraor-dinary success, any more than you or I could choose to be another Michael Jordan, Tiger Woods, or Monet or Picasso. It's impossible to put down on paper what makes any genius a genius, and I'm certainly not going to say I can give you the step-by-step approach to mimicking Buffett's oversized returns. I can say, however, with great certainty, that my approach is extremely similar to Buffett's in a number of ways, so much so that I've jokingly said Buffett reads America's Finest Companies when making his stock picks. He himself often points out: "If the business does well, the stock eventually follows."

Let's look at the facts. His largest holding is Coca-Cola. He also owned a big slice of Gillette (in America's Finest at the time), which was acquired by Procter & Gamble, an AFC stalwart. He owns a lot of American Express and Washington Post Co., both of which have been in the AFC group. Four of America's Finest Companies at the time—GEICO, FlightSafety International, International Dairy Queen, and General Re—were all partially owned by Buffett before he bought out the rest of their stock and took them private. The same goes for Clayton Homes. Today he has investments in Lowe's Companies, Wells Fargo, Home Depot, Wal-Mart Stores, Bank of America, and U.S. Bancorp, all still among America's Finest.

If—and it's a humongous if—you'd invested $10,000 with Buffett at the beginning of 1965, it would be north of $30 million today. His annual rate of return has been more than 21 percent per year, a figure so outsized it's almost unbelievable.

Buffett has many quotable quotes, and each is an investment lesson unto itself. Here are four choice ones:

> If [any] Fed chairman . . . were to whisper to me what his monetary policy was going to be over the next two years, it wouldn't change one thing I do.
> It's easier to create money than to spend it.
> You have to think for yourself.
> There's no use running if you're on the wrong road.

Buffett believes in buying high quality at fair prices, buying more, and holding, sometimes for years if not decades. If that's not patient, I don't know what is.

My favorite holding period is forever.
—WARREN BUFFETT, 1994

John Liscio, an astute columnist for *Barron's*, observed a decade ago that "even in the worst of times, buying and holding stocks beat bonds all hollow. If there is any lesson that investing through the years imparts, it is that the rising tide of compound interest lifts even the most lead-footed of market timers." I found his article unusually insightful.

Here's another example of just how much patience pays. From time to time, a bear market or sharp correction (quick drop) occurs and stock prices head south, sometimes violently. People without patience always panic and sell out of stocks at or near a bottom just before prices turn up. Patient investors continue to buy because they know share prices are on sale, so to speak, and who among us doesn't like to buy things on sale? In actuality, bear markets produce the best buying opportunities.

The 12 bear markets since 1968 lasted an average of 12 months (with a range of 1.5–23 months) and went through an average decline of 26.5 percent (range of 15.6–45.1 percent). After they ended, the typical stock price gain was 28.5 percent over the ensuing 12 months. Most, if not all, of the loss was recouped within two years, and stock prices then marched ahead to set new records. You have to be in to win.

I'm often asked about investing a lump sum: "Should I put it all into America's Finest Companies at once or scale in over the next few quarters?" Scaling in seems like the safer option, but it typically isn't. Let's say you have $500,000 to invest in stocks, and you're worried that the market is at an all-time high, which has been the case much of the time since the fall of 1990. I could respond by citing a 1994 Wright State University (Ohio) study that proves lump sum investing is better than easing in a little bit at a time, even though stock prices may appear to be overvalued. The odds of better returns would be two-to-one in your favor.

Also, easing into stocks works against you psychologically. As your money coach I tell you to put the entire amount into stocks. You respond, "I'm scared and I'm dropping my money into a money market fund and waiting for prices to fall. Stocks are way overpriced." Three months later the market is down 10 percent. You're right and I'm wrong. Another three months pass, and stocks drop another 10 percent. You're even more right and beginning to think you really know what you're doing and that I don't. Six more months zoom by, and this time stocks, in what turns out to be one of the most savage bear markets since 1900, fall another 20 percent. You're still in cash and smirking. Your money coach (me) looks like an idiot.

Suddenly and without warning, stock prices stop falling and quickly turn up. Some of the companies you wanted to buy, which went on sale in the bear market, are now up 20 to 40 percent over where they were just a few weeks ago. But you still don't buy. Four months later they're still climbing. You say smugly to yourself, "I'll wait for the pullback. Then I'll buy."

Four more months fly past with no pullback. Six months later, there is still no pullback. Stocks are soaring. All the business and stock market news is good and getting better. Another year rushes by in a hurry, and you're still in cash. Everything you wanted to purchase is up, in most cases dramatically. Some of your choices are even ahead of where they were before they started dropping, but you refused to buy.

This is not fiction. In 1987 during the Great Crash stock prices declined 36 percent (some even more) in less than two months—the steepest freefall in history. The patient investor who owned America's Finest Companies (the week before the crash) was even again in 18 months or less and then sailed to new highs in personal net worth.

What I recommend is easy, even with a lump sum:

1. Pick your portfolio of at least five companies, each in a different industry, from my latest America's Finest Companies directory.
2. Invest the same dollar amount into each.
3. Once a year, when the new edition list comes out, see if the stocks you bought the previous year are still included. If they are, buy more.
4. If one happens to have been dropped, sell and replace it with another company from the AFC list. Other than needing some cash, this is the only other reason to sell.

STEP 2: BUY MORE OF WHAT YOU ALREADY OWN

When you buy more of what you already own each year, you're employing the time-proven way to consistently buy shares at reasonable prices. This technique is one you'll seldom read about in investment books. It's the only way I know to make money in any stock environment, including the Great Depression. It demands 100 percent commitment to building a diversified portfolio of quality companies.

That technique is called dollar-cost averaging—buying the same dollar amount of common stocks periodically, monthly, quarterly, semiannually, or annually. I prefer once a year because that's easy to remember and requires less record keeping.

In dollar-cost averaging, there is absolutely no need to predict the short-term direction of stock prices because we already know that the long-term direction is up. If you continue buying highest-quality (especially AFC) stocks through good and bad years, dollar-cost averaging keeps the average cost of your purchases below their average market price—ensuring you a profit.

Here's why. If you buy a portfolio of stocks today and their prices fall every year for the next three years (as in the Great Depression or most recently in the period 2000–2002), each time you buy additional shares you'll purchase them at a lower price than before. Each time you buy more shares, you'll lower the average cost per share until the stocks bottom and begin to go up again.

Suppose you buy a $400 suit that goes on sale three months later for $300. You buy one in a different color because the price is so attractive. Your average cost per suit drops from $400 to $350. If you buy a third suit for $200, you drive the average cost per suit down again to $300. Each suit is still worth $400, but the average cost per suit is $100 less than that.

Assuming the companies you invest in are chosen from America's Finest Companies, their stock prices will stop falling at some point and start to move up again. Once the uptrends begin, you'll discover that your average cost per share is under the market value: you have a profit. On the other hand, if your stock portfolio goes up immediately and continues up, you have a profit, too. Either way, you make money. That's the extraordinary attraction of dollar-cost averaging using companies in America's Finest Companies.

In dollar-cost averaging, it's a mathematical certainty that you'll make money as long as the companies you buy don't go out of business. If you stick exclusively with America's Finest Companies, you won't have to worry about that. A company headed for serious trouble will be delisted well before it gets there.

In the nearly 20 years that my annual America's Finest Companies® investment directory has been published, no AFC company had gone bankrupt until 2008 when the financial crisis and panic of 2007–2008 forced Lehman Brothers into bankruptcy and put American International Group on the brink. Both have been deleted from the AFC Directory 2009 in the appendix at the end of this book. This is a first. I can't even recall any companies that were deleted ever having gone into bankruptcy although some got into serious financial trouble later on. This type of catastrophic market event usually occurs

TABLE 7.1   A Simple Example of Dollar Cost Averaging

Quarter	Stock Price	Quarterly Investment	Cumulative Shares Purchased	Average Cost per Share
1	10	$1,000	100.0	$10.00
2	9	1,000	111.1	9.47
3	8	1,000	125.0	8.93
4	7	1,000	142.9	8.35
5	6	1,000	166.7	7.74
6	5	1,000	200.0	7.09
7	6	1,000	166.7	6.91
8	7	1,000	142.9	6.92
9	8	1,000	125.0	7.03
10	9	1,000	111.1	7.19
11	10	1,000	100.0	7.38
Total		**$11,000**	**1491.4**	
Current value		**$14,914**		
Gain		**35.6%**		

Source: The Staton Institute® Inc.

near the ends of bear markets, but it may take quite a while longer for the financial system and economy to fully recover.

Assume you invest $1,000 at the beginning of 2009 in one of America's Finest at 10 per share, purchasing 100 shares. (In this example, I'm leaving out reinvesting dividends.) One quarter later, the stock has fallen to 9, and you spend another $1,000. The price is 10 percent lower than when you began. Instead of purchasing 100 shares, you get to buy 111.1 shares. In the next quarter, the price falls to 8. Then to 7, 6, and 5 in subsequent quarters. Every three months you buy $1,000 of stock even though the stock keeps falling like a stone.

After six installments over 15 months you've invested $6,000 of your hard-earned money. The stock has collapsed 50 percent in price from 10 to 5. Even though you are very discouraged and thinking Bill Staton is the dumbest financial advisor you know, you continue to add to your holdings because the company is sound. You know that because it's one of America's Finest. You believe the stock will eventually come back because the company isn't going to go out of business.

It's hard to beat a person who never gives up.
—BABE RUTH, THE FIRST MAN TO HIT THREE HOME RUNS
IN ONE GAME, THE 1926 WORLD SERIES. RUTH ENDED
HIS CAREER WITH A SLUGGING PERCENTAGE AT 0.69,
STILL THE HIGHEST IN HISTORY.

The stock finally turns around and slowly climbs to 7. At this point, the average cost of all shares purchased is $6.92, and you have a small profit. From here the profits grow larger as the stock rebounds toward the original price at which you first purchased it.

Eventually the stock recovers to 10 after 11 quarters (33 months). By now you have invested $11,000 total. The stock, first purchased for 10 per share, is still only 10. It has zero price appreciation. That's the bad news.

The good news is that you paid an average of $7.38 for each share. Your profit is $2.62 per share (excluding dividends, which could possibly boost profits dramatically if included). The shares are valued at $14,914, a handsome return of 35.6 percent in 2.75 years, 11.7 percent annualized. And the stock is no higher than when you started.

Dollar-cost averaging worked great even during the most hostile stock market environment in American history: the Great Depression. Nineteen twenty-nine had to be the worst time ever to start an investment program. How did dollar-cost averaging leave you if you'd been unfortunate enough to begin investing, even in the soundest of companies, on the eve of the Great Depression?

Assume you invested $1,000 on December 31, 1929. Stock prices had already crashed and begun to come down, but the worst was yet to come. Standard & Poor's 500 Index was 21.45. With $1,000 you would have bought 46.6 shares of the index. (They're not really shares, but the term is convenient and good enough for our purposes.) These shares produced $46 in annual dividends, which were set aside until December 31 the following year. By then the S&P had fallen 28.5 percent to 15.34. You acquired 68.2 more shares for $1,046 (your annual $1,000 plus the $46 in dividends).

The next December you invested another $1,000, plus $94 in dividends, and bought 134.7 shares of the S&P. It plunged 47.1 percent in 1931 for a dreadful 62.1 percent cumulative loss because you started just two years earlier. Time really flies when you're losing money—almost as fast as hackers like me losing golf balls. At the end of 1932, the market was down a whopping 67.9 percent. You shelled out $4,265, and your portfolio was worth $2,844, for a dismal 33.3 percent loss, but only half that of the S&P.

Because you knew dollar-cost averaging demanded total devotion (at this point it seemed more like total insanity), you continued to plunk down $1,000, plus dividends, at the end of each year. By December 31, 1935, you'd invested a total of $7,995. Your gain was 27.3 percent, while the S&P index was down 37.4 percent from the end of 1929. One year later you'd made a 52.7 percent profit ($14,563 divided by $9,540), while the index was still almost 20 percent under water.

Dollar-cost averaging is mechanical and overcomes one of the investor's worst enemies: emotion. Emotion encourages people to buy stocks at exorbitant highs and to dump them at ruinous lows. Dollar-cost averaging puts emotion on the back burner, where it belongs, and gives every investor the opportunity to amass the shares of highest-quality companies—America's Finest—at reasonable (and sometimes bargain) prices. Dollar-cost averaging unfailingly produces superior results even if you have the misfortune always to buy at market peaks.

What would happen if you bought at the high every year? T. Rowe Price, a large mutual fund company, proved that the commitment to invest is far more important than timing the investment. Said another way, *time in* the market is much more valuable than *timing* the market (unless you're in the very small minority who know how to do it). Their study calculated the growth of a $2,000 annual IRA contribution invested in shares of Standard & Poor's 500 index at its highest level each year from 1969 through 1988.

On July 31, 1989 (following one of the worst 20-year periods in history for stocks), the account was worth $171,757, more than four times the total investment of $40,000 spread over two decades. The compound annual total return was 12.4 percent. At that rate, money doubles every 7 years, quadruples in 14, and expands eightfold in 21.

Another study came up with a similar conclusion. If a hypothetically hapless investor invested $10,000 each year at the market's high from 1979 through 1994, the $160,000 total investment would have grown to more than $540,000 by the end of June 1995. That's in excess of a 235 percent gain in just a little over 16 years. A portfolio of so-called safe Treasury bills, invested in similar fashion (at each year's market high), grew to less than $280,000.

SmartMoney magazine's September 1995 issue pointed out that during the preceding 25 years "the worst possible day" to have purchased stocks was January 11, 1973, one day before stock market indexes began a 45 percent plunge over the ensuing two years. Investing in the market on that day, holding on for dear life, reinvesting all dividends and never adding another penny to your portfolio would have required you to wait until April 1978 just to get back to break-even. Treasury bills and other cash equivalents would have looked much better in the short run, but in the long run they made for a miserable comparison. Through mid-1995, stocks racked up a 1,022 percent gain compared to only 380 percent for cash.

Even if you wanted to, you couldn't invest at the highest point for stock prices every year for 20 straight years. You probably couldn't do it even one year. But even if you did, your results would still be excellent—in fact, better than from other investments. With America's Finest Companies, they'd be exceptional.

STEP 3: PROPERLY DIVERSIFY YOUR HOLDINGS

How many stocks do you need in your portfolio? You can start with one, but I recommend saving enough money until you can purchase five, each in a different industry. Then you can work your way toward seven, eight, or ten, perhaps even twelve to fifteen. More than that is probably excessive if you're working with $100,000 or less. Warren Buffett's Berkshire Hathaway has major stakes in relatively few companies. He believes, as I do, that owning several dozen or several hundred companies leads to mediocrity for investors.

A number of studies show that you can achieve about 90 percent of the benefits of diversification with as few as seven to eight companies, so long as each is in a different industry. The diversification table shown in Table 7.2 was adapted from Richard A. Brealey's excellent (and thin) book, *An Introduction to Risk and Return from Common Stocks.* Others may be somewhat different, but all the ones I've studied reach the same conclusion.

Noted economist and successful investor John Maynard Keynes said in 1942: "I am quite incapable of having adequate knowledge of more than a very limited range of investments. To suppose that safety-first consists of having a small gamble in a large number of different directions as compared with a substantial stake in a company where one's information is adequate strikes me as a travesty of investment policy."

TABLE 7.2   Diversification

	Number of Stocks	Reduction in Risk as % of Potential
Underdiversified	2	46.3
	4	72.0
	6	81.0
Well diversified	8	85.7
	10	88.5
Overdiversified	20	94.2
	50	97.7
	100	98.8

Source: Richard A. Brealey, *An Introduction to Risk and Return from Common Stocks* (Cambridge, MA: MIT Press, 1969). Copyright 1969 by The Massachusetts Institute of Technology. Reprinted by permission of the MIT Press.

Keynes knew then and Buffett knows now that scattering your money across dozens and dozens of stocks (as most mutual funds do) must lead to mediocrity. *Dow Theory Forecasts,* a popular financial newsletter that's been around since 1946, concluded: "A well-constructed portfolio of 15 stocks is not significantly riskier than a 100-stock portfolio. And your chances of beating the market are much higher with a focused portfolio."

A 10-stock portfolio provides 88.5 percent of the possible advantages of diversification. Five stocks provide 77.4 percent, 20 stocks 94.2 percent. Once you own 8 to 10 stocks, each in a different industry, adding others reduces risk almost imperceptibly. It's hardly worth the time and effort to own lots of stocks. Warren Buffett has proved it.

STEP 4: BUY ONLY SHARES OF AMERICA'S FINEST COMPANIES

On a visit to see our daughter Gracie in San Diego, the family toured Balboa Park with its 13 museums. Mary and Gracie went to the art museums, and I visited the Sports Hall of Fame, wherein I saw a video about one of my sports heroes, the Splendid Splinter, Ted Williams.

Here's a guy who hit 521 home runs, won the Triple Crown twice, and was the last person to bat more than .400 in a season (four hits in 10 times at bat). He did that in 1941. The record still stands.

When World War II broke out, Williams voluntarily served in the Army Air Corps for three years, right in the heart of his outstanding baseball career. When the Korean War started, he served nearly two more years as a Marine fighter pilot. Thus, almost five years of his career were spent defending our country. There is no telling what he could have accomplished if those years hadn't been taken away. Known for his ability to actually see the seams of a pitched baseball when it came at him, Ted Williams, on his last at bat, hit the ball out of the park.

Ted Williams can teach us a lot about investing because successful investing requires consistency, and few players were more consistent than he was. Williams never changed his style or his approach to baseball. Regardless of the opposing team or its pitchers, he stuck to what he knew worked.

And so do I. That's why America's Finest Companies continually outdistance the market, and so does my *Baker's Dozen Guided Portfolio®* in *$taton$ E-Money Digest,* which is always 100 percent invested in just 13 AFC companies. (In the next chapter I detail the results and construction of this handpicked portfolio and its current components.)

There's no special skill to making above-average profits in stocks if you:

1. Are patient and have an investment horizon of at least 5 to 10 years
2. Add to your holdings regularly.
3. Diversify properly.
4. Invest only in the shares of companies that will remain in business and have rising earnings and dividends. I think AFCs are your best bet.

Virtually anyone, even a young person, can name at least 20 to 30 companies that fit this mold.

When Gracie was 10 she picked a market-beating portfolio of eight stocks without my help. In the spring of 1988, about six months after the biggest stock crash in history, I wanted her to learn a little something about investing her own funds. She had slightly more than $4,000 cash in her college fund; the remainder was already invested in stocks.

I asked her to pick eight companies she'd like to own and purchased $500 of each through our stockbroker. It took her only a few minutes to come up with eight names. One was a private company that made stuffed animals, and another was a yogurt chain, which neither of us knew much about. She scotched those two names and came up with two more.

1. One was Pizza Hut, which at the time was owned by PepsiCo. So she bought PepsiCo.
2. She loved Coca-Cola, too, and bought $500 of that.
3. She also loved Jeep, which was then owned by Chrysler.
4. She was using the copier at my office, so Xerox was one stock to buy.
5–6. Gracie reasoned electricity and phones would always be in vogue. She purchased Duke Power and BellSouth.
7–8. She also added McDonald's, and NCNB (now Bank of America, headquartered here in Charlotte).

That was a great portfolio at the time. It was high quality and well diversified, even though Coca-Cola and PepsiCo were in the same business. All eight companies were likely to survive the worst downturn in the economy any of us can imagine. How did I know that? Because all but one, McDonald's, survived the Great Depression. Even though the America's Finest Companies list wasn't in existence, five of the eight are still in it: Coca-Cola, McDonald's, Bank of America, and PepsiCo. BellSouth later became part of the "new" AT&T, also one of America's Finest. Even a 10-year-old knew then that you should always buy the finest companies.

There are several ways to pick a portfolio. Which technique you use is not nearly as important as that you invest in nothing but the companies in America's Finest Companies. Fewer than 2 percent of all U.S. public companies make that cut. Because they have the most consistent growth records, they're going to make money for you regardless of how you pick the portfolio. You can bank on it because their track records are superior.

Most people instinctively fill their portfolios with companies they've heard of. You probably will, too, from the full list of current AFCs provided in the appendix.

That's an excellent way to assemble your portfolio. If you need an eight-stock portfolio, you can probably identify eight companies you like that are in different industries before you get into the Gs.

If you feel you need a certain amount of dividend income, your search may be limited to stocks yielding 4 percent or more.

If you'd rather go for companies that pay little or nothing, you might choose from among the stocks yielding 1 percent or less. Maybe you like certain industries, such as banking, utilities, or consumer products. Instead of searching for companies by name, scan the list in the appendix and pay close attention to the industry categories.

Another method to build your portfolio is to choose stocks randomly but not by throwing darts or drawing names. For example, if you need eight stocks, start anywhere on the list and pick every fifth company until you have the number you require. Or pick one company from eight letter groups, such as the As, Cs, Es, Gs, Is, Ks, Ms, and Os. It really doesn't matter so much how you pick because you should end up with a great portfolio in any case. Just remember to pick your stocks so that each is in a different industry.

STEP 5: MAINTAIN THE SAME DOLLAR AMOUNT IN EACH STOCK

When you've chosen your portfolio of at least five companies, the next thing is to purchase approximately the same dollar amount of each. (We'll get into how to open an account and work with a broker in Chapter 10.) The first place to establish your portfolio is in a retirement plan because money grows there without tax consequences until it's withdrawn. For now, assume your retirement account is already open.

If you're buying five companies, put 20 percent of your money into each. (With eight companies, put 12½ percent into each; with ten, 10 percent into each.) Don't make the mistake that so many professionals make when they try to apportion their money among the so-called best companies and industries. That's speculation. You don't need to speculate.

For example, a portfolio manager believes that drug/health care stocks are undervalued; so he puts 25 percent of his funds into that sector. He also thinks utilities won't do nearly as well; so only 5 percent of his money goes there. When you allocate, you introduce guesswork into what otherwise is a simple process of spreading your money equally among all your holdings.

Anyone can guess which groups and individual companies have the most promising outlooks. They can't be sure they're going to be right until after the fact. You and I already know we can't peek into the future. I still don't understand why so many professionals believe they can. I know for certain that I can't.

Once you've purchased your portfolio, do nothing. You don't have to do anything for a year. Let dividends accumulate in your account or automatically reinvest them. On the first anniversary date of your initial purchases, put more money into your account and buy more of what you already own.

STEP 6: SELL RARELY

USA Today (October 24, 2002) reported that "the small investor—long ridiculed and now badly burned by the worst bear market [March 2000–October 2002] since 1974—has withstood waves of stock selling and enough uncertainty to make even the pros flinch." Yet, the article indicated, for the most part those individuals hung on to their stocks. Many lost a lot of money in the process and in a very short time, less than three years.

One reason for these losses is that they didn't know how or when to sell. Another was that so many portfolios were filled with dot-coms that ultimately became dot-bombs.

As an investment advisor and money manager for close to 40 years, I've learned that having an effective sell discipline is often more important (particularly as people near retirement) than trying to figure out what to buy. It's easy to buy. It's a lot tougher to sell and to sell well because a number of factors work against all of us as investors:

1. If we lose money, we want to get back to even before we start thinking about selling. One wit labeled it "getevenitis."
2. Almost everyone can buy a stock recommended by Wall Street, but only those who own it can sell it. Hence, the major bias on the Street is buying because that looks like the easiest way to generate commissions.
3. We in the profession spend most of our time advising clients what to buy, not what they should be selling.
4. Buying is optimistic. Selling is pessimistic.
5. Losses realized are difficult to accept. Losses on paper, even though they amount to the same thing, are much easier to live with.

Years ago I came up with a simple formula for what to buy and when to sell.

- I *buy* stocks with at least 10 years in a row of higher earnings or dividends per share (almost exclusively dividends per share) and spread my investment across a variety of industries.
- Whenever a company fails to meet that criterion—that is, gets cut from my America's Finest Companies—I *sell* it and replace it with another.

Those two rules are simple, and they work. Everyone can follow them.

THOSE RULES AGAIN

To recap:

- Start with a portfolio of at least five stocks in America's Finest Companies, the same dollar amount in each, each in a different industry.
- Each year check the latest directory of America's Finest Companies to see whether all the companies you own are still included. If they are, buy more. If one's been knocked out of the box, replace it with another on the list. The directory is published each July.

Using this simple approach, you'll sell infrequently and simultaneously accumulate shares of the finest companies on the market.

Stock market and investing books are chock-full of all sorts of information, much of it half-baked, about how to time the market and sell at the right times. It's much more difficult to know when a stock is overpriced than to know when it's underpriced. Spotting a cheap stock and buying it is easy for me. Finding one that's not going any higher and may be headed for a fall is a lot tougher.

That's why the last investing step is to sell rarely. Unless I'm managing a client account, I generally recommend selling for only two reasons:

1. To get rid of a stock that's been dropped from America's Finest Companies. In that case, sell all of it.
2. You need some money. You may sell part or all of your holdings depending on how much money is required.

Other than for these reasons, I recommend buying, buying more, and not selling.

I'm in the camp with Warren Buffett, who says he loves buying, but selling is a different story. He compares the pace of his selling activity with a traveler stranded in Podunk's lone hotel. With no TV in the room, the stranger faced a long, uneventful evening. However, he soon discovered a book on the night table called *Things to Do in Podunk*. Excitedly opening it, the traveler found only a single line: "You're doing it."

You can be your own successful money manager by following these seven easy steps:

1. Create your own personal portfolio of at least five to eight of *America's Finest Companies®* (AFCs).
2. Make sure each company is in a different industry.
3. Invest the same dollar amount into each company for proper diversity.
4. Buy more of what you already own at least once each year as long as it's still in *America's Finest Companies®*. Maintain roughly equal dollar weightings in each position.
5. Reinvest dividends quarterly.
6. Sell only when a company is deleted from AFCs or when you need the money.
7. Be patient. The longer you invest, the more successful you'll be.

Of course, you can complicate managing your money, as most professionals and ordinary folk seem to want to do. (I've done it myself, more than I care to recount.) But it's not necessary. Why make money the hard way if there's an easier way? That's what I've always asked myself.

By the time I was 31, I had earned my first million from investing in stocks. I spent a lot of time analyzing and agonizing over my portfolios. Within five years, I was worth more than $3 million. Getting to that point was easier because I was simplifying the process.

Today my personal investment process for do-it-yourselfers is this one. It's easy to understand, is simple to put into practice, and, most important, it works.

Opponents of my method will mention this or that mutual fund that has, according to some survey, beat the pants off the market in recent years. They'll wonder why you weren't investing in those funds. That's a good question. In Chapter 5, I showed that most funds fail even to equal the market every year, let alone beat it.

The percentage of stock funds that beat the market over any 10-year period is remarkably small: about 5 to 15 percent in most years. Will you be able to pick the market beaters from the more than 8,000 mutual funds? I'll give odds you won't, and I'll win more than enough bets to retire wealthy from the bets alone.

MAKING IT WORK

Now let's put the AFC method to work. At the start of each class with my Charlotte high school students, I ask them to pick at least 10 companies using just one criterion. If they theoretically buy it, they have to hold for 20 years and cannot sell. However, they can buy as much of any of the companies any time they want to with as much as they care to invest. Over the more than 20 years I've been instructing these classes, the students' five top picks—all in America's Finest even though they didn't know it—were:

1. Anheuser-Busch (acquired by InBev in 2008).
2. Bank of America.
3. Coca-Cola.
4. Nucor.
5. Wal-Mart Stores.

When I selected them for this example, I did not know how the results would turn out, but they turned out far better than I would ever have anticipated.

I assumed a $1,000 purchase of each of the five stocks on the first trading day of 2000. I did not add any money, nor did I do any selling. At the end of each year, I took dividends collected and bought more shares of the stock that had gone up the least. In other words, by dollar value the stock that was the most under-weighted. That's where new money should always go—into the most underweighted stock(s) in your portfolio—to maintain balance.

Table 7.3 shows what the portfolios looked like over the period from the beginning of 2000 through the end of 2007. That eight-year period was poor for stocks, as measured by the S&P 500 and Dow Jones industrials, and it encompasses the gargantuan bear market that began in March 2000 and finally ended in October 2002. During that roughly 2½-year period, the total value of all U.S. stocks

TABLE 7.3   Portfolios from 2000–2008

January 2, 2000

	Price	Market Value	Yield (%)	Shares	Dividend	Income
Anheuser-Busch/BUD	28.91	1,012	2.21	35	0.64	22
Bank of America/BAC	17.41	992	5.92	57	1.03	59
Coca-Cola/KO	48.85	977	1.39	20	0.68	14
Nucor Corp./NUE	10.56	1,003	1.42	95	0.15	14
Wal-Mart Stores/WMT	50.65	1,013	0.45	20	0.23	5
Total		4,997				114
Yield			2.27			

January 2, 2001

	Price	Market Value	Yield (%)	Shares	Dividend	Income
Anheuser-Busch/BUD	37.75	1,321	1.83	35	0.69	24
Bank of America/BAC	20.21	1,152	5.64	57	1.14	65
Coca-Cola/KO	49.97	999	1.44	20	0.72	14
Nucor Corp./NUE	8.93	964	1.90	108	0.17	18
(bought 13 NUE)						
Wal-Mart Stores/WMT	52.80	1,056	0.51	20	0.27	5
Total		5,493				127
Yield			2.32			9.92%

January 2, 2002

	Price	Market Value	Yield (%)	Shares	Dividend	Income
Anheuser-Busch/BUD	41.84	1,464	1.79	35	0.75	26
Bank of America/BAC	24.62	1,403	4.63	57	1.14	65
Coca-Cola/KO	38.12	877	2.10	23	0.80	18
(bought 3 KO)						

(*continued*)

TABLE 7.3   Continued

January 2, 2002 (continued)

	Price	Market Value	Yield (%)	Shares	Dividend	Income
Nucor Corp./NUE	13.10	1,415	1.45	108	0.19	21
Wal-Mart Stores/WMT	56.07	1,121	0.54	20	0.30	6
Total		6,281				136
Yield			2.17			14.30%

January 2, 2003

	Price	Market Value	Yield (%)	Shares	Dividend	Income
Anheuser-Busch/BUD	42.64	1,492	1.95	35	0.83	29
Bank of America/BAC	28.36	1,617	5.08	57	1.44	82
Coca-Cola/KO	35.83	967	2.46	27	0.88	24
	(bought 4 KO)					
Nucor Corp./NUE	8.88	959	2.25	108	0.20	22
Wal-Mart Stores/WMT	44.93	899	0.78	20	0.35	7
Total		5,934				163
Yield			2.76			−5.52%

January 2, 2004

	Price	Market Value	Yield (%)	Shares	Dividend	Income
Anheuser-Busch/BUD	46.33	1,622	2.01	35	0.93	33
Bank of America/BAC	34.27	1,953	4.96	57	1.70	97
Coca-Cola/KO	44.50	1,202	2.25	27	1.00	27
	(bought 3 WMT)					
Nucor Corp./NUE	12.74	1,376	1.88	108	0.24	26
Wal-Mart Stores/WMT	50.95	1,172	0.94	23	0.48	11
Total		7,324				193
Yield			2.64			23.40%

TABLE 7.3   Continued

January 2, 2005

	Price	Market Value	Yield (%)	Shares	Dividend	Income
Anheuser-Busch/BUD	45.74	1,601	2.25	35	1.03	36
Bank of America/BAC	40.58	2,313	4.68	57	1.90	108
Coca-Cola/KO	38.33	1,227	2.92	32	1.12	36
	(bought 5 KO)					
Nucor Corp./NUE	25.71	2,777	3.62	108	0.93	100
Wal-Mart Stores/WMT	50.05	1,151	1.16	23	0.58	13
Total		9,068				294
Yield			3.24			23.80%

January 2, 2006

	Price	Market Value	Yield (%)	Shares	Dividend	Income
Anheuser-Busch/BUD	39.43	1,380	2.74	35	1.08	38
Bank of America/BAC	40.36	2,301	5.25	57	2.12	121
Coca-Cola/KO	39.23	1,255	3.16	32	1.24	40
	(bought 7 WMT)					
Nucor Corp./NUE	39.01	4,213	5.51	108	2.15	232
Wal-Mart Stores/WMT	44.59	1,338	1.46	30	0.65	20
Total		10,487				450
Yield			4.29			15.64%

January 2, 2007

	Price	Market Value	Yield (%)	Shares	Dividend	Income
Anheuser-Busch/BUD	49.72	1,740	2.65	35	1.32	46
Bank of America/BAC	50.06	2,853	4.79	57	2.40	137
Coca-Cola/KO	46.68	1,494	2.91	32	1.36	44
	(bought 10 WMT)					

(*continued*)

TABLE 7.3   Continued

January 2, 2007 (continued)

	Price	Market Value	Yield (%)	Shares	Dividend	Income
Nucor Corp./NUE	62.00	6,696	3.95	108	2.45	265
Wal-Mart Stores/WMT	46.80	1,872	1.77	40	0.83	33
Total		14,655				524
Yield			3.58			39.74%

January 2, 2008

	Price	Market Value	Yield (%)	Shares	Dividend	Income
Anheuser-Busch/BUD	47.03	1,646	2.98	35	1.40	49
Bank of America/BAC	42.37	2,415	6.04	57	2.56	146
Coca-Cola/KO	57.40	2,353	2.58	41	1.48	61
	(bought 9 KO)					
Nucor Corp./NUE	56.35	6,086	4.44	108	2.50	270
Wal-Mart Stores/WMT	49.56	1,982	1.86	40	0.92	37
Total		14,483				562
Yield			3.88			-1.17%

Source: The Staton Institute® Inc.

declined 47 percent, the worst debacle since the Great Depression 1929–1932. Even though the period was overall bad for most stocks, that was not true of the five in our example. And, again, I emphasize that, before I calculated the numbers, I had no idea what the results would be.

The total annual return of the portfolio compared to the S&P 500 is shown in Table 7.4. Note that the S&P was down three consecutive

TABLE 7.4   Total Return Gains/Losses (%)

	2000	2001	2002	2003	2004	2005	2006	2007
S&P 500	-9.10	-11.89	-22.10	28.69	10.88	4.91	15.79	5.49
5 stocks	9.92	14.30	-5.52	23.40	23.80	15.64	39.74	-1.17

Source: The Staton Institute® Inc.

years in 2000, 2001, and again in 2002. The five stocks were down 5.5 percent in 2002 and off a little more than one percent in 2007. They outperformed the market in all but two years, 2003 and 2007. They clobbered the S&P 500 in each of the other six.

Remember that one of the keys to profitable investing is to keep your stock positions roughly equally dollar weighted as time goes on. In our example, we didn't add any money. Presumably you will, as much as you can and as often as you can. When you do add money, simply buy more of the most underweighted stocks to bring them closer to those that are overweighted.

In this case, Nucor (on January 2, 2008) represents 42 percent of the total value of the portfolio, whereas Anheuser-Busch is underweighted at 11.4 percent. Wal-Mart is next most underweighted at 13.7 percent. If you had added, say, $3,000, at the beginning of 2008, you could have brought BUD and WMT up to equal weightings. That in turn would have reduced Nucor's weighting from 42 percent to 34.8 percent. That's still too high, but you see that over time you can bring it down without selling any NUE shares through buying more of the others.

GETTING STARTED WITH A LITTLE OR A LOT

The maximum annual contribution allowed by law to an IRA is $5,000. But you may have a lot less than that to begin with, or you may have much more.

Suppose you're 18 and starting college. You get a job, as I did when I was in school, and earn $2,500 each of the four years you're there. You need most of that money for living expenses, but you can invest $50 each month. Since you have earned income, you're allowed to contribute to an IRA.

You open an account with a discount brokerage firm (whose commissions are cheaper) and mail them a $50 check monthly for 12 months; this is invested in a money market fund earning, let's say, a paltry two percent. At the end of the year you've saved $600 and earned about $7 interest.

Now pick one stock you like from those in America's Finest Companies and buy it. Deducting the $10 estimated commission (because you're using a discount broker), you'll put roughly $590 to work. Follow the same routine each of the next three years you're in school and buy a different stock every time, making sure each is in a different industry.

When you graduate, you'll have invested $2,400 (after commissions) and will own a few shares of four different companies. Since you're armed with a college degree, you should soon start earning far more than $2,500 and be able to contribute your maximum of $4,000 per year (you're too young for the $5,000 maximum), assuming your employer doesn't offer a 401(k) plan. If your employer does, you should invest in the company plan first because you can put away far more than $4,000 per year. For this example, I'm assuming you're not covered at work.

You're now 22, and your little IRA has grown to $4,000. No doubt it's out of balance. When you make your first $4,000 annual contribution, you'll have more than enough money to add a fifth stock in a different industry. Follow the same technique outlined earlier to invest $4,000 annually and maintain balance. It sounds simple, and it is.

Now let's say you did not get started early in life, and you're self-employed. No one else works for you. You realize you've got zero dollars set aside for life after work (retirement) and need help; so you rush out and purchase a copy of this book. Smart move!

After completing Chapter 6 on retirement plans, you open a simplified employee pension (SEP) plan or Keogh. Take your pick. You fund it with a $10,000 contribution at age 50 and bump up the contribution each year by 10 percent. By age 60, you're up to $25,937 annually, which is $20,063 less than the maximum $46,000 you're allowed to contribute under today's law. By the time you're 60, the limit is probably going to be significantly higher. Your money grows at 12 percent each year in America's Finest Companies.

After 11 annual contributions (at the beginning of each year), you've put $185,310 into your SEP or Keogh. As shown in Table 7.5, when you are age 65, that amount will have grown to $551,112 (nearly tripled) and five years later will be approaching a million dollars (more than quintupled).

If you can start a portfolio with as much as $10,000 and add at a rate similar to this, you should eventually spread the money equally among a dozen or so companies rather than only five.

A BIT OF EXTRA ADVICE

I didn't set out in life to become the assistant leader of a cult.
—CHARLIE MUNGER'S WELCOMING STATEMENT TO
SHAREHOLDERS TO THE 2007
WESCO FINANCIAL CORP. ANNUAL MEETING

TABLE 7.5   A SEP/KEOGH Grows Rapidly Even When You Start Late

Start Age	Annual $ Contribution, Increased by 10% Annually, Earns 12% Tax Deferred
50	$ 10,000
51	11,000
52	12,100
53	13,310
54	14,641
55	16,105
56	17,716
57	19,487
58	21,436
59	23,579
60	25,937
Total contributions	$185,310
Worth at age 65	$551,112
Worth at age 70	$971,248
Worth at age 75	$1,711,671

Source: The Staton Institute® Inc.

Charlie Munger grew up in Omaha and worked in Warren Buffett's grandfather's grocery store as a teenager. Buffett says, "Charlie is rational, very rational" and has the "best 30-second mind in the world. He goes from A to Z in one move. He sees the essence of everything before you even finish the sentence."

Wesco is one of America's Finest Companies with 37 consecutive years of higher annual dividends through 2008. The so-called cult is the loyal throng of value investors that invade both Omaha, Nebraska, and Pasadena, California, each spring to learn at the feet of Munger and his legendary partner Warren Buffett. Munger is also vice chairman of Berkshire Hathaway Corp. The rabid fans hope, as Munger says, "to leave a little wiser than they came."

Munger's talk focused on the reasons Buffett and Berkshire have become such a "lollapalooza" success. Munger identified several factors that, working in concert, have led to one of the most spectacular investment and business records in the history of business. Every investor can learn from them, and I have:

- *Mental aptitude:* Warren Buffett is obviously a very smart man, but Munger stated he probably overachieved given his innate mental ability. For example, Buffett could not "beat all comers playing chess blindfolded" like U.S. chess champion Patrick Wolff. (Wolff beats multiple opponents simultaneously while blindfolded at Berkshire Hathaway annual meetings.)
- *Intense interest:* Munger noted that Buffett was keenly engaged in business and investing from a very young age. "There is no substitute for a very intense interest."
- *Early start:* With Buffett's early start in investing (age 19), he was able to use his skills to consistently compound capital over many decades.
- *Constant learning:* Munger described Buffett as one of the nation's best "learning machines." Continue learning throughout your life with a voracious appetite. The best way to gain wisdom, Munger said, is "sitting on your [behind] and reading all day."
- His book recommendations include *The Martians of Science: Five Physicists Who Changed the Twentieth Century* by Istvan Hargittai and *Einstein: His Life and Universe* by Walter Isaacson. Munger said he had read every Einstein biography, and this new one by Isaacson was the best.
- *Concentration:* Another factor in Berkshire's success is the latitude Buffett has been given to lead. "It's hard to think of committees that have been successful," Munger pointed out. He used the analogy of John Wooden's player-rotation strategy. The great UCLA basketball coach would play only 7 out of his 12 young men, so as to concentrate the experience into his 7 best players.
- Similarly, most of Berkshire's work is given to its best mind, Buffett's, although I think Munger underestimates his own abilities, as I witnessed personally when Buffett tossed Munger some of the hardest shareholder questions at the Berkshire 2004 annual meeting.
- *Be willing to change your mind:* One questioner asked whether Munger had ever changed his mind about a closely held belief. After some thinking, he responded that Berkshire's recent purchase of railroad stocks marked a 180-degree change in thinking about the industry. According to Munger, railroads now have a

huge competitive advantage over trucking because of innovations such as double-stacked cars and computer modeling of routes.

- Munger said he and Buffett were too late in recognizing the changes and could have made much more money buying earlier. Apparently, Bill Gates figured it out at least two years earlier and made "multiples of his money" with railroad stocks.
- *Watch for inefficient markets:* There are two kinds of inefficient markets: ones that are small and neglected and ones where people do crazy things. The latter happens from time to time, one of the latest examples being the dotcoms, most of which turned into dot-bombs. One of our money management clients lost more than 95 percent of his money in that fiasco. I'm happy to say none was ever in my AFC universe, nor did I ever recommend dot-coms to my private clients.

With humor and clarity, Munger also dispensed advice for living a well-examined life:

- *Don't go to extremes:* Many smart people handicap themselves with "nuttiness." One example is being an "extreme ideologue," which is the equivalent of "having taken your brain and started pounding it with a hammer." You can get away with more than you deserve in life by being slightly more rational, Munger says. Your life must focus on the "maximization of objectivity."
- *It may not be fair, but that's the way it is:* It is totally unproductive to think the world has been unfair to you. Munger believes, "Every tough stretch is an opportunity."
- And last but not least, *be grateful:* "I'm not going to complain about my age," he says, "because without it, I'd be dead."

8

The Unbeatable Power of Dependable and Rising Annual Dividends

There are ways for the individual investor to make money in the securities markets. Buying value and holding long term while collecting dividends has been proven over and over again.
— ROBERT M. SHARP, AUTHOR OF *THE LORE AND LEGENDS OF WALL STREET*

POINTS TO REMEMBER

- Higher dividends predict growth.
- Higher payouts equal higher returns.
- Dividend payouts help companies excel.

WHY DIVIDENDS MATTER WHEN BUYING STOCKS

A dividend is a sum of money paid to shareholders of a corporation out of earnings. It's also anything received as a bonus or reward or something in addition to or beyond what is expected (as in an extra or special dividend). Far too many stock investors believe that price appreciation is the way to make the most money from equities, not dividends. The truth is just the opposite.

In 1937 British economist Lord John Maynard Keynes remarked, "In one of the greatest investment markets in the world, namely, New York, the influence of speculation is enormous. It is rare for an American to 'invest for income,' and he will not readily purchase an investment except in the hope of capital appreciation." But John D. Rockefeller, the American industrialist, investor, and philanthropist who founded Standard Oil in 1870 and who was the world's richest person (measured in today's dollars) said, "Do you know the only thing that gives me pleasure? It's to see my dividends coming in."

A lot of smart people (including many professional money managers) have opined for years that dividends don't matter or, at best, matter little; it's really earnings growth and price appreciation that count.

Table 8.1 shows the S&P 500's compounded annual price growth rate (CAGR) from 1950 through 2000. Note that, during all five periods ranging from 10 to 50 years, dividends comprised no less than 14 percent to as much as 31 percent of the annual total return.

Many advisers shun higher-yielding stocks for high-tax-bracket investors because they focus only on how much the government will take of that income. They ignore the historic total return numbers and the fact that higher-yielding stocks generally go down less in a bear market. Thus, the overall return of the portfolio—dividends with appreciation—is almost always higher than from price appreciation alone.

Global markets analyst Mike Burnick sums it up this way, "Smart investing is about making money the old-fashioned way . . . earning it. This includes buying undervalued blue-chip companies [America's Finest Companies certainly qualify] with attractive dividend yields. That's one of the best investment strategies I know of."

TABLE 8.1   S&P 500 Annual Returns 1950–2000 (%)

	CAGR	With Dividends	Percentage Return from Dividends
1990–2000	14.9	17.3	14
1980–2000	12.0	15.4	22
1970–2000	9.3	13.0	29
1960–2000	8.1	11.8	31
1950–2000	8.7	12.5	30

Source: The Staton Institute® Inc.

I had the distinct pleasure of spending about 10 minutes one on one with John Neff (also a CFA like me) in 2004 at a Chartered Financial Analyst conference in Philadelphia. Neff was one of the most successful money managers in U.S. history while at the helm of Vanguard's Windsor Fund. His book, *John Neff On Investing* (Wiley) is well worth a read. Quoting Benjamin Franklin, "He that waits upon Fortune is never sure of a dinner," Neff writes, "As I see it, a superior yield at least lets you snack on hors d'oeuvres while waiting for the main meal."

Neff also writes, "Can you be confident about the yield? You can, unless the company lowers the dividend under extraordinary duress. In fact, good companies are much more apt to increase the dividend, which is like learning that your bank plans to increase its passbook rate."

Widely known as "the professional's professional," Neff's fund stayed within the top five percent of all mutual funds for more than three decades. By the end of his 32-year run (in 1995), he had compiled an annual return of 13.7 percent versus 10.6 percent for the S&P 500. He beat the market by an enormous margin.

To put his return into perspective, $10,000 invested in the S&P 500 grew to approximately $251,000. In Windsor, it rose to almost $609,000, or 2.4 times more. That's an incredible margin by any standards.

Like Mary and me, John Neff has always focused on value. He always attempted to buy quality issues at a discount to true worth. Also like us, he focused on solid and growing dividends first and moderate capital appreciation to a lesser degree. It has been said that he modeled his investment style based on the works of Benjamin Graham

Cash dividends have accounted for roughly 40 percent of the total return on stocks dating all the way back to the inception of the S&P 500 at the end of 1925. Dividends were *the* sole reason that stock returns were positive for the 10 years from the beginning of 1930 through the end of 1939, the period that encompassed the Great Depression.

Many money managers mimic the S&P 500 because it represents about 80 percent of the U.S. stock market value. And millions of individual investors regularly pour their money into index funds that are supposed to replicate the market. That said, it's no wonder so many people have made so little money since the dawn of this new millennium.

TABLE 8.2   S&P 500 Percentage Gains/Losses

	2000	2001	2002	2003	2004	2005	2006	2007
S&P 500	−9.10	−11.89	−22.10	28.69	10.88	4.91	15.79	5.49

Source: The Staton Institute® Inc.

Though the S&P 500 was down fractionally from the beginning of 2000 through the end of 2007, the total return, including dividends, was 14.0 percent, which works out to a pathetic 1.65 percent per year (see Table 8.2). With AFCs, the story was completely different as you will see shortly.

THE BAKER'S DOZEN GUIDED PORTFOLIO®

I started writing *$taton$ E-Money Digest* in early 2000 and put together The Baker's Dozen Guided Portfolio® on June 18 of that year, investing a theoretical $1,000 into each of 13 America's Finest Companies. Although The Baker's Dozen was down for the first year ever in 2007, by December 31 of that year it had climbed 168 percent in value from inception. The compound annual return was 14.0 percent. And that nearly eight-year period encompassed the worst stock market decline since the 1930s, in which stocks overall fell nearly 50 percent from peak to trough. (Note: The Baker's Dozen does not represent any account managed by Bill Staton or his firm, Staton Financial Advisors LLC, nor does the return stated above take into account client risk factors, advisory fees, and commissions.)

Since The Baker's Dozen inception, I have closed out 32 positions but have always kept 13 in the portfolio: no more, no less. I reinvest theoretical dividends at the end of each quarter into the stock with the smallest market value. No money has been added or taken out. I keep each stock about the same in market value over time and tend to rebalance once a year, usually in December.

The Baker's Dozen is the quintessential example of a portfolio constructed from America's Finest Companies®.

Table 8.3 represents how The Baker's Dozen Guided Portfolio® has performed since its inception on June 18, 2000, starting with $13,000. The table also shows the S&P 500 excluding dividends, whereas the Guided Portfolio includes dividends reinvested quarterly. The S&P dropped 10 points from inception to year-end 2007. The table does not show total return figures for the S&P starting from June 18, 2000, but does show them for the eight years January 1, 2000,

TABLE 8.3   The Baker's Dozen Guided Portfolio Performance

Date	S&P 500	Change (%)	Guided Portfolio	Change (%)
6/17/00	1479		$13,000	
12/29/00	1320	–10.8	$14,271	9.8
1/4/02	1173	–11.1	$19,315	35.3
1/10/03	928	–20.9	$19,572	1.3
1/9/04	1122	20.9	$27,093	38.4
12/31/04	1212	8.0	$29,895	10.3
12/30/05	1248	3.0	$30,230	1.1
12/29/06	1418	13.6	$37,969	25.6
12/31/07	1469	3.6	$34,834	–8.3
Net Change	**–10**	**–0.7**	**$21,834**	**168.0**

Source: The Staton Institute® Inc.

through December 31, 2007. The total return was 14.0 percent, which works out to a pitiful 1.65 percent per year.

The Baker's Dozen was down for the first time in 2007 but remains up 168 percent. The compound annual return is 14.0 percent. The Baker's Dozen has provided followers with an annual advantage of approximately 12 percentage points or more over the past 7.6 years. We'd pit that record against almost any domestic equity fund or independent money manager who specializes in American companies like us.

Investing exclusively in (1) U.S.–based companies that (2) hike their dividends each year (3) for a minimum of 10 years is the secret to making *big* money in stocks while sailing through even the worst of economic and stock market environments.

Mark Skousen, author of *Investing in One Lesson,* has observed that investing only in dividend-paying stocks will (1) help you avoid making big mistakes, (2) increase your chance of beating the market, and (3) typically do that with less volatility than the overall market.

Way back in early 1989, it occurred to me that there should be a simple way to identify the highest-quality companies that make the most money over long periods of time. I had an ah-hah, a blinding glimpse of the obvious. All I needed to do was to identify all U.S.–based companies with at least 10 years in a row of higher dividends and/or earnings per share. No one else was doing it, and to this day no one else does. Only me.

Earnings have always been somewhat tricky because there is so much wiggle room on every line from the top (revenue) to the bottom (net income after taxes). But with dividends, there are no tricks. Either a company pays a cash dividend or it doesn't. If it doesn't, I don't look at it.

A dividend can go in one of three directions: up, down or sideways. If it's not going up every single year without fail, I'm not interested. By that simple rule of thumb, I eliminate about 98 percent of all public U.S. companies. But that leaves more than 300 companies from which to choose, and that is more than plenty in which to invest and make solid returns.

When I first came up with this concept in late 1989, a research assistant and I took 18 months to compile the original database, which at that time was about 425 companies. Way before the Internet, I trudged to the library virtually every day to pore over— one page at a time—roughly 5,000 *Standard & Poor's Fact Sheets* and more than 1,800 pages of *The Value Line Investment Survey*.

We wrote hundreds of letters asking for annual reports and other necessary information, and we talked with about the same number of companies. It was a mammoth effort but well worth the time and trouble because my experience had taught me that consistency—as measured by long strings of rising earnings and dividends—is a hallmark of above-average stock performance whether you're a buy-and-holder, a market timer, or a combination of both.

AFC companies (fewer than 2 percent of all publicly traded U.S.–based corporations) are the prime choice in American industry, just as is prime beef, which is sold in only about 2 percent of America's finest restaurants. Isn't that an interesting analogy?

When I first started publishing my annual America's Finest Companies investment directory, now in its eighteenth edition, there was little evidence about investing in companies that pay dividends rather than those that don't. Now more and more research seems to be popping up to support my case.

HIGHER PAYOUTS EQUAL HIGHER RETURNS

My money management clients, with below-average risk, have generally performed consistently well simply because we focus on quality, dividend-paying stocks with above-average yields. Study after study has proved beyond the shadow of anyone's doubt that this approach is a long-term moneymaker. And it's easy to understand and implement.

In March 2003 *AIMR Digest*[1] carried a sophisticated article that originally appeared in *The Financial Analysts Journal* titled "Surprise! Higher Dividends = Higher Earnings Growth," by Robert D. Arnott (former global equity strategist for Salomon Brothers) and by hedge fund manager Clifford S. Asness. The article studied the payout ratio (the percentage of earnings paid as dividends) and its relationship to subsequent earnings growth stretching back for 130 years, with particular emphasis on the post–World War II era.

The authors concluded that higher payout ratios predicted faster earnings growth over the ensuing 10 years. The top 25 percent of S&P 500 stocks with the highest payouts enjoyed average inflation-adjusted earnings growth of 4.2 percent per year. Conversely, the lowest 25 percent reported profits shrinking by 0.4 percent per year. Even over the finest 10-year period, earnings growth was never higher than 3.2 percent annually.

Jack Hough, in *SmartMoney*, observed, "An old adage holds that investors in dividend stocks are being 'paid to wait for the stock to appreciate.' Academic research suggests they may not have to wait very long. Dividends, it turns out, can actually forecast earnings growth. And earnings growth, of course, drives stock gains." *SmartMoney* stated:

> These findings challenge investor assumptions that the only companies that can afford fat dividend payments are those that have run out of good ideas to fund. Fast growers are supposed to plow their profits back into their businesses, not send big quarterly payments to shareholders. And yet the numbers say it's the big dividend payers that grow the fastest.
>
> Arnott and Asness came up with two possible explanations for their findings. One holds that since managers hate cutting dividends, high payout ratios suggest extraordinary confidence in future earnings. Another says that high payout ratios prevent "empire building." That's the well-documented tendency of managers with too much cash on their hands to waste it on ill-advised acquisitions.

---

[1] AIMR is the Association of Investment Management and Research.

Continually paying and increasing dividends forces CEOs and managers to excel. The famous Hollywood actor Edward G. Robinson once opined: "Live beyond your means; then you're forced to work hard, you have to succeed."

The March 2003 issue of *Worth* magazine said that "investing in stocks with rising dividends is a prescription for growth, not just income." *Worth* observed:

> While many investors like . . . cash payouts for safety and income, [money manager Donald Taylor's] attraction stems largely from the discipline they impose. Companies with long records of mostly uninterrupted dividend growth tend to think carefully about how they allocate capital. They are much more likely to grow and prosper than companies that try to fuel growth by reinvesting a large portion of retained earnings, which often end up being wasted on slow-growth businesses, poorly thought-out projects or ill-fated acquisitions.

Said another way, lots of cash can easily burn huge holes in corporate pockets. History proves it.

Worth noted, "Between 1946 and 2000, companies' earnings growth was fastest following periods in which they paid out a high proportion of their income as dividends." This is strongly supported by the research of Arnott and Asness, who write:

> Unlike optimistic new-paradigm advocates, we found that low payout ratios historically precede low earnings growth. This relationship is strong and robust. We found that the empirical facts conform to a world in which managers possess private information that causes them to pay out a large share of earnings when they are optimistic that dividend cuts will not be necessary and to pay out a small share when they are pessimistic, perhaps so that they can be confident of maintaining the dividend payouts.

Standard & Poor's rating service has provided earnings and dividend rankings, commonly referred to as quality rankings, on common stocks since 1956. The quality ranking from A+ on down to D reflects the long-term growth and stability of a company's earnings and dividends. Portfolios of stocks with high quality rankings outperformed S&P's own 500 Index over the 1986–2002 period, just as did America's Finest Companies overall.

The portfolio with the highest ranking (A+) beat the S&P 500 by almost 1.5 percentage points per year during that 17-year span. (This encompassed one of the longest strongest bull markets in history as well as one of the most severe bear market declines.) On a risk-adjusted basis, the all-A portfolio outperformed the all-B portfolio by almost four percentage points per year.

S&P's quality ranking is derived by means of a complicated computer program with statistics from the previous 10 years, the same period I use to measure whether a company deserves to be in America's Finest. Their analysis shows that "high-quality companies provide high and stable growth in earnings and dividends," which dovetails nicely with my requirement that each AFC member deliver a minimum of 10 years in a row of higher earnings and/or dividends per share.

As has always been the case, the overwhelming majority of companies qualify because of rising dividends. Charles E. Babin of State Street Global Advisors, author of the 1999 business book, *Investing Secrets of the Masters*, observes:

> There's a school of thought that says dividends are strictly for old fogies and tax-exempt entities, and that smart investors should think only about capital gains. I don't subscribe. I think dividends do matter and that paying attention to them will improve your odds of getting capital gains.
>
> The key is to find stocks that consistently raise dividends year after year. Dividend hikes are the kind of news that feeds appreciation.

Laurence H. Sloan, the man who founded Standard & Poor's, noted way back in 1931, "An unbeatable combination is a stock with a hefty payout and an ability to keep raising it."

Regardless of what anyone says, *dividends matter*. The Dow Jones Industrial Average (DJIA) of just 30 stocks began with 12 in 1896 at the level of 42. In 2007 it passed 14,000 for the first time, but that's without dividends. With dividends reinvested, the DJIA would be well past 1 million today. Wow!

Money magazine said:

> The very fact that a company pays and regularly increases a dividend is a sign that the top managers lean toward traditional

ideas of sound financial management—they believe in return-
ing a growing stream of cash to shareholders and aren't betting
every cent they can borrow on future expansion. Stocks with
the fastest dividend growth tend to have the biggest gains.

According to Standard & Poor's:

> Investing in stocks that pay dividends is like betting on the tor-
> toise in Aesop's fable. Even though the hare is faster, slow and
> steady wins the race."
>   Most investors who try their hands at hot stocks only get
> burned. Dividends, on the other hand, are real. They represent
> a tangible return to you, the shareholder. Dividends are money
> in the bank. For as long as anyone can remember, investors
> have intuitively understood that dividend-paying stocks pro-
> vide a higher degree of price stability than non-dividend-paying
> issues [particularly in a market drop].

> *Steady plodding brings prosperity. Hasty speculation brings poverty.*
>   —PROVERBS 21:5

Peter Lynch, the renowned money manager adds to that: "The
dividend is such an important factor in the success of many stocks
that you could hardly go wrong by making an entire portfolio of companies that have raised their dividends for 10 or 20 years in a row."

Further on the subject of the power of dividends, refer to Figure 8.1.
On this chart of the S&P 500 (which represents more than 75 percent
of all U.S. stock market value), for the 20-year period 1987 through
the end of 2006, dividend-paying stocks in the index returned 10.11
percent annually (top line) compared to only 3.39 percent for nondividend payers (bottom line), a remarkable difference.

Figure 8.2 stretches all the way back to 1871 for the S&P 500
and its predecessor index. You can see that the broad area in the
middle (representing dividends) grew at a 4.8 percent compound-
annual rate whereas the bottom section (representing price appreciation) grew at 2.2 percent annually or less than half the return
of dividends. The top portion is the annual inflation rate. Together
inflation, dividends, and capital growth combined led to an annual
compound return of 9.2 percent with dividends contributing more
than half (52.2 percent) of the total amount.

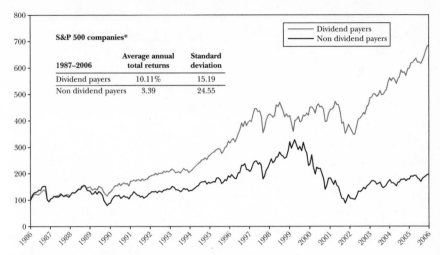

FIGURE 8.1   S&P 500 Companies: Dividend and Nondividend Payers

Source: The Staton Institute® Inc.

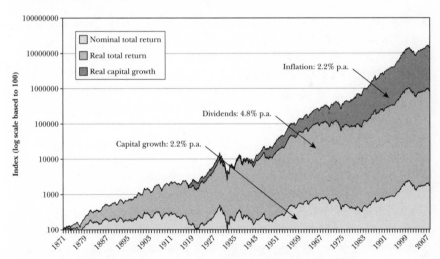

FIGURE 8.2   S&P 500 Components of Total Nominal Return (1871–2006)

Source: Plexus Asset Management (based on data from Prof. Robert Shiller and I-Net Bridge)

One final comment about dividends from the March–April 2007 *CFA Magazine:*

> Dividends have at least three functions. The first is to provide a predictable, low-risk, spendable and repeatable investment return to shareholders.

The second is to provide a metric for security analysts to value the stock.

The third function is signaling. A company that increases its dividend regularly is perceived by investors as a sound, growing company. If a company reduces its dividend the market takes this as evidence that the company is in trouble.

If a company has an annual reduction, we delete it from America's Finest Companies, unless annual earnings continue to rise.

The relationship between paying dividends and long-term performance is no mirage: Companies with long histories of rising annual dividends should be superior in any and every environment. They have in the past. They ought to in the future.

In a Twist, High Dividends Are Now a Predictor of Growth[2]

It may seem too good to be true, but companies that pay the highest dividends are also likely to grow the fastest.

For years, many finance professors have taught just the opposite. Reinvesting current earnings back into a company is supposed to promote earnings growth. Higher payout ratios are supposed to be followed by lower earnings growth. But research conducted by Robert D. Arnott of First Quadrant and Clifford S. Asness of AQR Capital Management reveals a very different picture. For the overall stock market between 1871 and 2001, corporate profits grew fastest in the 10 years following the calendar years in which companies had the highest average dividend payout ratio. In contrast, the 10-year real earnings growth rate was the lowest following years with the lowest average payout ratios.

Mr. Arnott and Mr. Asness, who both work for quantitative research firms, began circulating early versions of their study in academic circles earlier this year. In their latest version, which will be published in the January/February issue of *The Financial Analysts Journal*, they respond to several arguments posed by critics who have read their work.

---

[2] "In a Twist, High Dividends Are Now a Predictor of Growth," excerpted from *The New York Times*. From The New York Times, November 17, 2002. © 2002 The New York Times. All Rights Reserved. Used by permission and protected by the Copyright Laws of the United States. The printing, copying, redistribution or retransmission of the Material without express written permission is prohibited.

Critics say that while the researchers' conclusion may accurately describe the behavior of the overall market, it may not apply to individual companies. Mr. Arnott and Mr. Asness concede that this is possible.

But based on the preliminary results of additional research being conducted by Mr. Arnott, he believes it is likely that the pattern that he and Mr. Asness found at the level of the overall market applies to the individual firm as well. He notes in this regard another study that appeared in last December's *Journal of Finance* by two Columbia Business School accounting professors, Doron Nissim and Amir Ziv ("Dividend Changes and Future Profitability"). This other research found that between 1963 and 1997, earnings per share grew for two years at an above-market rate for the average company that increased its dividends.

Other critics worried that the research by Mr. Arnott and Mr. Asness may have been skewed by firms' share repurchases. Mr. Arnott and Mr. Asness reject that objection. They found that the period since 1980 fit the same pattern as did the prior period back to 1871, during which share repurchase programs were relatively rare.

Mr. Arnott and Ms. Asness believe that the primary cause of their surprising result is the poor job that the average company does when investing the cash that it would pay out as dividends. Therefore it is better for the company to distribute its earnings to shareholders.

With less cash on hand, a company interested in building its empire is forced to resort to the debt or equity markets to secure needed financing. That directly subjects its business to market discipline, reducing the likelihood that management will pursue unprofitable ventures.

Their research provides strong evidence in favor of a theory first advanced in 1986 by Michael C. Jensen, currently an emeritus professor of business administration at Harvard Business School. Writing in *The American Economic Review*, Professor Jensen speculated that the more cash that companies have now (beyond what is needed for current projects) the less efficient they will be in the future.

Professor Jensen said managers had incentives to use this excess cash to expand their firms beyond what was most profitable because "growth increases managers' power by increasing the resources under their control." So shareholders need to determine "how to motivate managers to disgorge the cash," he said.

The common theme that emerges from these various studies is a very unflattering portrait of corporate management: give executives lots of rope and they too often end up hanging themselves. It would appear that a high dividend payout ratio is an effective way to reduce the length of that rope.

9

How to Dodge Uncle Sam Outside Your Life-after-Work Plan

You've got to hand it to the IRS. If you don't, they'll come get it.

—ANONYMOUS

POINTS TO REMEMBER

- Buy only no- or low-dividend-paying stocks.
- Sell rarely.
- Offset gains with losses, if any.

Money inside a retirement—or life-after-work—plan receives preferential treatment because it grows without taxes until withdrawn. If you sell appreciated stock in your retirement plan, you never have to pay any capital gains taxes. You pay taxes only when you withdraw money, beginning as early as 59½; and no later than 70½.

Money outside a retirement plan is taxed both by the federal government and by all the states with income taxes. Taxes on dividends and capital gains must be paid in the years they're realized. Although losses can be used to offset gains, that's not much of a benefit, since taxes can knock a Titanic-sized hole in your financial ship.

Because capital gains taxes can take a chunk out of profits in a taxable account, it usually makes the most sense to lock away every investment dollar possible in a retirement plan. However, the government makes it hard to get money out of a retirement plan without triggering a 10 percent penalty, plus requiring ordinary income taxes. If you're building a stock portfolio for something other than life after work, you'll probably do it in a taxable account. Then you can get your hands on your money penalty free anytime you want.

MINIMIZING TAXES

To minimize taxes, you can build a portfolio of low-yielding stocks (2 percent or less is my criterion) and sell rarely. Selling rarely (and therefore avoiding capital gains taxes) is what has allowed many self-made millionaires and billionaires, members of the Forbes 400, to establish such incredible fortunes: Warren Buffett of Berkshire Hathaway, Bill Gates of Microsoft (formerly one of America's Finest), Leon Levine of Family Dollar Stores, the Waltons of Wal-Mart Stores, to name four.

Here's an example of how to minimize taxes. An attorney, who was very well to do, came by for one of my personal coaching sessions. He already had a substantial buildup in his retirement plan and was making the maximum annual contribution each year, but he still earned a lot of extra money to invest in his taxable portfolio. That portfolio contained a number of low-quality stocks with no companies in the AFC universe except Sysco Corp., the nation's largest food distributor with 15 percent market share.

There were capital gains in some issues, losses in the others, and no particular rhyme or reason as to what he purchased or sold. In addition, he had dozens of stocks, far too many to keep up with. My recommendation was to sell everything but Sysco, offsetting gains with losses where possible, and to assemble a portfolio of 15 companies within the AFC universe (including Sysco), with roughly 6–7 percent of the money in each.

The client was in the highest possible tax bracket, so keeping taxes minimal was important. Without revealing what he bought, the thought process went something like this:

If you want to invest in relatively high-yielding stocks [real estate investment trusts (REITs), for example], those stocks should be in your retirement plan, where dividends won't be taxed. When you invest outside the retirement plan and to keep taxes down, the focus should be (1) selling infrequently and (2) low yields.

Picking such a portfolio is easy and takes no more than a couple of minutes. Turn to the alphabetical listing of companies in the

America's Finest Companies universe in the Appendix and start skimming the list. For this example, I'm sticking with all companies yielding no more than 2.0 percent, and I want to end up with 14 on top of Sysco. So I picked the first 14 from the AFC list meeting that sole criterion.

Now I buy the portfolio and invest 6–7 percent of my money into each. One year from the purchase date, I add additional money to the portfolio and bring the bottom two or three laggard positions into line with the others. If one stock runs way ahead of the rest of the pack and becomes dramatically overweighted, I don't sell part of it to bring it into line with the others because I don't want to pay capital gains taxes. I let my profits ride as long as the company remains within the AFC universe.

If it's booted out, it becomes an automatic sell. As long as I don't realize gains, my money continues to grow tax-deferred, with the exception of the taxes I'll pay on annual dividends. That won't be a lot because the yield is comparatively skimpy.

If I want to pay no taxes, I need companies that don't pay dividends. However, only five America's Finest Companies qualify and are shown in Table 9.1. By including picks from this short list of companies, there are almost no taxable dividends—just as in a retirement plan—and no capital gains as long as I don't sell.

In a taxable account, you should sell only if the stock is deleted from America's Finest Companies or you need the money. Otherwise, there is no good reason to sell in a taxable account unless you'd like to use a loss to offset other income. (In a nontaxable account, the loss wouldn't matter for tax purposes.)

Especially in a taxable account, always picture yourself as a buyer, not as a seller. Once your portfolio is set up, keep buying more of what you've got, and keep all stock positions in as near equal dollar proportion as possible. Sell only when necessary. Otherwise Uncle Sam (and probably the state where you reside) will come calling to claim their "fair" share of your profits.

Why Pay Taxes When You Don't Have to?

Avoid taxes by letting your portfolio continue to appreciate over the next 5, 10, 15, 20 years, or more.

Multibillionaire Warren Buffett is a buyer of quality, and he rarely sells. Inasmuch as he's worth more than $60 billion and one of

TABLE 9.1   20 Lowest Annual Dividend Yields in AFC

Company	Ticker	Industry	Yield
Moog Inc.	MOG-A	Manufacturing	0.0%
O'Reilly Automotive	ORLY	Auto Parts	0.0%
Patterson Cos. Inc.	PDCO	Medical Supplies	0.0%
Sonic Corp.	SONC	Restaurant	0.0%
Starbucks Corp.	SBUX	Restaurant	0.0%
UnitedHealth Group	UNH	Health Care	0.1%
Danaher Corp.	DHR	Metal Products	0.2%
Universal Forest Products Inc.	UFPI	Wood Products	0.2%
Wesco Financial Corp.	WSC	Financial	0.4%
Roper Industries Inc	ROP	Manufacturing	0.4%
DENTSPLY International Inc.	XRAY	Medical Supplies	0.4%
Matthews International Corp.	MATW	Miscellaneous	0.5%
Stryker Corp.	SYK	Medical Prods.	0.5%
SEI Investments Co.	SEIC	Investment Bank.	0.6%
Church & Dwight Co. Inc.	CHD	Cleaning Products	0.6%
Progressive Corp.	PGR	Insurance/Prop.	0.6%
Expeditors International	EXPD	Air Freight	0.6%
Energen Corp.	EGN	Natural Gas	0.6%
C.R. Bard Inc.	BCR	Medical Prods.	0.7%
Questar Corp.	STR	Natural Gas	0.7%

Source: The Staton Institute® Inc.

the world's top three wealthiest individuals, what he knows is worth knowing. Buffett says: "Buying only the best is something that . . . is very simple and very obvious." The AFC universe is not just the best. It's the finest!

As of December 31, 2007, Buffett's four largest stock investments were American Express (formerly one of America's Finest Companies®), Coca-Cola, Procter & Gamble, and Wells Fargo. Coke, Procter & Gamble, and Wells Fargo are in America's Finest. Buffett points out that both American Express and Wells Fargo were organized by Henry Wells and William Fargo in 1850 and 1852. Coke got its start in 1886, and P&G was formed in 1837.

The other stocks he owns that are also among America's Finest are Anheuser-Busch (acquired by InBev), Bank of America, Home Depot, Johnson & Johnson, Lowe's, US Bancorp (he's the largest shareowner), Wal-Mart Stores, Wesco Financial (run by Buffett's partner Charles Munger), Gannett, General Electric, M&T Bank Corp. and SunTrust Bank.

If you invest strictly in America's Finest Companies, if you continue to buy more of what you own, and if you rarely sell, you are modeling Buffett, the finest example of a successful long-term investor in history. Maybe you won't be worth $60+ billion before you die (or maybe you will), but you could easily become a millionaire, even a multimillionaire, given enough time and patience. And you could do it early enough in your life to enjoy some of the financial rewards of wise investing.

In his February 2008 letter to Berkshire Hathaway shareholders, Buffett wrote:

> I should emphasize that we do not measure the progress of our investments by what their market prices do during any given year. [Nor should you.] Rather, we evaluate their performance by the two methods we apply to the businesses we own.
>
> The first test is improvement in earnings, with our making due allowance for industry conditions. [If a company's dividends are rising year after year, it's proof positive that earnings must be growing as well.]
>
> The second test, more subjective, is whether their 'moats'—a metaphor for the superiorities they possess that make life difficult for competitors—have widened during the year.

I think the fact that Buffett owns various sized "pieces" of 15 different America's Finest Companies®, plus the fact that over the years he bought 100 percent of the shares of other AFCs including Geico, General Re, International Dairy Queen, FlightSafety International and Clayton Homes, to name but five, shows that America's Finest as a whole meet his moat criteria.

To start building a secure financial future with a portfolio of stocks in America's Finest Companies, to continue buying them, and to hold them for a long time is such a simple, no-brainer strategy you have to wonder why more investors don't do it. I surely do.

CHAPTER

10

Don't Delay! Get Started Now—It's Easy

Don't delay! A good plan, violently executed now, is better than a perfect plan next week. War is a very simple thing [like profitable investing], and the determining characteristics are self-confidence, speed, and audacity.
—GENERAL GEORGE S. PATTON, JR., U.S. ARMY FIELD
COMMANDER IN WORLD WAR II (1885–1945)

POINTS TO REMEMBER

- Use discount brokers, online or in person.
- Or use direct company investment plans and dividend reinvestment plans (DRPs).
- Starting now takes only a few bucks.

If you've invested before, you already have a brokerage account and know how it works, and you're familiar with the commissions and fees involved. But if you're just beginning, the prospect of opening an account can be intimidating, particularly if you've got only a few hundred or a few thousand dollars to invest. (While proofing this chapter, I talked via phone with someone starting out to invest $3,000 in five AFCs.)

You may think you're such a small investor nobody will want to do business with you. Certainly, a lot of brokers aren't interested in small accounts because they think they don't make enough in commissions. These brokers fail to realize that often large accounts don't start large; they start small. For example, my largest managed account came as the result of doing a good job for one of my smallest accounts.

Discount brokers offer lower commission rates than full-service brokers because they seek investors who want to save money and who, like you, make their own investment decisions.

Every year *Smart Money* magazine conducts a survey of the major discount brokers. Here's what they wrote in August 2007:

> For our 15th annual survey, we searched for the best combination of 21st-century features with old-fashioned service. As we usually do, we set up our own accounts, and bought and sold both big and small stocks. We also scrutinized how easy it was to fill out and make a trade.

To find an excellent listing of them and other useful comments, go to http://www.smartmoney.com/brokers/index.fm?story=august2007.

Here's another web site worth checking out with a very comprehensive list of brokers and necessary contact information: http://www.dfin.com/ldisc_brokers.htm.

Because you're now confident to be your own money manager and comfortable with your own decisions about what and when to buy and sell, where you open a brokerage account isn't nearly as important as it would be if you had no idea what you were doing. But you do know what you're doing; you're in control, not the broker.

There's no need to worry about a salesperson selling you something you don't want. What is important is that the firm is reputable and has the services you need. Perhaps as important is how much they charge, but you won't trade a lot under my investment strategy, so finding the cheapest commission isn't that big a deal.

ELIMINATING EVERY COST POSSIBLE

When you begin an investment program with as little as $500, commissions, transaction fees, and other charges can be a real burden because they can take a good chunk out of principal. But as you continue to add to your portfolio every six months to a year and your assets multiply, they become less and less of an albatross.

Although reducing or eliminating every cost possible is important, it's of far greater importance to have your portfolio invested strictly in America's Finest Companies, to keep the holdings properly weighted, and to buy more of what you already own every chance you get.

In my nearly 40 years in the investment business, I've seen people fail to make a lot of money because they spent too much time shopping for the best broker, trying to unearth the best brokerage firm, attempting to cut commissions to the bone, or all three. They were putting the cart before the horse, and that's not a profitable strategy.

Investing for maximum profits requires patience, a simple strategy like the one explained in these pages, and at least a ten-year horizon to give the strategy ample time to work. Keeping costs minimal improves your overall return—no doubt—but it won't improve your return nearly as much as planning to beat Wall Street with America's Finest Companies, implementing your plan, and sticking to it.

Investing Directly in a Company

One of the great innovations for do-it-yourself investors is online direct investing, and companies like General Electric (GE) are leading the way. GE offers investors the opportunity to buy its stock at a special web site. This type of web site is especially useful if you're starting out for yourself or for your children or grandchildren with a small amount of money, say $500 to $1,000. At GE's special web site, you can see your account balance and current transaction and disbursement check history, all the while being able not only to buy shares online but also to sell them, with small fees either way. For more information, visit www.ge.com/investor or phone (800) STOCK-GE.

By investing directly, you can make a small amount of money go a long way and build an excellent, well diversifed portfolio. Table 10.1 shows an example. For just under $1,000, the portfolio in Table 10.1 is diversified into eight different industries. You simply go to each company's individual web site and look for Company Info, Investor Relations, Investors, Shareholder Services, or some such link.

Gather information about each company's direct stock purchase plan and dividend reinvestment plan. Or go to the company's transfer agent's web site and look for Invest Online, Direct Investing, or Direct Purchase, (or something similar) and find the company you

TABLE 10.1   Investing Directly in a Company

Company	Minimum Dollar Amount	Industry	Web Site
New Jersey Resources	$25	Natural gas	*njresources.com*
Walgreen Co.	$50	Drug stores	*walgreens.com*
Eli Lilly & Co.	$50	Pharmaceutical	*lilly.com*
Badger Meter	$100	Manufacturing	*badgermeter.com*
Kimco Realty Corp.	$100	Real estate investment trust	*kimcorealty.com*
Otter Tail Corp.	$100	Electric utility	*ottertail.com*
ExxonMobil Corp.	$250	Oil	*exxon.com*
General Electric	$250	Electrical equipment	*ge.com*
Total	$975		

Source: The Staton Institute® Inc.

are looking for. Many firm's plans are administered through their transfer agent such as:

- Computershare (www-us.computershare.com)
- American Stock Transfer & Trust Company (www.amstock.com)
- BNY Mellon Shareowner Services (www.mellon.com/mis)

You can then sign up online or call the toll-free number that each provides for an information packet.

For additional information about buying shares of America's Finest Companies® in small-dollar amounts, please check out these two excellent web sites: www.sharebuilder.com and www.oneshare.com.

DIVIDEND REINVESTMENT STATEMENT

As an old-school investor from the early 1970s, I am not the most adept computer user, but when grandson Austin was born, I went online and bought him shares of two America's Finest Companies.

It took about 10 minutes per company and was very easy to do, even for me. If I can do it, anyone can.

Almost all companies that pay dividends pay once per quarter. Only a few, like McDonald's, pay annually. After you've signed on for a company's DRP, the next time a dividend is paid it will be used to buy whole and fractional shares (to the third and fourth decimal points) of stock instead of being sent to you.

Every quarter you'll receive a dividend reinvestment statement from each of your companies showing how many shares or fractions of shares you bought and at what price. The companies hold the shares; you don't have to keep track of them.

At or near the end of every calendar year (after the fourth quarterly dividend has been reinvested), you'll get a final DRP statement documenting all the purchases made during the year and how many shares you were able to acquire. Be sure these statements are kept in a safe place. You'll need them for tax purposes when you sell some or all of your shares in the future.

The quarterly form in Figure 10.1 is typical of the kind you'll receive. The backside describes all pertinent details of the front side, which makes this statement particularly easy to read. Some statements don't have such a description, but they all look pretty much the same.

Each quarterly DRP statement has a blank for you to fill in, indicating how much money you'd like to invest, if any, that period. In most cases, the minimum amount is $25–$50 (although it can be as low as $10), with a typical maximum of $3,000–$5,000 and more per quarter. In our example, that option is at the bottom of the statement (lower right corner) with a range of $25–$1,000 per investment.

Believe it or not, some companies have no maximums. You could almost drive a Brink's truck up to the front door, unload a million dollars or more, and say, "Here's my money. Buy me more shares."

These quarterly statements are your personal calls to action to send in more money (unless you sign up for bank drafts) to buy more shares, thus increasing your ownership in every company you own, which is the whole purpose of investing wisely.

Let's say you've made your share purchases of five companies and are saving $50 a month. After three months, you'll have saved $150. Mail that to company 1 using its DRP statement. After three more months, you'll have saved another $150. Mail that amount to company 2. The next $150 saved goes to 3, then to 4 and finally to 5.

KIMCO REALTY
CORPORATION

c/o The Bank of New York
P.O. Box 1958
Newark, N.J. 07101-9774

NOTE: This is not a Proxy

Please mark ☒ the appropriate box to enroll or change your current plan option. **DO NOT RETURN THIS CARD UNLESS YOU HAVE SELECTED ONE OF THE FOLLOWING OPTIONS:**

To help the government fight the funding of terrorism and money laundering activities, Federal law requires all financial institutions to obtain, verify, and record information that identifies each person who opens an account. What this means for you: When you complete and enrollment application, we will ask for your name, address, date of birth, and other information that will allow us to identify you. Please be aware that we will verify the information you provide and may also ask for copies of your driver's license or other identifying documents.

☐ FULL DIVIDEND REINVESTMENT: I wish to reinvest all dividends for this account. I may also make optional cash payments of a minimum of $50 up to a maximum of $250,000 per year.

☐ PARTIAL DIVIDEND REINVESTMENT: I with to receive cash dividends on ____ shares of common stock, ____ shares of Class A Preferred Stock, ____ shares of Class B Preferred Stock, and ____ shares of Class C Preferred Stock. (Indicate only whole shares.) The remaining dividends as well as any optional cash payments I make will be invested in additional shares of common stock.

Name: _____
Address:_____
_____
_____

☐ OPTIONAL CASH ONLY: I wish to make any optional cash payments to the Plan. I will receive a dividend check for all shares. Please make check or money order payable to The Bank of New York - Kimco Realty Corporation.

Date of Birth _____ / _____ / _____
           month   day   year

If you have an address change, please mark the box to the right and indicate the change on the reverse side of this form.   ☐

Taxpayer I.D. No.:_____

_____ ___/___/___
Signature(s) of Registered Owner(s) — all registered owners MUST sign   Date

▲ Detach Card Here ▲

PLEASE READ CAREFULLY BEFORE SIGNING. TEAR ALONG PERFORATION AND RETURN THE TOP PORTION TO THE BANK OF NEW YORK IN THE ENVELOPE PROVIDED. KEEP THE BOTTOM PORTION FOR YOUR REFERENCE.

INVESTMENT OPTIONS FOR THE KIMCO REALTY CORPORATION DIVIDEND REINVESTMENT AND DIRECT PURCHASE PLAN.

FULL DIVIDEND REINVESTMENT—The dividends on all Kimco Realty Corporation shares you hold as well as dividends on shares credited to your account under the Plan will be invested to purchase additional shares. You may also invest by making optional cash payments of minimum of $50 up to a maximum of $250,000 per calendar year.

PARTIAL DIVIDEND REINVESTMENT—The dividends on less than all your Kimco Realty Corporation shares may be reinvested in the Plan. For example, if you own 300 shares of common stock and want to receive cash dividends on 100 shares of common stock, check the "Partial Dividend Reinvestment" box and write 100 on the appropriate blank line. (The cash dividends you wish to receive must be on full shares.) Dividends on the remaining 200 shares of common stock will be reinvested to purchase additional shares. You may also invest by making option al cash payments of a minimum of $50 up to a maximum of $250,000 per calendar year.

OPTIONAL CASH ONLY—You may make optional cash payments of a minimum of $50 up to a maximum of $250,000 per calendar year without reinvesting dividends on the shares you hold. Any shares purchased through optional cash payments will be credited to your account under the plan. Dividends on all Kimco Realty Corporation shares credited to your account under the Plan will be paid to you in cash automatically.

QUESTIONS—If you have any questions, please write to Kimco Realty Corporation, c/o The Bank of New York at P.O. Box 1958, Newark, N.J. 07101-9774 or call toll-free: 1-856-557-8695.

Your participation in the Plan is subject to the terms set forth in the accompanying Prospectus. you may terminate participation in the Plan any time by writing to The Bank of New York, P.O. Box 1958, Newark, N.J. 07101-9774 or calling toll-free: 1-866-557-8695.

Do not return this form unless you intend to participate in the Plan since this form authorizes The Bank of New York to enroll your account in the Plan. If this form is signed by no box checked, you will be enrolled in the Plan under the Full Dividend Reinvestment option.

FIGURE 10.1   DRP form

Source: KIMCO Realty Corporation.

By this time, 15 months have elapsed and you've acquired an additional $750 of stock in five companies, on top of your initial investment. Now it's time to mail your next quarterly savings to company and start the process all over again. In time, you'll be bumping up the amount to $60 a month, then to $70, and so on as your income rises. This method enables you to become a multi-millionaire even faster.

If you change addresses, be sure to notify all your companies. There's a place on the quarterly DRP statement to do that. See the bottom right corner of the page in Figure 10.1.

Naturally, some stocks will perform better than others in any given year. To keep the portfolio in balance (i.e., 20 percent of your money in each company if there are five companies, 16.7 percent if there are six, 14.3 percent with seven, 12.5 percent with eight), it is necessary to invest more in the laggards and less in the leaders, but that's simple enough to do. If one stock is worth $2,000 and the other is worth $2,500, invest an extra $500 in the former to make it equal to the latter.

Don't make the mistake of sending more money only to your top stocks. Portfolio balance helps shield you from fluctuations in the stock market and maintains constant diversity.

Go for Singles, Not Home Runs

Whenever we talk to a money-management prospect at Staton Financial Advisors, we're often asked what we think about the direction of the stock market. Our general answer is: "We don't know. A lot depends on factors over which we have no control. Whatever the market does, we believe we can do better. Given enough time and patience on your part, we believe you're not going to lose money. And when you don't lose money, you have a much better chance of making great profits."

We tell anyone who cares to listen; it's really easy to lose a lot of money in a hurry. But it's difficult to make a lot of money in a hurry. Therefore, you should not rush. There are only two ways to end up with a lot of money quickly: marry it or inherit it. Unfortunately, most of us don't qualify for either and never will.

Would you like to earn 18–20 percent a year with lots of ups and downs, or does something in the low double-digits with not as much fluctuation sound better? We bet you choose the latter rather than the former. Why? Because, when you need some or all of your money you don't want to be way down in value when you make a withdrawal.

Lou Gehrig is best remembered, not for his home runs a la Babe Ruth, Hank Aaron, Mark McGuire, Sammy Sosa, or Barry Bonds, but for his remarkable ability to get to first base. Percentagewise he did it better than any player in history. No wonder he was labeled the Iron Horse.

This book teaches you how to consistently get to first base with your money. From there, you can run on to second, then to third, and finally arrive at home plate.

11

Turning Your Children and Grandchildren into Millionaires

All a parent can give a child is roots and wings.
—CHINESE PROVERB

POINTS TO REMEMBER

- Encourage young people to work and save.
- Entice them with riches beyond the dreams of avarice.
- Make money a fun family activity.

STARTING EARLY

Custodial Accounts

The day after my daughter was born in 1978, I opened a custodial account for her at the brokerage firm where I was director of equity research. A custodial account is as simple to open as a regular brokerage account. An adult signs on as custodian until the child is 18, at which time the child, who, of course, by then is a young adult, assumes complete control of the account. Anyone can contribute up to $12,000 of cash, securities, or a combination of the two into a custodial account every year with no gift tax consequences.

Once the account was set up, my wife and I contributed a few thousand dollars, and then I made three very important phone calls to my father, my mother, and my aunt, who was like a second mother to me. Because this was their first grandchild by me, I told them I was certain they'd each want to help secure Gracie's financial future with gifts of cash or stock. Naturally, they couldn't say no.

It wasn't long before those gifts came in the mail, and I was able to add several thousand dollars of stock to Gracie's account. Before she was even six months old, she had a five-digit sum in her brokerage account, which I invested in a portfolio of growth stocks. There was no America's Finest Companies at that time, but I was still picking the same kind of top-quality stocks that consistently beat the market over the long haul. I knew Gracie was off on the right foot.

Later my father and aunt made some additional gifts of stock, but the account is worth what it is today primarily because her portfolio has performed so well. I don't know exactly how much money was withdrawn to pay for K–12 at a private school here in Charlotte and for four years at Hollins University (private), but it was certainly more than $250,000. Yet, there was still $25,000 left for her to begin the rest of her life after college with a sizable portfolio of fine companies.

IRAs (Individual Retirement Accounts)

You can also help your children set up IRA accounts as soon as they start working. The IRA is a powerful wealth builder for anyone, especially a child. The younger the child is, the more valuable the IRA will be.

Suppose a child begins to do odd jobs like mowing lawns (as I did) at 10 years of age and mows five each week during the summer (again as I did). I made $7 a week back in the 1950s. Today earnings are probably at least ten times that. Let's say the child rakes in $100 weekly ($20 per lawn) for 10 weeks each summer, starting at age 10 and ending at age 16. (At 16 the child will want to drive a car and will be much too old to want to mow lawns.)

After each of the seven years of work, the child puts the entire $1,000 into an IRA, earning 13 percent annually (using my AFC stocks) through age 65. That $7,000 grows to $4.15 million over 49 years. (See Table 11.1.) The child can become a millionaire from mowing five lawns a week for just seven summers. Because this money is in an IRA, the principal grows without being taxed until it starts to be withdrawn between ages 59½ and 70½.

Actually, children can make more than $100 each week over the summer and throughout the year for spending money and to build

TABLE 11.1   IRA Earnings

Years	Investment	Value Earning 13 Percent per Year	Age
1	$1,000	$1,000	
2	$1,000	$2,130	11
3	$1,000	$3,407	12
4	$1,000	$4,850	13
5	$1,000	$6,480	14
6	$1,000	$8,323	15
7	$1,000	$10,405	16
56	$7,000	$4,150,224	65

Source: The Staton Institute® Inc.

an incredible portfolio. They can add gift money as well. Getting kids to work may be harder these days, but they do love money and are fascinated by it.

So, if you show them how much money they can make over the years by explaining what you have done for yourself and through opening a custodial account for them, they will feel empowered by the money they make, proud of the great stocks they can and should help pick. This teaches them valuable lessons about life and money, and they can have fun investing with you as their partner while they watch their own wealth grow.

Some parents and grandparents argue against providing for their children's financial security, saying that doing so works to a child's detriment because the child doesn't learn how to fend for himself or herself in the "real" world.

My late friend Eddie Graham felt exactly like that. He grew up poor and worked hard all his life to make ends meet. His house was paid for, and he still managed to set aside a little extra money each month. He and his wife liked to junket to Las Vegas and Atlantic City to enjoy, in his words, "the good life." When I asked Eddie about his children, he said he planned to leave nothing to them. It was up to them to "work hard and provide for themselves," just as he'd done. That's one view.

Another argument is that parents and grandparents should offer some financial aid but not, even if they can afford to do so, provide everything a child needs monetarily. Warren Buffett, for example, has stated that he wants his children to have enough to do whatever they want to do, but not enough to loll around and do nothing.

Still a third view is mine. I wanted to enable my children to be as financially comfortable as possible before they entered the workplace, which Gracie, Tate, and Whitney have achieved to a degree. (Our fourth, Will, is still at New York University studying to become an actor.) I wanted them to have the opportunity to enjoy the kinds of careers they can sink their teeth into and not have to worry so much about whether the job pays enough.

Using my children as examples, I'm demonstrating the relative ease with which all children can build small fortunes, or even large ones. They can do so without your help if they have the knowledge contained in these pages, but it will be considerably easier with your assistance. Almost anywhere is a great starting place: a custodial account at a brokerage house, an IRA containing part-time wages and gift money invested in stocks, a dividend reinvestment plan (DRP), or all of the above.

If you're worried that your children or grandchildren will be foolish with their money after they reach 18, you can, for modest fees, establish trust accounts that are very flexible yet have restrictions preventing the assets from being abused. You can be the trustee and invest the money however you like. Whether in a custodial or a trust account, you should invest strictly in American's Finest Companies. A child or grandchild who is eight or older will most likely want to participate in assembling the portfolio. Sometimes children even younger than that willingly cooperate. All you need to do is ask them.

When Gracie invested in eight companies that she chose herself in 1988, she was excited about having the chance to pick companies. Money is fun for most young people (as it should be for us adults); so why not take advantage of that characteristic? Just the idea of making a lot of money can encourage youngsters to earn some for themselves and save some for their future, perhaps for a car when they get their license.

The lawn mowing child in my earlier example would have more than $10,000 at age 16 to put toward a car. All you have to do is encourage youngsters to save money, help them set up their accounts, and teach them how to pick stocks out of America's Finest Companies.

The interest of young people is evident when I teach applied economics to juniors and seniors (where my daughter went to school) through the Junior Achievement (JA) Program. I'm the real-life consultant who takes practical experiences and knowledge into the classroom and (hopefully) brings economics to life for these bright young people.

They want to learn about making money. They do it well and have even taught me a thing or two. Junior Achievement writes its own economics text, which is revised and updated every three years. If you've ever hankered to learn more about the so-called "dismal science" but couldn't find an interesting text, JA's is it.

BUY LESS, INVEST MORE

Mary and I recently read an intriguing article about consuming less while conserving more, especially energy. The article stated: "Energy is consumed in the manufacturing and transport of everything you buy. A good way to reduce the amount of energy you use is simply to buy less. Before making a purchase, ask yourself if you really need it."

As a family, we work at wasting less of everything, including money, but we've never thought much about saving energy simply by buying fewer things produced with energy. That line of thinking leads us to see how much we can gain by wasting a few dollars less and investing them into America's Finest Companies.

As an example, we started investing small amounts of "saved dollars," through DRPs, upon the birth of our grandson Austin, now almost 6. Already he's well north of $6,000, and the amount is growing.

If you have a newborn child or grandchild, you can get started right away. At $50 per month until age 30, with compounding at 13 percent each year, the child can have $221,032, $3.0 million at age 50, and $10.9 million by age 60. Fifty dollars a month for 60 years is a total investment of only $36,000, but it can turn into more than 300 times that.

Everybody we know, including us, easily wastes a lot more than $50 every month. We believe you probably do as well.

For many of you, however, your parents or grandparents did not set up a portfolio when you were born nor help you set up your own portfolio as a youngster. Now let's say you're 40 and have done nothing for retirement. Could you invest $200 a month? If so, by age 70 it'd be worth $884,128, and at age 80 $3.27 million.

Just remember: It's never too late to start. And, the sooner you start, the better off you'll be.

Bill,

I have never met you, but feel like I've known you if that makes any sense. I purchased your *7 Secrets to Becoming a Multimillionaire* a few months ago. I am turning 51. So I am still 9 years from midlife as heard on your program. I'm in that category of only having a whopping $1,150.00 saved for retirement. I'm in that group that has been in the mode of living high. I was in the scouts growing up and am a 1972 Eagle. I graduated from East Mecklenburg in 1975 and was given the outstanding student award in 3 of my classes. I graduated from Cleveland State College in Cleveland, TN and was given the outstanding student award in Dental Technology in 1980. I am a Dental Technician here in Charlotte and own my own business. But in all this time, the point I'm trying to make is that I wished I had been an outstanding student in my personal finances! I am totally on board in using your methods on America's Finest Companies®. I will be turning my life around financially.

Thank You,

Roy A. P., CDT

Hello to you both,

I have been a huge fan of Bill since reading his *The America's Finest Companies® Investment Plan* in '95. At that time I was 61 and still working as an RN with a small IRA "managed" by a broker (load as well!). I didn't have the courage to put the money in stocks—even though I knew Bill was right. I gave your book to some of my 7 children and begged them to invest for the future but I was talked out of being my own manager and let it ride for too many years. I called you at home because I was so "paralyzed" about what to do and wanted your thoughts about buying 3 REITs in a 6 stock pick. You were so kind and helpful and I did it—used Share Builder as you suggested and **doubled my money in 3 years**. I called you again when we moved back east to be nearer family to get help caring for my beloved Bob before he died. We used much of our savings on alternative treatments which was helping the cancer but the eye pain from the shingles wore him down. I am now, at 73, back in school to become a certified holistic health counselor and looking forward to investing again. I have been "talking you up" to #2 son and just sent him your *Worry Free* book and he is about ready to "do it"! I just want to thank you both for your wisdom and kindness. You told me once "the hand that gives, gathers" (when you asked for input into son Will's side effects from acne medicine). If I were younger Bill, I would probably qualify as one of your "groupie" fans, hanging on to every word. This rambling "note" was originally to request a 3-issue trial of your e-digest. Just looked at my survey answers—did well because you and Mary are such good teachers. God bless you both and keep you well.

Thank you.

Sincerely,

Angela J.

CHAPTER 12

Using America's Finest Companies
for Maximum Profits

Chance favors only the mind that is prepared.
—LOUIS PASTEUR, FRENCH CHEMIST, FOUNDER
OF MICROBIOLOGY (1822–1895)

POINTS TO REMEMBER

- You can start small.
- Pick the finest stocks anyway you like.
- Just do it!

This book shows you a simple, time-proven way to make your money grow at above-average rates with sharply reduced risk. By investing solely in America's Finest Companies, you could potentially double your money every five to seven years. If so, you will outperform at least 75 percent of all investment professionals 100 percent of the time.

All that is possible because, as explained throughout this book, a diversified portfolio invested into America's Finest Companies (AFCs), with enough time and patience, should earn you a 12 to 15 percent (certainly not every year), compound annual return, compared to 10 percent plus, the market's rate for the past 50 or so years. That 20–50 percent incremental advantage over a long period of time could be worth hundreds of thousands of extra dollars.

You can maximize the effects of this method by doing just three simple things:

1. Earn as much as you can (honestly) in any way that you can.
2. Diversify your AFC companies.
3. Believe you can do it!

EARN AND INVEST AS MUCH AS YOU CAN

If you invest $50 per month at 13 percent per year for your children at birth and continue through age 20, the money will grow to $57,276. With no additional contributions from you or the child, that $57,276 will be worth $3.0 million when he or she is 50, and $10.9 million by age 60.

These are staggering numbers, and you might ask, "Isn't $10.9 million at age 60 more than enough for anyone?" It sure is, probably by many millions.

However, there is no reason not to earn more if you can. My mission is to enable you to earn as much money as you can on your investments, as safely as you can, and in as little time as you can. I'd rather see you earn 13 percent per year than 12 percent. Fourteen percent would be even better and 15 percent better still. Even so, I believe 13 percent is not only reasonable but also possible, again giving yourself enough time, hopefully at least 10 years. Beyond 15 percent, we go into the never-never land of returns that may never materialize but that I have seen promoted by others in the financial arena.

Why not earn as much money as you can? The more you earn, the more you'll have to spend on things you need, on things you want, and as important if not more so, on helping others. Yet I'm not unreasonable or impractical. I know most of us don't save and invest every extra dollar. Mary and I save and invest in a manner that lets us spend part of our principal each year while leaving the balance to grow for the future.

DIVERSIFY INTO QUALITY COMPANIES

Any way I've measured them, diversified portfolios, invested in America's Finest Companies, have generally outperformed the market over the past 10 years. They've whomped most of the pros, too, because the market indexes beat three-quarters of them year in and year out. It's easy to see why AFCs are market beaters. Each of the more than 300 companies qualifying for listing has increased dividends and/or earnings for at least 10 straight years.

It's easy to explain how America's Finest Companies are above-average performers. They're growing, and the values of their businesses are on a consistent uptrend. As the values of the businesses rise, the stock prices rise also. They have to. Here's why.

Any one of America's Finest Companies is like a staircase that begins at the left and rises one step at a time toward the right. Every step represents an increase in the value of the AFC company's business. Now picture a curve that follows the staircase upward and that represents the AFC stock price over the years. It goes up and down in value (randomly) in the short run, but the path is always in only one direction–upward. Sometimes the stock price is above what the company is really worth. At other times it's valued about correctly. And at still other times it's undervalued.

If you're dollar-cost averaging—purchasing the stock of an AFC company on a regular timeframe over 5, 10, 15 years, and more— you'll buy at different points along the staircase. Sometimes you'll pay too much. When you do, you'll buy fewer shares per dollar invested because the price is high. Often you'll buy shares on the cheap, buying more shares for the same number of dollars invested. Given enough time, dollar-cost averaging will automatically produce superior results over a buy-and-hold strategy, as demonstrated in Chapter 7.

One of the keys to such high returns is to diversify your investments. You can use the data in my America's Finest Companies listing in various ways to end up with a well-balanced portfolio to meet your needs. However, you should be a winner regardless of how you select your portfolio.

An excellent portfolio to use as a model for picking consists of the 16 Dow stocks that make the AFC cutoff (see Table 12.1). (Thirty companies make up the venerable Dow Jones industrial average.) The companies in the table are some of the oldest, strongest, most respected names in American business. They've been around a long time, and you can rest assured they'll be around a lot longer. All have roots stretching back before the Great Depression, with the exception of Home Depot and McDonald's, the rookies of the group.

TABLE 12.1   America's Finest Companies in Dow Jones Industrials

Ticker	Company	Industry	Consecutive Years Higher Earnings	Consecutive Years Higher Dividends
BAC	Bank of America Corp.	Banking	0	30
CAT	Caterpillar Inc.	Manufacturing	5	14
CVX	Chevron Corp.	Oil	5	20
GE	General Electric Co.	Electrical Equipment	32	32
HD	Home Depot Inc.	Retail	0	20
IBM	International Business Machines	Computers	3	12
JNJ	Johnson & Johnson	Health care	24	45
KO	Coca-Cola Co.	Soft drink	5	45
MCD	McDonald's Corp.	Restaurant	0	33
MMM	3M Co.	Manufacturing	6	49
PFE	Pfizer Inc.	Health care	0	40
PG	Procter & Gamble Co.	Household Products	7	52
T	AT&T Inc.	Telephone	2	23
UTX	United Technologies	Aviation	7	14
WMT	Wal-Mart Stores Inc.	Retail	46	33
XOM	ExxonMobil Corp.	Oil	5	25

Source: The Staton Institute® Inc.

BELIEVE YOU CAN

When Gracie was five, one of her favorite books was *The Value of Believing in Yourself: The Story of Louis Pasteur* by Spencer Johnson, MD, who also penned the best seller, *Who Moved My Cheese?* (Few people seem to know that Johnson coauthored *The One-Minute Manager* with Ken Blanchard.) It remains one of my favorite books to this day. I know it almost by heart, having read it aloud to her (and years later her brother Will) many times.

Pasteur (1822–1895), as you may recall, was a French chemist and bacteriologist whose scientific exploits were widely ignored, principally because he was not a medical doctor. He taught at Dijon, Strasbourg, and Lille. He also taught in Paris at the École Normale Supérieure as well as the Sorbonne (1867–1889). His early research consisted of chemical studies of the tartrates, in which he discovered molecular dissymmetry (1848). Pasteur had the firm conviction that diseases were caused by invisible enemies called germs or bacteria.

In the 1860s he discovered that undesired fermentation could be prevented in wine and beer by heating it to 135° Fahrenheit (57° Celsius) for a few minutes. That discovery led him to learn that the partial sterilization of liquids such as milk, orange juice, wine, as well as cheese, would destroy disease-causing and other undesirable organisms. Milk is now pasteurized by heating it to about 145° Fahrenheit (63° Celsius) for 30 minutes or by the flash method of heating it to 160° Fahrenheit (71° Celsius) for 15 seconds, followed by rapid cooling to below 50° Fahrenheit (10° Celsius), at which temperature it is stored. Harmless lactic acid bacteria survive the process, but, if milk is not kept cold, they multiply rapidly, causing it to sour.

Of great economic value also was his solution for the control of silkworm disease, his study of chicken cholera, and his technique of vaccination against anthrax, which led to his successful administration of a human rabies vaccine in 1885, the first ever for that killer.

In 1888, the Pasteur Institute was founded in Paris. As the first director, Pasteur continued to work on rabies and provide a teaching and research center for virulent and contagious diseases. Even though many of the finest minds in the world had no faith in his work, Pasteur believed in himself.

In the book, as he vigorously hunts for the rabies cure, Louis Pasteur repeats to himself, "I believe I can, I believe I can." He had to believe in himself because few others did, other than his wife Marie. But Pasteur knew exactly what he was doing. Even when his work proved successful, some of his critics refused to acknowledge his great works because they thought he was just lucky. However, Pasteur knew luck had nothing to do with his outstanding accomplishments and said, "Let me tell you the secret that has led me to my goal. My strength lies solely in my tenacity."

There's another wonderful story about a believing minister who was pastor of Marble Collegiate Church (the Dutch-founded institution "Where Good Things Happen" with roots back to 1628) on Fifth Avenue in New York City for 52 years. In the early 1950s, he wrote the manuscript for what he thought would be an instant bestseller, a book he was certain would help everyone who read it.

The minister shopped publisher after publisher, yet could find none to print it. So one evening, after another day of shopping with no success, he came home in disgust and threw his manuscript into the trash can. He told his wife Ruth that it was no use wasting any more time. No one wanted his book.

Lovingly, she took out the crumpled manuscript and put it into her oversized purse. Some days later she bumped into a literary agent acquaintance, who then introduced them to Prentice-Hall Inc., which in turn published what became the runaway bestseller, *The Power of Positive Thinking*, in 1952. It was on The New York Times bestseller list for 186 straight weeks and has since sold more than seven million copies in 15 different languages. President Ronald Reagan presented Dr. Norman Vincent Peale with the Presidential Medal of Freedom (our country's highest civilian honor) in 1984 for his contributions to the field and study of theology. Peale died of a stroke the day before Christmas 1993, at age 95.

I have read his inspiring book a number of times and garner new insights each time. I keep the gift-edition version on my reading table upstairs in our bedroom. Chapter 1, appropriately enough, is entitled "Believe in Yourself." Peale quotes Ralph Waldo Emerson who "declared a tremendous truth": "They conquer who believe they can. Do the thing you fear and the death of fear is certain."

At the end of the chapter, Dr. Peale provides 10 points to build up self-confidence and positive self-belief. Point 2 reads, "Whenever a negative thought concerning your personal powers comes to mind, deliberately voice a positive thought to cancel it out." And in point 8, "Make a true estimate of your own ability; then raise it 10 percent. Do not become egotistical, but develop a wholesome self-respect. Believe in your own God-released powers."

The average man or woman on the street thinks investing in stocks is nothing but a game of chance, with the luckiest ones making money. The rest lose it. They don't realize that investing in stocks is usually the fastest way to accumulate wealth and that it can be done with virtually zero risk if given enough time, as I've demonstrated.

If you use the simple, rational method outlined on these pages, you'll have phenomenal success with your money regardless of the amount you begin with. In a sense, you'll be like Louis Pasteur because you'll ignore the advice commonly given by most financial experts, who want you to believe you need them to be successful. There aren't many of us who know you can do it yourself, have a lot of fun, and make a lot of money, too. Believe in yourself. You can do it!

In building a diversified portfolio of America's Finest Companies, you're doing far more than buying pieces of paper that change in price many times each day. You are actually buying pieces of American enterprises, the finest this country has to offer. As these companies grow and thrive in the future, so will you by virtue of your ownership.

It doesn't matter that the value of your shares goes down today and then bobs up tomorrow. Value is not created in a day. Value takes years to build. Daily fluctuations in stock prices are meaningless. They do not affect the long-term value of the Finest Companies.

What does affect the value is growth in revenue, earnings, dividends, and the asset values of the businesses. If you continually add to your portfolio of first-rate companies, you can be certain that over the years the value will increase faster than from any of the other investments—and keep you well ahead of inflation and the tax collector, too.

In the words of Charlie Munger: "There are huge advantages for an individual to get into a position where you make a few great investments and just sit back. You're paying less to brokers. You're listening to less nonsense."

There's nothing to wait for. You now have the knowledge you need for investing and stock-market success. Ancient Greek philosopher Epicurus warned, "Life is wasted in procrastination."

Procrastinate no longer. Start the steps to financial security today! Happy investing!

PS: Always remember the words of entrepreneur Luke Johnson: "Optimists have the last laugh. History shows they are always the long-run winners."

May the sun bring you new energy by day.
May the moon softly restore you by night.
May the rain wash away your worries.
May the breeze blow new strength into your being.
                                        —APACHE BLESSING

APPENDIX

America's Finest Companies® Directory 2009

Every effort has been made to ensure the accuracy of all data, but accuracy is not guaranteed. Past performance of any company is no assurance of future returns. Beginning on the next page, you will find the following information:

* America's Finest Companies® in the first column.
* Each company's stock symbol in column two.
* Next are the industry category, stock price, earnings per share (EPS), and dividend.
* The price/earnings (PE) ratio is calculated by dividing the latest 12 months' earnings per share into the stock price.
* Dividend yield is the annualized dividend rate divided by the stock price.
* Dividend coverage is the ratio of earnings to dividend. The higher the ratio is, generally the safer the dividend is.
* Every company with a dividend reinvestment plan (DRP) is indicated with an X. If the company's DRP allows an investor to buy shares at a discount, the percentage discount is shown in parentheses beside the X. Most—but not all—companies with DRPs allow investors to purchase additional shares at least quarterly (sometimes monthly or even more often) through an

optional cash payment (OCP) plan. Many pay all administrative fees and commissions and will let you begin investing by purchasing just one share. Check with each company for details about its DRP/OCP programs.

- In the next column, companies allowing initial stock purchases directly from the company are noted, and the required initial investment is shown.

A List of America's Finest Companies

Company	Ticker	Industry	5/31/08 Price	Earnings Per Share	Dividend	Price/ Earnings Ratio	Dividend Yield
Abbott Laboratories	ABT	Health Care	54.76	2.46	1.44	22.3	2.63%
ABM Industries Inc.	ABM	Special Services	21.94	0.99	0.50	22.2	2.28%
AFLAC Inc.	AFL	Insurance/Life	65.44	3.31	0.96	19.8	1.47%
Air Products & Chemicals	APD	Chemicals	103.06	4.80	1.52	21.5	1.47%
Albemarle Corp.	ALB	Chemicals	44.34	2.44	0.48	18.2	1.08%
Allstate Corp.	ALL	Insurance/ Prop.	50.03	7.77	1.62	6.4	3.24%
American Capital Strategies	ACAS	Financial	30.95	3.42	4.19	9.0	13.54%
American States Water Co.	AWR	Water Utility	34.44	1.61	1.00	21.4	2.90%
Anchor Bancorp Wisconsin	ABCW	Banking	12.46	1.59	0.72	7.8	5.78%
Anheuser-Busch Cos. Inc.	BUD	Alcoholic Bever.	57.28	2.79	1.32	20.5	2.30%
AptarGroup Inc.	ATR	Plastics	44.76	2.09	0.52	21.4	1.16%
Aqua America Inc.	WTR	Water Utility	17.71	0.68	0.50	26.0	2.82%

Source: The Staton Insitute®Inc.

- Then come the numbers of consecutive years of higher earnings and dividends.
- The last column shows the company address, including, as available, toll-free or other phone numbers that go direct to investor relations or corporate communications instead of the general switchboard. If a company has a web site, it is also included with "www." and ".com" omitted unless otherwise noted.

Dividend Coverage	Dividend Reinvestment Plan	Minimum Direct Investment	Consecutive Years Higher		Address/Phone/Web Site
			EPS	Dividends	
1.7	X		1	35	100 Abbott Park Rd./Abbott Park/IL/ 60064/847/937-7300/abbott
2.0			0	43	160 Pacific Ave., Ste. 222/San Francisco/CA/94111/415/ 733-4000/abm
3.4	X	1000	4	25	1932 Wynnton Rd./Columbus/ GA/31999/800/235-2667/aflac
3.2	X	500	4	25	7201 Hamilton Blvd./Allentown /PA/ 18195/800/247-6525 /airproducts
5.1	X		3	13	PO Box 1335/Richmond/VA/ 23219/804/788-6000/albemarle
4.8	X	50	0	14	2775 Sanders Rd./Northbrook/ IL/60062/847/402-5000/allstate
0.8			4	10	2 Bethesda Metro Center/Bethesda/ MD /20184/301/951-6122/ american-capital
1.6	X	500	1	55	630 E. Foothill Blvd. /San Dimas/ CA/91773/909/394-3600/aswater
2.2			0	14	25 W. Main St./Madison/WI/53703/ 608/252-8700/anchorbank
2.1	X	100	2	33	One Busch Place/St. Louis/MO/ 63118/314/577-2000/ anheuser-busch
4.0			5	14	475 W. Terra Cotta Ave./Crystal Lake/IL/60014/815/477-0424/ aptargroup
1.4	X(5)	500	0	16	762 W. Lancaster Ave./Bryn Mawr/PA/19010/610/525-1400/ aquaamerica

(*continued*)

A List of America's Finest Companies (Continued)

Company	Ticker	Industry	5/31/08 Price	Earnings Per Share	Dividend	Price/ Earnings Ratio	Dividend Yield
Archer-Daniels-Midland Co.	ADM	Foods	37.20	2.65	0.52	14.0	1.40%
Artesian Resources Corp.	ARTNA	Water Utility	18.50	0.90	0.71	20.6	3.86%
Associated Banc-Corp.	ASBC	Banking	25.44	2.18	1.28	11.7	5.03%
Astoria Financial Corp.	AF	Banking	22.66	1.30	1.04	17.4	4.59%
Atmos Energy Corp.	ATO	Natural Gas	27.06	1.77	1.30	15.3	4.80%
AT&T Inc.	T	Telephone	38.21	2.06	1.60	18.5	4.19%
Automatic Data Processing	ADP	Computer Soft.	42.39	2.05	1.16	20.7	2.74%
Avery Dennison Corp.	AVY	Manufacturing	49.05	2.96	1.64	16.6	3.34%
Avon Products Inc.	AVP	Toiletries	37.21	1.28	0.80	29.1	2.15%
Badger Meter Inc.	BMI	Manufacturing	48.45	1.51	0.36	32.1	0.74%
BancFirst Corp.	BANF	Banking	43.71	3.39	0.80	12.9	1.83%
Bancorp South Inc.	BXS	Banking	22.17	1.70	0.88	13.0	3.97%
Bank of America Corp.	BAC	Banking	30.50	2.37	2.56	12.9	8.39%
Bank of Granite Corp.	GRAN	Banking	9.85	def.	0.52	def.	5.28%
Bank of Hawaii Corp.	BOH	Banking	53.00	3.83	1.76	13.8	3.32%
BankAtlantic Bancorp,	BBX	Banking	1.77	def.	0.17	def.	9.60%

Dividend Coverage	Dividend Reinvestment Plan	Minimum Direct Investment	Consecutive Years Higher		Address/Phone/Web Site
			EPS	Dividends	
5.1			4	33	Box 1470/Decatur/IL/62525/217/424-4647/admworld
1.3	X		0	15	664 Churchmans Rd./Newark/DE/19702/800/332-5114/artesianwater
1.7	X		0	37	1200 Hansen Rd./Green Bay/WI/54304/800/236-2722 /associatedbank
1.3	X		0	12	One Astoria Federal Plaza/Lake Success/NY/11042/516/327-7877/astoriafederal
1.4	X(5)	1250	5	20	3 Lincoln Center. Ste. 1800, 5430 LBJ Freeway/Dallas/TX/75240/972/934-9227/atmosenergy
1.3	X	500	2	23	175 East Houston/San Antonio/TX/78205/210/821-4105/sbc
1.8			3	33	One ADP Boulevard/Roseland/NJ/07068/973/974-5858 /adp
1.8	X	500	0	32	PO Box 7090/Pasadena/CA/91109/626/304-2000 /averydennison
1.6	X		1	17	1345 Ave. of Americas/New York/NY/10105/212/282-5623/avon
4.2	X	100	1	15	PO Box 245036/Milwaukee/WI/53224/414/355-0400/badgermeter
4.2			0	14	101 N. Broadway/Oklahoma City/OK/73102/405/270-1086/bancfirst
1.9	X		3	25	One Mississippi Pl., 201 S. Spring St./Tupelo/MS/38804/662/680-2000/bancorpsouth
0.9	X	1000	0	30	Bank of America Corp. Center/Charlotte/NC/28255/704/386-8486/bankofamerica
0.0	X		0	54	PO Box 128/Granite Falls/NC/28630/828/496-2022 /bankofgranite
2.2	X		7	30	130 Merchant St./Honolulu/HI/96813/888/643-3888/boh
0.0			0	11	2100 West Cypress Creek Rd./Ft. Lauderdale/FL/33309/954-940-5000/bankatlantic

(continued)

A List of America's Finest Companies (Continued)

Company	Ticker	Industry	5/31/08 Price	Earnings Per Share	Dividend	Price/ Earnings Ratio	Dividend Yield
Banner Corp.	BANR	Banking	16.13	2.41	0.80	6.7	4.96%
Bard, C.R. Inc.	BCR	Medical Prods.	89.43	3.84	0.60	23.3	0.67%
BB&T Corp.	BBT	Banking	28.06	3.14	1.84	8.9	6.56%
Beckman Coulter, Inc.	BEC	Medical Prods.	69.95	3.19	0.68	21.9	0.97%
Becton, Dickinson & Co.	BDX	Medical Prods.	82.53	4.11	1.14	20.1	1.38%
Bemis Co.	BMS	Containers	25.48	1.74	0.88	14.6	3.45%
Black Hills Corp.	BKH	Electric Utility	35.15	2.64	1.36	13.3	3.87%
Bowl America Inc.	BWL-A	Recreation	14.00	0.81	0.60	17.3	4.29%
Brady Corp.	BRC	Chemicals	37.72	2.12	0.60	17.8	1.59%
Brown & Brown Inc.	BRO	Insurance	19.34	1.30	0.28	14.9	1.45%
Brown-Forman Corp.	BF-B	Alcoholic Bever.	77.25	3.28	1.36	23.6	1.76%
Buckeye Partners LP	BPL	Natural Gas	45.40	3.03	3.40	15.0	7.49%
California Water Service Group	CWT	Water Utility	35.54	1.50	1.17	23.7	3.29%
Capital City Bank Group Inc.	CCBG	Banking	26.48	1.71	0.70	15.5	2.64%
Carlisle Companies Inc.	CSL	Manufacturing	31.47	1.87	0.58	16.8	1.84%
Cardinal Health Inc.	CAH	Health Care	55.98	3.00	0.48	18.7	0.86%

Dividend Coverage	Dividend Reinvestment Plan	Minimum Direct Investment	Consecutive Years Higher		Address/Phone/Web Site
			EPS	Dividends	
3.0			2	11	10 S. First Avenue/Walla Walla/WA/99362/509-527-3636/banrbank
6.4	X	250	1	36	730 Central Ave./Murray Hill/NJ/07974/908/277-8000/crbard
1.7	X		1	36	PO Box 1250/Winston-Salem /NC/27102/336/733-3058/bbandt
4.7			0	16	2300 N. Harbor Blvd./Fullerton/CA/92834/714/871-4848/beckmancoulter
3.6	X	250	9	36	1 Becton Dr./Franklin Lakes/NJ/07417/201/847-6800/bd
2.0	X		2	24	PO Box 669/Neenah/WI/54957/920/727-4100/bemis
1.9	X	250	2	37	PO Box 1400/Rapid City/SD/57709/605/721-1700 /blackhillscorp
1.4			1	35	PO Box 1288/Springfield/VA/22151/703/941-6300/bowl-america
3.5	X		0	22	PO Box 571/Milwaukee/WI/53201/414/438-6940/bradycorp
4.6			15	14	220 S. Ridgewood Ave./Daytona Beach/FL/32114/368/252-9601/bbinsurance
2.4	X		3	23	850 Dixie Hwy./Louisville/KY/40210/502/585-1100/brown-forman
0.9		250	1	12	5002 Buckeye Road/Emmaus/PA/18049/800/422-2825/buckeye
1.3	X	250	1	40	1720 N. First St./San Jose/CA/95112/800/750-8200/calwater
2.4			0	14	PO Box 11248/Tallahassee/FL/32302/850/671-0300/mycapitalcitybank
3.2	X		0	31	13925 Ballantyne Corp. Plaza, Ste. 400/Charlote/NC/28277/704/501-1100/carlisle
6.3			1	14	7000 Cardinal Place/Dublin/OH/43017/614/757-5000/cardinal-health

(continued)

A List of America's Finest Companies (Continued)

Company	Ticker	Industry	5/31/08 Price	Earnings Per Share	Dividend	Price/ Earnings Ratio	Dividend Yield
Caterpillar Inc.	CAT	Manufacturing	79.99	5.51	1.44	14.5	1.80%
CBL & Assoc. Properties Inc.	CBL	RE Invest. Trust	25.61	0.90	2.18	28.5	8.51%
Cedar Fair L.P.	FUN	Entertainment	22.05	def.	1.92	def.	8.71%
CenturyTel Inc.	CTL	Telephone	35.92	3.72	0.27	9.7	0.75%
Chemical Financial Corp.	CHFC	Banking	23.30	1.65	1.17	14.1	5.02%
Chevron Corp.	CVX	Oil	99.50	8.77	2.60	11.3	2.61%
Chubb Corp.	CB	Insurance/ Prop.	53.12	7.07	1.32	7.5	2.48%
Church & Dwight Co. Inc.	CHD	Cleaning Products	54.97	2.61	0.32	21.1	0.58%
Cincinnati Financial Corp.	CINF	Insurance/ Prop.	33.30	4.97	1.56	6.7	4.68%
Cintas Corp.	CTAS	Business Services	28.12	2.14	0.46	13.1	1.64%
City National Corp.	CYN	Banking	47.30	4.52	1.92	10.5	4.06%
CLARCOR Inc.	CLC	Manufacturing	41.62	1.78	0.32	23.4	0.77%
Clorox Co.	CLX	Household Prods.	53.91	3.29	1.60	16.4	2.97%
Coca-Cola Co.	KO	Soft Drink	55.80	2.67	1.52	20.9	2.72%
Colgate-Palmolive Co.	CL	Household Prods.	72.69	3.20	1.60	22.7	2.20%
Colonial Properties Trust	CLP	RE Invest. Trust	23.62	7.28	2.72	3.2	11.52%
Comerica Inc.	CMA	Banking	35.31	4.43	2.64	8.0	7.48%

Dividend Coverage	Dividend Reinvestment Plan	Minimum Direct Investment	Consecutive Years Higher		Address/Phone/Web Site
			EPS	Dividends	
3.8	X	250	5	14	100 NE Adams St./Peoria/ IL/61629/309/675-1000/CAT
0.4	X		0	13	2030 Hamilton Place Blvd./ Chattanooga/TN/37421/423/ 855-0001/cblproperties
0.0	X		0	21	One Cedar Point Drive/Sandusky/ OH/44870/419/627-2233/cedarfair
13.8	X		5	34	100 CenturyTel Drive/Monroe/LA/ 71203/800/833-1188 /centurytel
1.4	X	50	0	33	PO Box 569/Midland/MI/48640/ 989/839-5350/chemicalbankmi
3.4	X	250	5	20	6001 Bollinger Canyon Rd./San Ramon/CA/94583/925/842-1000/ chevrontexaco
5.4	X		6	43	PO Box 1615/Warren/ NJ/07061/908/903-2000 /chubb
8.2			7	10	469 North Harrison St./Princeton/ NJ/08543/609-683-5900/ churchdwight
3.2	X		0	47	PO Box 145496 /Cincinnati/ OH/45250/513/870-2639 /cinfin
4.7			39	25	PO Box 625737/Cincinnati/ OH/45262/513/459-1200/cintas
2.4			0	13	400 North Roxbury Drive/Beverly Hills/CA/90210/310/888-1037/cnb
5.6	X		15	24	840 Crescent Ctr. Dr. #600/Franklin / TN/37067/615/771-3100/clarcor
2.1	X	250	2	30	1221 Broadway/Oakland/ CA/94612/510/271-7000/clorox
1.8	X		5	45	One Coca-Cola Plaza /Atlanta/GA/ 30313/404/676-2121/coca-cola
2.0	X	500	3	45	300 Park Ave./New York/ NY/10022/800/850-2654/colgate
2.7			1	13	2101 Sixth Ave. N. #750/ Birmingham/AL/35203/866/ 897-1807/colonialprop
1.7	X		0	64	500 Woodward Ave./Detroit/ MI/48226/313/222-9743/comerica

(*continued*)

A List of America's Finest Companies (Continued)

Company	Ticker	Industry	5/31/08 Price	Earnings Per Share	Dividend	Price/ Earnings Ratio	Dividend Yield
Commerce Bancshares Inc.	CBSH	Banking	42.77	3.19	1.00	13.4	2.34%
Community Bank System Inc.	CBU	Banking	23.59	1.42	0.83	16.6	3.52%
Community Trust Bancorp Inc.	CTBI	Banking	30.02	2.43	1.16	12.4	3.86%
Connecticut Water Service	CTWS	Water Utility	24.65	1.05	0.87	23.5	3.53%
Consolidated Edison Inc.	ED	Electric Utility	40.04	3.47	2.34	11.5	5.84%
Corus Bankshares Inc.	CORS	Banking	4.99	1.85	1.00	2.7	20.04%
Courier Corp.	CRRC	Printing	22.37	1.65	0.76	13.6	3.40%
Cullen/Frost Bankers Inc.	CFR	Banking	53.49	3.55	1.60	15.1	2.99%
CVB Financial Corp.	CVBF	Banking	10.90	0.74	0.36	14.7	3.30%
Danaher Corp.	DHR	Metal Products	79.19	4.19	0.12	18.9	0.15%
DENTSPLY International Inc.	XRAY	Medical Supplies	39.10	1.68	0.16	23.3	0.41%
Diebold Inc.	DBD	Ofc. Equip/ Supp	39.21	1.02	1.00	38.4	2.55%
Donaldson Co.	DCI	Manufacturing	50.14	1.87	0.44	26.8	0.88%
Dover Corp.	DOV	Manufacturing	51.93	3.22	0.80	16.1	1.54%

Dividend Coverage	Dividend Reinvestment Plan	Minimum Direct Investment	Consecutive Years Higher		Address/Phone/Web Site
			EPS	Dividends	
3.2			23	38	PO Box 419248/Kansas City/ MO/64141/800/892-7100/ commercebank
1.7	X	250	1	16	5790 Widewaters Pkwy./DeWitt/ NY/13214/800/724-2262/ communitybankna
2.1	X		0	27	PO Box 2947/Pikeville/ KY/41502/606/432-1414/ctbi
1.2	X	100	1	38	93 W. Main St./Clinton/ CT/06413/800/428-3985 /ctwater
1.5	X		3	33	4 Irving Place/New York/NY/ 10003/800/522-5522/conedison
1.9			0	21	3959 N. Lincoln Ave./Chicago/ IL/60613/773/832-3088/corusbank
2.2			0	14	15 Wellman Ave./N. Chelmsford/ MA/01863/978/251-6000/courier
2.2			6	14	100 W. Houston St./San Antonio/ TX/78205/210/220-4011/frostbank
2.1			0	17	701 N. Haven Ave. Ste. 1600/ Ontario/CA/91764/909/980-4030/ cbbank
34.9			6	14	2099 Pennsylvania Ave. NW/ Washington/DC/20006/202/ 828-0850/danaher
10.5			2	13	221 W. Philadelphia St./York/ PA/17405/717/845-7511/dentsply
1.0	X	500	0	54	PO Box 3077/N. Canton/ OH/44720/800/766-5859/diebold
4.3	X		18	14	PO Box 1299/Minneapolis/MN/ 55440/800/468-9716/donaldson
4.0	X	500	5	51	280 Park Ave./New York/NY/ 10017/212/922-1640 / dovercorporation

(*continued*)

A List of America's Finest Companies (Continued)

Company	Ticker	Industry	5/31/08 Price	Earnings Per Share	Dividend	Price/ Earnings Ratio	Dividend Yield
Duke Realty Corp.	DRE	RE Invest. Trust	24.60	2.70	1.92	9.1	7.80%
EastGroup Properties Inc.	EGP	RE Invest. Trust	46.62	3.12	2.08	14.9	4.46%
Eaton Vance Corp.	EV	Financial	41.01	1.50	0.60	27.3	1.46%
Ecolab Inc.	ECL	Business Services	44.41	1.76	0.50	25.2	1.13%
Emerson Electric Co.	EMR	Electrical Equip.	55.93	2.48	1.20	22.6	2.15%
Energen Corp.	EGN	Natural Gas	75.07	4.28	0.48	17.5	0.64%
Erie Indemnity Co.	ERIE	Insurance	49.56	3.43	1.68	14.4	3.39%
Essex Property Trust Inc.	ESS	RE Invest. Trust	120.21	5.01	4.08	24.0	3.39%
Expeditors International	EXPD	Air Freight	45.58	1.21	0.28	37.7	0.61%
ExxonMobil Corp.	XOM	Oil	86.79	7.28	1.60	11.9	1.84%
1st Source Corp.	SRCE	Banking	19.25	1.28	0.56	15.0	2.91%
FactSet Research Systems	FDS	Special Services	63.79	2.21	0.48	28.9	0.75%
Family Dollar Stores Inc.	FDO	Retail	22.20	1.62	0.50	13.7	2.25%
Farmer Brothers Co.	FARM	Foods	23.72	0.12	0.46	197.7	1.94%

Dividend Coverage	Dividend Reinvestment Plan	Minimum Direct Investment	Consecutive Years Higher		Address/Phone/Web Site
			EPS	Dividends	
1.4	X	250	1	14	600 E. 96th St. #100/Indianapolis/ IN/46240/317/808-6005/ dukerealty
1.5			3	15	300 One Jackson Pl., 188 E. Capitol St./Jackson/MS/39201/601/ 354-3555/eastgroup.net
2.5			1	27	255 State St./Boston/MA/ 02109/617/482-8260 /eatonvance
3.5			6	15	370 Wabasha St. N./St. Paul/ MN/55102/651/293-2233/ecolab
2.1	X	250	0	51	PO Box 4100/St. Louis/MO/ 63136/314/553-2197 /emerson
8.9	X	250	12	25	605 Richard Arrington Jr. Blvd. N./ Birmingham/AL/35203/800/ 654-3206 /energen
2.0			1	12	100 Erie Insurance Place/Erie/ PA/16530/814/870-2000/ erieinsurance
1.2	X	100	1	13	925 East Meadow Drive/Palo Alto/CA/94303/650/849-1600/ essexpropertytrust
4.3			14	14	1015 Third Ave., Ste. 1200/ Seattle/WA/98104/206/674-3400/ expeditors
4.6	X	250	5	25	PO Box 140369/Irving/ TX/75014/972/444-1157/ exxonmobil
2.3			0	19	PO Box 1602/South Bend/ IN/46634/574/235-2702/1stsource
4.6			25	9	One Greenwich Plaza/Greenwich/ CT/06830/203/863-1500/factset
3.2			1	31	PO Box 1017/Charlotte/ NC/28201/704/847-6961/ familydollar
0.3			1	19	20333 S. Normandie Ave./Torrance/ CA /90502/310/787-5200/ farmerbroscousa

(continued)

A List of America's Finest Companies (Continued)

Company	Ticker	Industry	5/31/08 Price	Earnings Per Share	Dividend	Price/ Earnings Ratio	Dividend Yield
Federal Realty Inv. Trust	FRT	RE Invest. Trust	79.35	3.60	2.44	22.0	3.07%
Fidelity National Financial	FNF	Financial	15.69	0.59	1.20	26.6	7.65%
Fifth Third Bancorp	FITB	Banking	16.74	1.93	1.76	8.7	10.51%
First Bancorp Inc.	FBNC	Banking	16.74	1.51	0.76	11.1	4.54%
First Busey Corp.	BUSE	Banking	18.12	1.39	0.80	13.0	4.42%
First Charter Corp.	FCTR	Banking	30.02	1.18	1.10	25.4	3.66%
First Community Bancshares, Inc.	FCBC	Banking	32.41	2.62	1.12	12.4	3.46%
First Financial Corp.	THFF	Banking	32.95	1.94	0.88	17.0	2.67%
First Financial Holdings	FFCH	Banking	22.65	1.87	1.01	12.1	4.46%
FirstMerit Corp.	FMER	Banking	19.10	1.53	1.16	12.5	6.07%
First Midwest Bancorp Inc.	FMBI	Banking	25.01	1.55	1.21	16.1	4.84%
First State Bancorporation	FSNM	Banking	7.21	1.20	0.36	6.0	4.99%
Florida Public Utilities	FPU	Electric Utility	11.45	0.54	0.45	21.2	3.93%
Flushing Financial Corp.	FFIC	Banking	19.47	1.10	0.50	17.7	2.57%
F.N.B. Corp.	FNB	Banking	14.74	1.14	0.96	12.9	6.51%
FPL Group Inc.	FPL	Electric Utility	64.01	3.27	1.70	19.6	2.66%

Dividend Coverage	Dividend Reinvestment Plan	Minimum Direct Investment	Consecutive Years Higher		Address/Phone/Web Site
			EPS	Dividends	
1.5	X	250	6	40	1626 E. Jefferson St./Rockville/ MD/20852/301/998-8100/ federalrealty
0.5			0	20	17911 VonKarman Ave. Ste. 300/ Irvine/CA/92614/949/622-4333 /fnf
1.1	X	250	0	35	38 Fountain Sq. Plaza/Cincinnati/ OH/45263/513/534-5300/53
2.0			2	11	341 North Main Street/Troy/ NC/27371/910-576-6171/ firstbancorp
1.7			9	16	201 West Main Street/Urbana/ IL/61801/217/365-4556/busey
1.1			0	15	10200 David Taylor Dr./Charlotte/ NC/28262/704/688-4300/ firstcharter
2.3			2	11	One Community Place/Bluefield/ VA/24605/276-326-9000/fcbinc
2.2			2	11	One First Financial Plaza/Terre Haute/IN/47807/812-238-6000/ first-online
1.9	X	250	0	15	34 Broad St./Charleston/ SC/29401/843/529-5933/ firstfinancialholdings
1.3	X		1	26	III Cascade Plaza/Akron/OH/ 44308/330/996-6300 /FirstMerit
1.3	X		0	16	One Pierce Place #1500/Itasca/IL/ 60143/630/875-7463/firstmidwest
3.3			8	12	7900 Jefferson NE/Albuquerque/ NM/87109/505/241-7500/fsbnm
1.2	X		0	18	PO Box 3395/West Palm Beach/ FL/33402/561/832-0872/fpuc
2.2			0	11	144-51 Northern Blvd./Flushing/NY/ 11354/718-961-5400/ flushingsavings
1.2	X	50	2	35	2150 Goodlette Rd. N./Naples/FL/ 34102/239/262-7600/ fnbcorporation
1.9	X		2	12	700 Universe Blvd./Juno Beach/ FL/33408/800/222-4511/fplgroup

(*continued*)

A List of America's Finest Companies (Continued)

Company	Ticker	Industry	5/31/08 Price	Earnings Per Share	Dividend	Price/ Earnings Ratio	Dividend Yield
Franklin Electric Co. Inc.	FELE	Electrical Equip.	39.99	1.36	0.50	29.4	1.25%
Franklin Resources Inc.	BEN	Investment Bank.	99.63	7.48	0.80	13.3	0.80%
Fuller, H.B. Co.	FUL	Chemicals	23.98	1.68	0.26	14.3	1.10%
Fulton Financial Corp.	FULT	Banking	11.72	0.88	0.60	13.3	5.12%
Gallagher, Arthur J. & Co.	AJG	Insurance/ Brokers	25.00	1.16	1.28	21.6	5.12%
Gannett Co. Inc.	GCI	Publishing	27.75	4.46	1.60	6.2	5.77%
General Dynamics	GD	Aerospace	86.65	5.43	1.40	16.0	1.62%
General Electric Co.	GE	Electrical Equip.	30.02	2.00	1.24	15.0	4.13%
General Growth Properties	GGP	RE Invest. Trust	39.73	3.50	1.95	11.4	4.91%
Genuine Parts Co.	GPC	Auto Parts	41.88	2.98	1.56	14.1	3.72%
Glacier Bancorp	GBCI	Banking	19.20	1.30	0.52	14.8	2.71%
Gorman-Rupp Co.	GRC	Manufacturing	41.00	1.50	0.40	27.3	0.98%
Grainger, W.W., Inc.	GWW	Electrical Equip.	89.22	5.20	1.60	17.2	1.79%
Harley-Davidson Inc.	HOG	Automotive	39.79	3.74	1.32	10.6	3.32%
Harleysville Group Inc.	HGIC	Insurance/ Prop.	38.85	3.19	0.76	12.2	1.96%

Dividend Coverage	Dividend Reinvestment Plan	Minimum Direct Investment	Consecutive Years Higher		Address/Phone/Web Site
			EPS	Dividends	
2.7			0	14	400 E. Spring St./Bluffton/IN/46714/260/824-2900/franklin-electric
9.4	X		5	27	One Franklin Pkwy./San Mateo/CA/94403/800/342-5236/franklintempleton
6.4	X(3)		0	39	PO Box 64683/St. Paul/MN/55164/800/214-2523/hbfuller
1.5	X		0	34	One Penn Sq., PO Box 4887/Lancaster/PA/17604/717/291-2411/fult
0.9		250	2	23	Two Pierce Place/Itasca/IL/60143/630/773-3800/ajg
2.8	X		1	37	7950 Jones Branch Dr./McLean/VA/22107/800/778-3299/gannett
3.9			9	16	2941 Fairview Park Drive #100/Falls Church/VA/22042/703/876-3000/generaldynamics
1.6	X	250	32	32	3135 Easton Turnpike/Fairfield/CT/06828/203/373-2211/ge
1.8	X	200	1	14	110 N. Wacker Dr./Chicago/IL/60606/312/960-5000/generalgrowth
1.9	X		5	51	2999 Circle 75 Pkwy./Atlanta/GA/30339/770/953-1700 /genpt
2.5	X	250	11	21	49 Commons Loop /Kalispell/MT/59901/406/756-4200/glacierbancorp
3.8	X	500	3	35	PO Box 1217/Mansfield/OH/44901/419/755-1294/gormanrupp
3.3			6	36	100 Grainger Pkwy./Lake Forest/IL/60045/847/535-1000/grainger
2.8	X	500	0	14	3700 W. Juneau Ave./Milwaukee/WI/53208/414/342-4680/harley-davidson
4.2	X		0	21	355 Maple Ave./Harleysville/PA/19438/215/256-5000/harleysvillegroup

(continued)

A List of America's Finest Companies (Continued)

Company	Ticker	Industry	5/31/08 Price	Earnings Per Share	Dividend	Price/ Earnings Ratio	Dividend Yield
Harleysville National Corp.	HNBC	Banking	13.23	0.90	0.80	14.7	6.05%
Harsco Corp.	HSC	Industrial Services	61.20	3.12	0.78	19.6	1.27%
Harte-Hanks Inc.	HHS	Publishing	13.59	1.21	0.28	11.2	2.06%
Hartford Financial Services Group Inc	HIG	Insurance	70.93	9.24	2.12	7.7	2.99%
HCC Insurance Holdings Inc.	HCC	Insurance	23.76	3.22	0.44	7.4	1.85%
HCP Inc.	HCP	RE Invest. Trust	33.76	1.82	1.80	18.5	5.33%
Heartland Financial USA Inc.	HTLF	Banking	22.75	1.58	0.40	14.4	1.76%
Hershey Corp.	HSY	Foods	37.46	0.93	1.19	40.3	3.18%
Hilb, Rogal & Hobbs Co.	HRH	Insurance Brokers	30.89	2.11	0.56	14.6	1.81%
HNI Corporation	HNI	Ofc. Equip/ Supp	23.27	2.57	0.86	9.1	3.70%
Holly Corp.	HOC	Oil & Gas	43.72	5.98	0.60	7.3	1.37%
Home Depot Inc.	HD	Retail	27.18	2.37	0.90	11.5	3.31%
Home Properties Inc.	HME	RE Invest. Trust	51.47	3.20	2.64	16.1	5.13%
Horizon Financial Corp.	HRZB	Financial	10.08	1.51	0.54	6.7	5.36%

Dividend Coverage	Dividend Reinvestment Plan	Minimum Direct Investment	Consecutive Years Higher		Address/Phone/Web Site
			EPS	Dividends	
1.1	X		0	33	483 Main St./Harleysville/ PA/19438/215/256-8851/hncbank
4.0			1	14	350 Poplar Church Road/Camp Hill/PA/17001/717/7975-5677/ harsco
4.3			0	12	200 Concord Plaza Drive/San Antonio/TX/78216/210/ 829-9000/harte-hanks
4.4			2	11	Hartford Plaza/Hartford/ CT/06115/860-547-5000/ thehartford
7.3			2	11	13403 Northwest Freeway/Houston / TX/77040/713-690-7300/hcch
1.0	X	750	1	22	3760 Kilroy Airport Way, Ste. 300/ Long Beach/CA/90806/562/ 733-5100 /hcpi
4.0			2	11	1398 Central Avenue/Dubuque/ IA/52004/563-589-2100/htlf
0.8	X	250	0	33	PO Box 810/Hershey/ PA/17033/800/539-0261/hersheys
3.8			0	20	4951 Lake Brook Dr., Ste. 500/ Glen Allen/VA/23060/804/ 747-6500 /hrh
3.0			1	23	PO Box 1109 /Muscatine/ IA/52761/563/264-7400/honi
10.0		250	5	14	100 Crescent Ct./Dallas/ TX/75201/214/871-3555/hollycorp
2.6	X	500	0	20	2455 Paces Ferry Rd. NW /Atlanta/ GA/30339/770/433-8211/ homedepot
1.2		1000	3	13	850 Clinton Square/Rochester/ NY/14604/877/305-4111/ homeproperties
2.8	X		0	20	PO Box 580 /Bellingham/ WA/98227/360/733-3050/ horizonbank

(*continued*)

A List of America's Finest Companies (Continued)

Company	Ticker	Industry	5/31/08 Price	Earnings Per Share	Dividend	Price/ Earnings Ratio	Dividend Yield
Hormel Foods Corp.	HRL	Foods	36.85	2.17	0.74	17.0	2.01%
IBERIABANK	IBKC	Banking	50.50	3.27	1.36	15.4	2.69%
Illinois Tool Works Inc.	ITW	Manufacturing	50.16	3.36	1.12	14.9	2.23%
Independent Bank Corp.	IBCP	Banking	4.90	1.08	0.84	4.5	17.14%
Integrys Energy Group	TEG	Electric Utility	51.16	2.48	2.68	20.6	5.24%
International Business Machines	IBM	Computers	124.94	7.18	2.00	17.4	1.60%
Investors Real Estate Trust	IRETS	RE Invest. Trust	10.36	0.40	0.67	25.9	6.47%
Irwin Financial Corp.	IFC	Banking	4.18	def.	0.48	def.	11.48%
Jack Henry & Associates	JKHY	Special Services	23.12	1.16	0.30	19.9	1.30%
Johnson & Johnson	JNJ	Health Care	65.76	3.63	1.84	18.1	2.80%
Johnson Controls Inc.	JCI	Manufacturing	31.54	2.09	0.52	15.1	1.65%
KeyCorp	KEY	Banking	17.30	2.32	1.50	7.5	8.67%
Kimberly-Clark Corp.	KMB	Household Prods.	62.11	4.15	2.32	15.0	3.74%
Kimco Realty Corp.	KIM	RE Invest. Trust	37.89	2.59	1.60	14.6	4.22%
Kinder Morgan Energy Partners	KMP	Oil & Gas	59.34	1.75	3.52	33.9	5.93%

Dividend Coverage	Dividend Reinvestment Plan	Minimum Direct Investment	Consecutive Years Higher		Address/Phone/Web Site
			EPS	Dividends	
2.9	X		4	41	1 Hormel Place/Austin/ MN/55912/507/437-5611/hormel
2.4			0	12	200 West Congress St./Lafayette/ LA/70501/337/521-4003/ iberiabank
3.0	X		5	45	3600 West Lake Avenue/Glenview/ IL/60026/847/657-4929/itw
1.3			0	19	230 W. Main St./Ionia/ MI/48846/616/527-9450/ibcp
0.9	X	100	0	49	PO Box 19001/Green Bay/ WI/54301/800/228-6888/ integrysgroup
3.6	X	500	3	12	New Orchard Road/Armonk/ NY/10504/914/499-1900/ibm
0.6	X		0	37	PO Box 1988/Minot/ ND/58702/701/837-7106/iret
0.0			0	16	500 Washington St./Columbus/ IN/47201/812/376-1909/ irwinfinancial
3.9			4	17	PO Box 807/Monett/ MO/65708/417/235-6652/ jackhenry
2.0	X		24	45	One Johnson & Johnson Plaza/ New Brunswick/NJ/08933/ 800/950-5089 /jnj
4.0	X	250	6	32	PO Box 591/Milwaukee/ WI/53201/800/524-6220/ johnsoncontrols
1.5	X	250	0	27	127 Public Sq./Cleveland/ OH/44114/216/689-6300/key
1.8	X		1	35	PO Box 619100 /Dallas/TX/ 75261/800/639-1352/kimberly-clark
1.6	X	100	16	16	3333 New Hyde Park Rd. #100/ New Hyde Park/NY/11042/ 516/869-7288/kimcorealty
0.5			1	11	500 Dallas St. Suite 1000/Houston/ TX/77002/713-369-9000/ kindermorgan

(*continued*)

A List of America's Finest Companies (Continued)

Company	Ticker	Industry	5/31/08 Price	Earnings Per Share	Dividend	Price/ Earnings Ratio	Dividend Yield
Lancaster Colony Corp.	LANC	Foods	32.43	1.43	1.12	22.7	3.45%
Leggett & Platt Inc.	LEG	Household Furn.	18.60	def.	1.00	def.	5.38%
Legg Mason Inc.	LM	Investment Bank.	52.92	4.48	0.96	11.8	1.81%
Liberty Property Trust	LRY	RE Invest. Trust	35.63	1.69	2.48	21.1	6.96%
Lilly, Eli & Co.	LLY	Health Care	48.42	3.21	1.88	15.1	3.88%
Lincoln National Group	LNC	Insurance/Life	52.62	4.43	1.64	11.9	3.12%
Linear Technology Corp.	LLTC	Semiconductors	35.11	1.44	0.72	24.4	2.05%
Lowe's Companies Inc.	LOW	Retail	23.52	1.88	0.32	12.5	1.36%
LSI Industries Inc.	LYTS	Manufacturing	9.56	1.01	0.60	9.5	6.28%
M&T Bank Corp.	MTB	Banking	81.18	6.20	2.80	13.1	3.45%
Macerich Co.	MAC	RE Invest. Trust	69.45	1.00	3.20	69.5	4.61%
MainSource Financial Group Inc	MSFG	Banking	16.90	1.22	0.56	13.9	3.31%
Marshall & Ilsley Corp.	MI	Banking	21.28	1.60	1.28	13.3	6.02%
Martin Marietta Materials	MLM	Bldng. Materials	112.85	6.06	1.38	18.6	1.22%

Dividend Coverage	Dividend Reinvestment Plan	Minimum Direct Investment	Consecutive Years Higher		Address/Phone/Web Site
			EPS	Dividends	
1.3	X		0	45	37 W. Broad St. /Columbus/ OH/43215/614/224-7141/ lancastercolony
0.0			0	36	PO Box 757/Carthage/MO/ 64836/417/358-8131 /leggett
4.7			0	26	100 Light St./Baltimore/MD/ 21202/410/539-0000 /leggmason
0.7	X	250	0	13	500 Chesterfield Parkway/Malvern/ PA/19355/610/648-1700/ libertyproperty
1.7	X	50	3	40	Lilly Corporate Center/ Indianapolis/IN/46285/317/ 276-2000/lilly
2.7	X	500	0	24	1500 Market St., 39th Flr./ Philadelphia/PA/19102/866/ 541-9693/lfg
2.0			4	15	1630 McCarthy Blvd./Milpitas/ CA/95035/408/432-1900/linear
5.9	X	250	0	27	1000 Lowe's Blvd./Mooresville/ NC/28117/888/345-6937/lowes. com/investor
1.7	X		1	18	10000 Alliance Road/Cincinnati/ OH/45242/513/793-3200/ lsi-industries
2.2	X		0	27	One M&T Plaza/Buffalo/ NY/14203/716/842-5445/ mandtbank
0.3	X	250	0	13	401 Wilshire Blvd. #700/Santa Monica/CA/90401/310/394-6000/ macerich
2.2			0	11	201 North Broadway/Greensburg/ IN/47240/812-663-0157/ mainsourcefinancial
1.3	X(1)		0	35	770 North Water St./Milwaukee/ WI/53202/800/642-2657/micorp
4.4			5	13	2710 Wycliff Road/Raleigh/ NC/27607/919/781-4550/ martinmarietta

(continued)

A List of America's Finest Companies (Continued)

Company	Ticker	Industry	5/31/08 Price	Earnings Per Share	Dividend	Price/ Earnings Ratio	Dividend Yield
Masco Corp.	MAS	Bldng. Materials	17.18	1.03	0.92	16.7	5.36%
Matthews International Corp.	MATW	Miscellaneous	46.61	2.16	0.22	21.6	0.47%
McCormick & Co.	MKC	Foods	37.76	1.79	0.88	21.1	2.33%
McDonald's Corp.	MCD	Restaurant	56.95	2.17	1.50	26.2	2.63%
McGrath RentCorp	MGRC	Special Services	26.96	1.67	0.80	16.1	2.97%
McGraw-Hill Companies Inc.	MHP	Publishing	44.36	2.94	0.88	15.1	1.98%
MDU Resources Group Inc.	MDU	Electric Utility	33.70	2.36	0.54	14.3	1.60%
Media General Inc.	MEG	Publishing	14.29	def.	0.92	def.	6.44%
Medtronic Inc.	MDT	Medical Prods.	50.37	1.94	0.50	26.0	0.99%
Mercury General Corp.	MCY	Insurance/ Multi.	51.30	4.34	2.32	11.8	4.52%
Meredith Corp.	MDP	Publishing	31.91	3.36	0.72	9.5	2.26%
Meridian Bioscience Inc.	VIVO	Biotechnology	30.21	0.73	0.64	41.4	2.12%
MGE Energy	MGEE	Electric Utility	34.25	2.27	1.42	15.1	4.15%
Middlesex Water Co.	MSEX	Water Utility	18.53	0.87	0.70	21.3	3.78%

Dividend Coverage	Dividend Reinvestment Plan	Minimum Direct Investment	Consecutive Years Higher		Address/Phone/Web Site
			EPS	Dividends	
1.1	X	50	0	49	21001 Van Born Rd./Taylor/ MI/48180/515/274-7400 /masco
9.8			0	13	Two Northshore Center/ Pittsburgh/PA/15212/412/ 442-8200/matw
2.0	X	250	1	21	18 Loveton Circle/Sparks/ MD/21152/800/424-5855/ mccormick
1.4	X	500	0	33	McDonald's Plaza/Oak Brook/ IL/60523/630/623-3000/ mcdonalds
2.1			5	16	5700 Las Positas Rd./Livermore/ CA/94551/925/606-9200/mgrc
3.3	X	500	6	34	1221 Ave. of Americas/New York/ NY/10020/866/436-8502/ mcgraw-hill
4.4	X	250	5	17	PO Box 5650/Bismarck/ ND/58506/800/437-8000/mdu
0.0	X(5)		0	13	333 East Grace St./Richmond/ VA/23219/804/649-6000/ mediageneral
3.9	X	250	0	30	710 Medtronic Parkway/ Minneapolis/MN/55432/763/ 514-4000/medtronic
1.9			1	21	4484 Wilshire Blvd. /Los Angeles/ CA/90010/800/524-4458/ mercuryinsurance
4.7	X		4	14	1716 Locust St./Des Moines/ IA/50336/515/284-3000/meredith
1.1			6	15	3471 River Hills Dr./Cincinnati/ OH/45244/513/271-3700/ meridianbioscience
1.6	X	250	2	32	PO Box 1231/Madison/ WI/53701/800/356-6423/ mgeenergy
1.2	X(5)		2	34	PO Box 1500/Iselin/ NJ/08830/732/634-1500/ middlesexwater

(continued)

A List of America's Finest Companies (Continued)

Company	Ticker	Industry	5/31/08 Price	Earnings Per Share	Dividend	Price/ Earnings Ratio	Dividend Yield
Mine Safety Appliances Co.	MSA	Health Care	42.00	1.86	0.88	22.6	2.10%
3M Co.	MMM	Manufacturing	74.86	5.60	2.00	13.4	2.67%
Moog Inc.	MOG-A	Manufacturing	41.50	2.51	0.00	16.5	0.00%
Myers Industries Inc.	MYE	Manufacturing	11.37	1.56	0.24	7.3	2.11%
NACCO Industries Inc.	NC	Manufacturing	81.91	10.33	2.00	7.9	2.44%
National Fuel Gas Co.	NFG	Natural Gas	58.97	4.12	1.24	14.3	2.10%
National Penn Bancshares Inc.	NPBC	Banking	16.43	1.31	0.68	12.5	4.14%
National Retail Properties Inc.	NNN	RE Invest. Trust	22.00	1.87	1.50	11.8	6.82%
National Security Group Inc.	NSEC	Insurance/ Multi.	16.40	2.45	0.90	6.7	5.49%
New Jersey Resources Corp.	NJR	Natural Gas	33.46	3.18	1.12	10.5	3.35%
New York Times Co.	NYT	Publishing	16.82	1.28	0.92	13.1	5.47%
Nordson Corp.	NDSN	Manufacturing	73.07	2.81	0.73	26.0	1.00%
Nordstrom Inc	JWN	Apparel	33.99	2.88	0.64	11.8	1.88%
Northern Trust Corp.	NTRS	Banking	71.37	4.11	1.00	17.4	1.40%
NSTAR	NST	Electric Utility	33.79	2.18	1.30	15.5	3.85%

Dividend Coverage	Dividend Reinvestment Plan	Minimum Direct Investment	Consecutive Years Higher		Address/Phone/Web Site
			EPS	Dividends	
2.1			1	37	PO Box 426/Pittsburgh/ PA/15230/412/967-3046/msanet
2.8	X(1)		6	49	3M Center/St. Paul/ MN/55144/651/733-1110/3m
0.0			13	0	East Aurora/NY/14052/716/ 687-4225/moog
6.5	X		1	33	1293 South Main St./Akron/ OH/44301/330/253-5592/ myersind
5.2			0	29	5875 Landerbrook Dr./Cleveland/ OH/44124/440/449-9669/nacco
3.3	X	1000	1	37	6363 Main Street/Williamsville/ NY/14221/716/857-7000/ nationalfuelgas
1.9	X		30	29	PO Box 547/Boyertown/ PA/19512/800/822-3321/ nationalpennbancshares
1.2	X(1)	100	6	18	450 S. Orange Ave. #900/Orlando/ FL/32801/800/265-7348/nnnreit
2.7			2	29	661 East Davis St. /Elba/ AL/36323/334/897-2273/ nationalsecuritygroup
2.8	X	25	16	12	1415 Wyckoff Rd./Wall / NJ/07719/732/938-1229/ njresources
1.4			1	12	229 West 43rd Street/New York/ NY/10036/212/556-1234/nytco
3.8	X		5	44	28601 Clemens Rd./Westlake/ OH/44145/440/414-5344/nordson
4.5			6	10	1617 Sixth Avenue Suite 500/ Seattle/WA/98101/206-628-2111/ nordstrom
4.1			4	21	50 S. La Salle St./Chicago/ IL/60675/312/630-6000/ northerntrust
1.7	X	500	6	17	800 Boylston St./Boston/ MA/02199/617/424-2000/ nstaronline

(continued)

A List of America's Finest Companies (Continued)

Company	Ticker	Industry	5/31/08 Price	Earnings Per Share	Dividend	Price/ Earnings Ratio	Dividend Yield
Nucor Corp.	NUE	Steel	78.20	4.94	2.48	15.8	3.17%
NW Natural Gas Co.	NWN	Natural Gas	45.84	2.76	1.50	16.6	3.27%
Old National Bancorp	ONB	Banking	17.16	1.27	0.92	13.5	5.36%
Old Republic Intl. Corp.	ORI	Insurance/ Multi.	14.79	1.18	0.64	12.5	4.33%
Old Second Bancorp Inc.	OSBC	Banking	19.23	1.88	0.60	10.2	3.12%
O'Reilly Automotive	ORLY	Auto Parts	25.22	1.67	0.00	15.1	0.00%
Otter Tail Corp.	OTTR	Electric Utility	38.38	1.78	1.19	21.6	3.10%
Park National Corp.	PRK	Banking	68.15	1.76	3.76	38.7	5.52%
Patterson Cos. Inc.	PDCO	Medical Supplies	33.27	1.63	0.00	20.4	0.00%
Paychex Inc.	PAYX	Computer Soft.	33.17	1.50	1.20	22.1	3.62%
Pentair Inc.	PNR	Manufacturing	36.32	2.10	0.68	17.3	1.87%
Peoples Bancorp Inc.	PEBO	Banking	23.71	1.76	0.88	13.5	3.71%
PepsiCo Inc.	PEP	Soft Drink	65.52	3.41	1.50	19.2	2.29%
Pfizer Inc.	PFE	Health Care	17.96	1.20	1.28	15.0	7.13%

Dividend Coverage	Dividend Reinvestment Plan	Minimum Direct Investment	Consecutive Years Higher		Address/Phone/Web Site
			EPS	Dividends	
2.0	X		0	35	1915 Rexford Road/Charlotte/ NC/28211/704/366-7000/nucor
1.8	X	250	5	52	220 NW 2nd Ave./Portland/ OR/97209/800/422-4012 / nwnatural
1.4	X(3)	500	3	20	PO Box 718/Evansville/ IN/47705/812/464-1366/ oldnational
1.8	X		0	27	307 N. Michigan Ave. /Chicago/ IL/60601/312/346-8100/ oldrepublic
3.1			1	13	37 South River Street/Aurora/ IL/60507/630/892-0202/ 02bancorp
0.0			16	0	233. S. Patterson/Springfield/ MO/65802/417/874-7165/ oreillyauto
1.5	X	100	1	32	PO Box 496/Fergus Falls/ MN/56538/800/664-1259/ottertail
0.5	X		0	47	PO Box 3500/Newark/ OH/43058/740/349-3927/ parknationalcorp
0.0			15	0	1031 Mendota Heights Rd./St. Paul/MN/55120/651/686-1775/ pattersoncompanies
1.3	X	250	18	19	911 Panorama Trail South/ Rochester/NY/14625/585/ 383-3406/paychex
3.1	X		6	31	5500 Wayzata Blvd., Ste. 800/ Golden Valley/MN/55416/763/545-1730/pentair
2.0	X		0	42	PO Box 738/Marietta/ OH/45750/800/374-6123/ peoplesbancorp
2.3	X	250	2	35	700 Anderson Hill Rd./Purchase/ NY/10577/914/253-3035/pepsico
0.9	X	500	0	40	235 East 42nd Street/New York/ NY/10017/212/573-2323/pfizer

(continued)

A List of America's Finest Companies (Continued)

Company	Ticker	Industry	5/31/08 Price	Earnings Per Share	Dividend	Price/ Earnings Ratio	Dividend Yield
Piedmont Natural Gas Co.	PNY	Natural Gas	27.45	1.56	1.04	17.6	3.79%
Pinnacle West Capital Corp.	PNW	Electric Utility	32.37	3.05	2.10	10.6	6.49%
Pitney Bowes Inc.	PBI	Ofc. Equip/ Supp	36.08	1.66	1.40	21.7	3.88%
Polaris Industries Inc.	PII	Recreation	46.83	3.28	1.52	14.3	3.25%
PPG Industries	PPG	Chemicals	61.23	5.03	2.08	12.2	3.40%
Praxair Inc.	PX	Chemicals	96.12	3.77	1.50	25.5	1.56%
Procter & Gamble Co.	PG	Household Prods.	65.37	3.26	1.60	20.1	2.45%
Progress Energy Inc.	PGN	Electric Utility	42.17	1.96	2.46	21.5	5.83%
Progressive Corp.	PGR	Insurance/ Prop.	20.08	1.51	0.12	13.3	0.60%
ProLogis Trust	PLD	RE Invest. Trust	58.66	4.61	2.07	12.7	3.53%
Protective Life Corp.	PL	Insurance/Life	40.93	4.20	0.90	9.7	2.20%
Questar Corp.	STR	Natural Gas	66.04	3.17	0.49	20.8	0.74%
Quixote Corp.	QUIX	Construction	9.00	0.28	0.20	def.	2.22%
Raven Industries Inc.	RAVN	Textile/ Apparel	36.38	1.53	0.52	23.8	1.43%

Dividend Coverage	Dividend Reinvestment Plan	Minimum Direct Investment	Consecutive Years Higher		Address/Phone/Web Site
			EPS	Dividends	
1.5	X(5)	250	1	29	PO Box 33068/Charlotte/ NC/28233/704/731-4438/ piedmontng
1.5	X	50	0	14	PO Box 53999/Phoenix/ AZ/85004/602/250-5668/ pinnaclewest
1.2	X		1	25	One Elmcroft Rd./Stamford/ CT/06926/203/356-5000/ pitneybowes
2.2	X		1	12	2100 Highway 55/Medina/ MN/55340/763/542-0500/ polarisindustries
2.4	X	500	2	36	One PPG Place/Pittsburgh/ PA/15272/412/434-3131/ppg
2.5	X		5	15	39 Old Ridgebury Rd./Danbury/ CT/06810/203/837-2000/praxair
2.0	X	250	7	52	PO Box 599/Cincinnati/OH/ 45201/800/764-7483/pg.com/ investor
0.8	X	250	0	19	PO Box 1551/Raleigh/ NC/27602/866/290-4388/ progress-energy
12.6			0	38	6300 Wilson Mills Rd./Mayfield Village/OH/44143/440/461-5000/ progressive
2.2	X	200	4	13	14100 E. 35th Pl. /Aurora/ CO/80011/303/375-9292/prologis
4.7	X		6	18	2801 Highway 280 S./Birmingham/ AL/35223/205/268-1000/ protective
6.5	X	250	5	30	180 E. 100 South St./Salt Lake City/ UT/84145/801/324-5000/questar
1.4			0	14	35 East Wacker Drive/Chicago/ IL/60601/312/467-6755/ quixotecorp
2.9	X		5	21	PO Box 5107/Sioux Falls/ SD/57117/605/336-2750/ ravenind

(continued)

A List of America's Finest Companies (Continued)

Company	Ticker	Industry	5/31/08 Price	Earnings Per Share	Dividend	Price/ Earnings Ratio	Dividend Yield
Realty Income Corp.	O	RE Invest. Trust	23.84	1.73	1.65	13.8	6.91%
Regency Centers Corp.	REG	RE Invest. Trust	65.21	2.65	2.64	24.6	4.05%
Regions Financial Corp.	RF	Banking	15.45	1.79	1.52	8.6	9.84%
Renasant Corp	RNST	Banking	21.99	2.20	0.68	10.0	3.09%
RLI Corp.	RLI	Insurance/ Prop.	51.84	7.12	1.00	7.3	1.93%
Robinson Worldwide, C.H. Inc.	CHRW	Special Services	61.07	1.94	0.88	31.5	1.44%
Rohm & Haas Co.	ROH	Chemicals	52.90	3.13	1.48	16.9	2.80%
Roper Industries Inc	ROP	Manufacturing	65.61	2.80	0.26	23.4	0.40%
Ross Stores Inc.	ROST	Retail	36.55	1.90	0.38	19.2	1.04%
RPM International Inc.	RPM	Chemicals	24.33	1.66	0.76	14.7	3.12%
S.Y. Bancorp Inc.	SYBT	Banking	24.00	1.66	0.68	14.5	2.83%
S&T Bancorp Inc.	STBA	Banking	31.11	2.26	1.24	13.8	3.99%
Sandy Spring Bancorp Inc.	SASR	Banking	23.70	2.02	0.96	11.7	4.05%
SEI Investments Co.	SEIC	Investment Bank.	24.54	1.28	0.14	19.2	0.57%
Sherwin-Williams Co.	SHW	Bldng. Materials	50.19	4.51	1.40	11.1	2.79%

Dividend Coverage	Dividend Reinvestment Plan	Minimum Direct Investment	Consecutive Years Higher		Address/Phone/Web Site
			EPS	Dividends	
1.0			13	13	600 La Terraza Boulevard/ Escondido/CA/92025/888/ 811-2001/realtyincome
1.0	X		0	13	One Independent Dr. #114/ Jacksonville/FL/32202/800/ 950-6333/regencycenters
1.2	X	1000	0	36	PO Box 10247/Birmingham/ AL/35202/205/944-1300/regions
3.2			2	10	209 Troy Street/Tupelo/ MS/38802/662-680-1001/renasant
7.1	X		9	31	9025 N. Lindbergh Dr./Peoria/ IL/61615/800/331-4929 /rlicorp
2.2			10	9	8100 Mitchell Road/Eden Prairie/ MN/55344/952/937-8500/ chrobinson
2.1			0	30	100 Independence Mall W./ Philadelphia/PA/19106/215/ 592-3000/rohmhaas
10.8			4	15	6901 Professional Pkwy. East #200/ Sarasota/FL /34240/941/556-2601/ roperind
5.0			3	14	4440 Rosewood Drive/Pleasonton/ CA/94588/925/965-4400/rossstores
2.2	X		3	34	PO Box 777/Medina/ OH/44258/800/776-4488/rpminc
2.4			2	10	1040 East Main Street/Louisville/ KY/40206/502-582-2571/syb
1.8		250	1	18	43 S. Ninth St./Indiana/ PA/15701/724/465-1466/stbank
2.1	X	250	0	12	17801 Georgia Avenue/Olney/ MD/20832/800/399-5919/ssnb
9.1			15	16	PO Box 1100/Oaks/ PA/19456/610/676-1000/seic
3.2	X		5	28	101 Prospect Avenue NW/ Cleveland/OH/44115/866/ 537-8703/sherwin

(continued)

A List of America's Finest Companies (Continued)

Company	Ticker	Industry	5/31/08 Price	Earnings Per Share	Dividend	Price/ Earnings Ratio	Dividend Yield
Sigma-Aldrich Corp.	SIAL	Chemicals	58.12	2.42	0.52	24.0	0.89%
Simmons First National Corp.	SFNC	Banking	30.71	2.09	0.76	14.7	2.47%
SJW Corp.	SJW	Water Utility	31.38	1.04	0.65	30.2	2.07%
Smith, A.O. Corp.	AOS	Electric Equipment	34.56	2.92	0.72	11.8	2.08%
Sonic Corp.	SONC	Restaurant	18.45	1.01	0.00	18.3	0.00%
Sonoco Products Co.	SON	Containers	33.16	2.10	1.04	15.8	3.14%
South Financial Group Inc. (The)	TSFG	Banking	5.05	def.	0.76	def.	15.05%
Southwest Bancorp Inc.	OKSB	Banking	16.35	1.51	0.37	10.8	2.26%
Southwest Water Co.	SWWC	Water Utility	10.29	def.	0.24	def.	2.33%
Sovran Self Storage Inc.	SSS	RE Invest. Trust	43.53	3.38	2.52	12.9	5.79%
Stanley Works	SWK	Hdware. & Tools	47.44	4.00	1.24	11.9	2.61%
Starbucks Corp.	SBUX	Restaurant	17.67	0.89	0.00	19.9	0.00%
State Auto Financial Corp.	STFC	Insurance/ Prop.	27.76	1.81	0.60	15.3	2.16%
State Street Corp.	STT	Banking	68.02	3.73	0.92	18.2	1.35%
Stepan Co.	SCL	Chemicals	41.75	1.79	0.84	23.3	2.01%

Dividend Coverage	Dividend Reinvestment Plan	Minimum Direct Investment	Consecutive Years Higher		Address/Phone/Web Site
			EPS	Dividends	
4.7			5	36	3050 Spruce St./St. Louis/MO/63103/314/771-5765/sigma-aldrich
2.8			0	16	501 Main St./Pine Bluff/AR/71601/870/541-1000/simmonsfirst
1.6			0	39	374 W. Santa Clara St./San Jose/CA/95196/800/250-5147 /sjwater
4.1	X		3	15	PO Box 245008/Milwaukee/WI/53224/414/359-4009/aosmith
0.0			13	0	101 Park Avenue/Oklahoma City/OK/73102/405/280-7654/sonicdrivein
2.0	X	250	6	25	1 North Second St./Hartsville/SC/29550/843/383-7000/sonoco
0.0			0	13	102 South Main Street/Greenville/SC/29601/864/255-7900/thesouthgroup
4.1			0	13	608 South Main Street/Stillwater/OK/74074/405/372-2230/oksb
0.0			0	12	624 South Grand Avenue/Los Angeles/CA/90017/213/929-1800/swwc
1.3	X	100	4	12	6467 Main Street/Buffalo/NY/14221/716/633-1850/sovranss
3.2	X	250	2	40	PO Box 7000/New Britain/CT/06053/860/225-5111/stanleyworks
0.0			15	0	2401 Utah Avenue South/Seattle/WA/98134/206/447-1575/starbucks
3.0	X		0	16	518 East Broad St./Columbus/OH/43215/614/464-5078/stateauto
4.1	X		4	29	One Lincoln Street/Boston/MA/02111/617/786-3000/statestreet
2.1			1	40	22 W. Frontage Rd./Northfield/IL/60093/847/446-7500/stepan

(continued)

A List of America's Finest Companies (Continued)

Company	Ticker	Industry	5/31/08 Price	Earnings Per Share	Dividend	Price/ Earnings Ratio	Dividend Yield
Sterling Bancshares Inc.	SBIB	Financial	9.97	0.72	0.21	13.8	2.11%
Stryker Corp.	SYK	Medical Prods.	63.94	2.44	0.33	26.2	0.52%
SunTrust Banks, Inc.	STI	Banking	46.32	3.92	3.08	11.8	6.65%
Susquehanna Bancshares Inc.	SUSQ	Banking	17.57	1.23	1.04	14.3	5.92%
SYSCO Corp.	SYY	Distributor	30.38	1.74	0.88	17.5	2.90%
Tanger Factor Outlet Ctrs	SKT	RE Invest. Trust	39.41	0.73	1.52	54.0	3.86%
Target Corp.	TGT	Retail	52.52	3.33	0.56	15.8	1.07%
Taubman Centers Inc.	TCO	Retail	53.51	0.80	1.66	66.9	3.10%
TCF Financial Corp.	TCB	Banking	15.25	1.85	0.96	8.2	6.30%
Teleflex Inc.	TFX	Electronics	58.27	3.73	1.36	15.6	2.33%
Telephone & Data Systems	TDS	Telephone	51.00	0.25	0.41	204.0	0.80%
Tennant Co.	TNC	Manufacturing	35.25	2.01	0.52	17.5	1.48%
TEPPCO Partners L.P.	TPP	Natural Gas	35.46	1.00	2.84	35.5	8.01%
Thomson Corp.	TRI	Publishing	35.43	6.20	1.27	5.7	3.58%
TJX Companies Inc	TJX	Retail	31.61	1.66	0.44	19.0	1.39%
Tompkins Financial	TMP	Banking	45.25	2.89	1.28	15.7	2.83%

| Dividend Coverage | Dividend Reinvestment Plan | Minimum Direct Investment | Consecutive Years Higher | | Address/Phone/Web Site |
			EPS	Dividends	
3.4			3	14	2550 North Loop W. #600/ Houston/TX/77092/713/ 466-8300/banksterling
7.4			8	16	PO Box 4085 /Kalamazoo/MI /49003/269/385-2600/strykercorp
1.3	X		0	32	PO Box 4418 Ctr. 645/Atlanta/ GA/30302/800/324-8093/suntrust
1.2	X	250	0	25	PO Box 1000/Lititz/ PA/17543/717/625-6305/ susquehanna.net
2.0	X		1	37	1390 Enclave Parkway/Houston/ TX/77077/281/584-1308/sysco
0.5			0	14	3200 Northline Ave./Greensboro/ NC/27408/336/292-3010/ tangeroutlet
5.9	X	500	2	34	1000 Nicollet Mall/Minneapolis/ MN/55403/612/304-6073/target
0.5			1	11	200 East Long Lake Rd. Suite 300 PO Box 200/Bloomfield Hills/ MI/48303/248-258-6800/taubman
1.9	X	250	1	16	200 Lake St. East/Wayzata/ MN/55391/612/661-6500/tcfbank
2.7	X	250	3	31	2917 Weck Dr./Research Triangle Park/NC/27709/800/334-9751/ teleflex
0.6	X(5)		0	33	30 N. LaSalle St., Ste. 400/Chicago/ IL/60602/312/630-1900 /teldta
3.9	X		3	36	PO Box 1452/Minneapolis/ MN/55440/800/553-8033/ tennantco
0.4			0	15	PO Box 2521/Houston/ TX/77252/713/759-3636/teppco
4.9			6	10	Three Times Square/New York/ NY/10036/646/223-4000/thomson
3.8			2	10	770 Cochinuate Road/ Framingham/MA/01701/ 508-390-1000/tjx
2.3	X	100	35	19	PO Box 460/Ithaca/NY/14851/ 607/273-3210 /tompkinstrustco

A List of America's Finest Companies (Continued)

Company	Ticker	Industry	5/31/08 Price	Earnings Per Share	Dividend	Price/ Earnings Ratio	Dividend Yield
Tootsie Roll Industries Inc.	TR	Foods	26.21	0.89	0.32	29.4	1.22%
Total System Services	TSS	Special Services	24.41	1.20	0.28	20.3	1.15%
Transatlantic Holdings Inc.	TRH	Insurance/ Multi.	63.30	6.53	0.64	9.7	1.01%
T. Rowe Price Group Inc.	TROW	Financial	58.37	2.40	0.96	24.3	1.64%
Trustmark Corp.	TRMK	Banking	19.45	1.88	0.92	10.3	4.73%
UDR Inc.	UDR	RE Invest. Trust	24.85	1.53	1.32	16.2	5.31%
UGI Corp.	UGI	Natural Gas	26.61	2.05	0.77	13.0	2.89%
United Bankshares Inc.-WV	UBSI	Banking	27.16	2.15	1.16	12.6	4.27%
UMH Properties Inc.	UMH	RE Invest. Trust	8.88	0.25	1.00	35.5	11.26%
UnitedHealth Group	UNH	Health Care	33.03	3.42	0.03	9.7	0.09%
United Technologies	UTX	Aviation	67.01	4.27	1.28	15.7	1.91%
Universal Corp.	UVV	Tobacco	49.90	3.95	1.80	12.6	3.61%
Universal Forest Products Inc.	UFPI	Wood Products	32.63	1.09	0.06	29.9	0.18%
Universal Health Realty Income	UHT	RE Invest. Trust	35.00	2.45	2.32	14.3	6.63%
U.S. Bancorp Inc.	USB	Banking	32.07	2.60	1.70	12.3	5.30%
Valley National Bancorp	VLY	Banking	17.25	1.12	0.84	15.4	4.87%

Dividend Coverage	Dividend Reinvestment Plan	Minimum Direct Investment	Consecutive Years Higher		Address/Phone/Web Site
			EPS	Dividends	
2.8			0	44	7401 S. Cicero Ave./Chicago/ IL/60629/773/838-3400 /tootsie
4.3	X	250	0	14	PO Box 2567/Columbus/GA/ 31902/706/649-5220/tsys
10.2			2	17	80 Pine St./New York/ NY/10005/212/770-2040/transre
2.5			5	22	100 E. Pratt St./Baltimore/MD/ 21202/888/648-8155/troweprice
2.0	X		0	34	PO Box 291/Jackson/MS/ 39205/601/354-5111/trustmark
1.2	X		1	32	1745 Shea Center Dr., Ste. 200/Highland Ranch/ CO/80129/720/283-6120/udrt
2.7	X		7	21	PO Box 858/Valley Forge/ PA/19482/800/844-9453 /ugicorp
1.9	X		1	17	300 United Center, 500 Virginia St. E./Charleston/ WV/25301/304/424-8800/ubsi-wv
0.3			0	17	3499 Rte. 9 N., Ste. 3-C/Freehold/ NJ/07728/732/577-9997/umh
114.0			11	0	9900 Bren Road East/Minnetonka/ MN/55343/952/936-1300/ unitedhealthgroup
3.3	X	250	7	14	United Technologies Bldg./ Hartford/CT/06103/860/ 728-7000/utc
2.2	X		1	37	PO Box 25099/Richmond/VA/ 23260/804/359-9311/universalcorp
18.2			0	14	2801 East Beltline NE/Grand Rapids/MI/49525/616/ 364-6161/ufpi
1.1			1	20	PO Box 61558/King of Prussia/ PA/19406/610/265-0688/uhrit
1.5	X(5)	250	0	36	800 Nicollet Mall/Minneapolis/ MN/55402/866/775-9668/usbank
1.3	X		0	16	1455 Valley Rd./Wayne/ NJ/07470/800/522-4100/ valleynationalbank

(*continued*)

A List of America's Finest Companies (Continued)

Company	Ticker	Industry	5/31/08 Price	Earnings Per Share	Dividend	Price/ Earnings Ratio	Dividend Yield
Valspar Corp. (The)	VAL	Bldng. Materials	21.23	1.50	0.56	14.2	2.64%
Vectren Corp.	VVC	Natural Gas	30.37	1.79	1.30	17.0	4.28%
VF Corp.	VFC	Textile/ Apparel	72.78	5.35	2.32	13.6	3.19%
Vulcan Materials Co.	VMC	Bldng. Materials	70.95	4.54	1.96	15.6	2.76%
Wal-Mart Stores Inc.	WMT	Retail	58.37	3.13	0.95	18.6	1.63%
Walgreen Co.	WAG	Retail Drug	35.53	2.11	0.38	16.8	1.07%
Washington Federal Inc.	WFSL	Savings & Loan	21.57	1.57	0.84	13.7	3.89%
Washington REIT	WRE	RE Invest. Trust	32.95	2.04	1.69	16.2	5.13%
Webster Financial Corp.	WBS	Savings & Loan	20.67	1.61	1.20	12.8	5.81%
Weingarten Realty Investors	WRI	RE Invest. Trust	33.32	3.06	2.10	10.9	6.30%
Wells Fargo & Co.	WFC	Banking	25.42	2.38	1.24	10.7	4.88%
WesBanco Inc.	WSBC	Banking	20.70	2.09	1.12	9.9	5.41%
Wesco Financial Corp.	WSC	Financial	420.01	15.33	1.50	27.4	0.36%
Westamerica Bancorporation	WABC	Banking	53.63	3.14	1.40	17.1	2.61%

Dividend Coverage	Dividend Reinvestment Plan	Minimum Direct Investment	Consecutive Years Higher		Address/Phone/Web Site
			EPS	Dividends	
2.7	X	1000	0	30	PO Box 1461/Minneapolis/ MN/55440/612/332-7371/ valsparglobal
1.4			1	47	20 NW 4th St./Evansville/ IN/47708/812/491-4209/vectren
2.3	X		5	35	105 Corporate Center Blvd./ Greensboro/NC/27408/336/ 547-6000 /vfc
2.3	X	250	0	15	1200 Urban Center Dr./ Birmingham/AL/35242/205/ 298-3000/vulcanmaterials
3.3	X	250	46	33	702 SW Eighth St./Bentonville/ AR/72716/479/273-4000/ walmartstores
5.6	X	50	33	31	200 Wilmot Rd./Deerfield/ IL/60015/847/914-2385/walgreens
1.9			0	24	425 Pike St./Seattle/ WA/98101/206/624-7930/ washingtonfederal
1.2	X	250	2	37	6110 Executive Blvd., #800/ Rockville/MD/20852/800/ 565-9748 /writ
1.3	X		0	15	Webster Plaza/Waterbury/ CT/06720/203/753-2921/ websterbank
1.5	X	250	18	23	PO Box 924133/Houston/ TX/77292/713/866-6000/ weingarten
1.9	X	250	0	20	420 Montgomery St./San Francisco/CA/94163/800/ 411-4932 /wellsfargo
1.9	X		1	22	1 Bank Plaza/Wheeling/WV/26003/ 304/234-9000/wesbanco
10.2			3	36	301 E. Colorado Blvd., Ste. 300/ Pasadena/CA/91101/626/585-6700/ wescofinancial
2.2	X	100	0	18	1108 Fifth Ave./San Rafael/ CA/94901/415/257-8000/ westamerica

(*continued*)

A List of America's Finest Companies (Continued)

Company	Ticker	Industry	5/31/08 Price	Earnings Per Share	Dividend	Price/ Earnings Ratio	Dividend Yield
West Coast Bancorp	WCBO	Banking	10.76	0.69	0.54	15.6	5.02%
West Pharmaceutical Services	WST	Health Care	46.80	2.05	0.56	22.8	1.20%
Weyco Group Inc.	WEYS	Shoes	27.60	1.91	0.56	14.5	2.03%
WGL Holdings Inc.	WGL	Natural Gas	35.11	2.19	1.42	16.0	4.04%
Whitney Holding Corp.	WTNY	Banking	21.17	2.13	1.24	9.9	5.86%
Wiley (John) & Sons Inc.	JW-A	Publishing	47.48	2.25	0.44	21.1	0.93%
Wilmington Trust Corp.	WL	Banking	31.10	2.64	1.38	11.8	4.44%
Wolverine World Wide Inc.	WWW	Leather Products	28.22	1.77	0.44	15.9	1.56%

Dividend Coverage	Dividend Reinvestment Plan	Minimum Direct Investment	Consecutive Years Higher		Address/Phone/Web Site
			EPS	Dividends	
1.3			0	10	5335 Meadows Road Suite 201/Lake Oswego/OR/97035/ 503-684-0884/wcb
3.7	X		3	15	PO Box 645/Lionville/ PA/19341/610/594-2900/ westpharma
3.4			2	27	PO Box 1188/Milwaukee/ WI/53201/414/908-1600/ weycogroup
1.5	X		1	31	1100 H St. NW/Washington/ DC/20080/202/624-6410/ wglholdings
1.7			3	14	228 St. Charles Ave./New Orleans/ LA/70130/504/586-7272/ whitneybank
5.1			4	14	111 River St./Hoboken/ NJ/07030/201/748-6000/wiley
1.9	X		1	26	1100 N. Market St./Wilmington/ DE/19890/888/456-9361/ wilmingtontrust
4.0			6	14	9341 Courtland Dr./Rockford/ MI/49351/616/866-5500/ wolverineworldwide

INDEX

Brealey, Richard A., 126
Brokers, 30, 165–166
Brown, Charles Farrar, 25
Buffett, Warren, 3, 17, 67, 69, 85,
    113, 114, 117–119
  on Ben Graham, 17–18
  charitable pursuits, 89–90
  largest stock investments, 162
  provisions for family of, 175–176
  sell discipline, 160, 161–162
  stock holdings, 119
  on stock performance
    evaluation, 163
  success factors, 142–143
Burnick, Mike, 146
Buttonwood Agreement, 30
Buy/sell formula, 131–132

Capital gains, 7, 159–160
Carnegie, Andrew, 96
Cash, 103, 105
Certificates of deposit (CDs), 43
Children, investing for, 173–178
  custodial accounts, 173–174
  IRAs, 174–177
  trust accounts, 176
Chopra, Deepak, 90
Cicero, Marcus Tullius, 23
Clements, Jonathan, 83–85
Coca-Cola, 134–138
Cohen, Jerome B., 35
Colgate, Joseph, 89
Commissions, 165
Common stock, 32. *See also* Stocks
Compound annual returns, 5–8,
    44–45, 93
Compounded annual price growth
    rate (CAGR), 146
"Conversation with Benjamin
    Graham" *(Financial Analysts
    Journal)*, 52–53
Cottle, Sydney, 48
Creditors, 107–109
Custodial accounts, 173–174

Dalai Lama, 96
Direct investing, 167–168
Discount brokers, 166
Diversification, 126–127, 180–182
Dividend reinvestment plan,
    165, 167
Dividend reinvestment statement,
    168–171
Dividends, 6–7, 129
  Baker's Dozen Guided
    Portfolio®, 148–150
  defined, 145
  dividend reinvestment statement,
    168–171
  functions of, 155–156
  higher returns with, 150–157
  importance of, 145–148
  payment of, 169
  as predictor of growth, 156
  S&P dividend and nondividend
    payers, 155
  taxes on, 159
Dodd, David, 17, 48
Dollar-cost averaging, 121–126, 181
Dot-coms, 39–40, 143
Dow, Charles Henry, 34
Dow Jones industrial average,
    34–37, 57–59
  in 1973–1974, 47–48
  America's Finest Companies® in,
    181, 182
  annualized return of, 59
  reinvested dividends and, 153
Dow Theory Forecasts, 127
Dreman, David, 75
Dulles, John Foster, 73
Dyer, Wayne W., 90

Early start, in investing, 142
Earnings per share, 150
Edelston, Marty, 82
Einstein, Albert, 45
Einstein: His Life and Universe
    (Isaacson), 142